INTERNATIONAL ORGANIZATION,
NATIONAL POLICIES
AND ECONOMIC DEVELOPMENT

CARNEGIE - ROCHESTER CONFERENCE SERIES ON PUBLIC POLICY

A supplementary series to the Journal of Monetary Economics

Editors

KARL BRUNNER
ALLAN H. MELTZER

Production Editor

ANGELA L. BARNES

VOLUME 6

NORTH-HOLLAND PUBLISHING COMPANY
AMSTERDAM · NEW YORK · OXFORD

INTERNATIONAL ORGANIZATION, NATIONAL POLICIES AND ECONOMIC DEVELOPMENT

Editors

KARL BRUNNER

Graduate School of Management
The University of Rochester

ALLAN H. MELTZER

Carnegie-Mellon University

1977

NORTH-HOLLAND PUBLISHING COMPANY
AMSTERDAM · NEW YORK · OXFORD

ISBN North-Holland for this volume: 0 7204 0744 3

Publishers:

NORTH-HOLLAND PUBLISHING COMPANY
AMSTERDAM · NEW YORK · OXFORD

Sole distributors for the U.S.A. and Canada:
ELSEVIER NORTH-HOLLAND, INC.
52 VANDERBILT AVENUE,
NEW YORK, N.Y. 10017

PRINTED IN THE NETHERLANDS

INTRODUCTION TO THE SERIES

The Carnegie-Rochester Conference on Public Policy was initiated several years ago through the efforts of the Center for Research in Government Policy and Business at the University of Rochester and the Center for the Study of Public Policy at Carnegie-Mellon University. This book is the sixth volume in the series which presents the papers prepared for the Conferences, plus the comments of discussants and participants.

Policies depend not only on theories and evidence, but on the structure of policymaking bodies and the procedures by which policies are made, implemented, and changed. The Conferences direct the attention of economists to major problems of economic policy and institutional arrangements. We hope that the papers and the Conferences will encourage further research on policy and on the effects of national agencies and international institutions on the choice of policies.

The Carnegie-Rochester Conference is an open forum. Participants are united by their interest in the issues discussed and by their belief that analysis, evidence, and informed discussion have lasting effects on the public and its institutions.

This sixth volume of the series, offered as a supplement to the Journal of Monetary Economics, contains papers presented at the April 1976 Conference. Future volumes of the Conference proceedings will be mailed to subscribers as a supplement to the journal. The editor of the journal will consider for publication comments on the papers published in the supplement.

We wish to acknowledge the unfailing assistance of Mrs. Jean Morris and Mrs. Jean Patterson in every aspect of the organization of the Conferences from their beginning, and in the production of the papers for the series.

K. BRUNNER
A.H. MELTZER
Editors

CONTENTS

INTERNATIONAL ORGANIZATION, NATIONAL POLICIES AND ECONOMIC DEVELOPMENT

Karl Brunner
University of Rochester

and

Allan H. Meltzer
Carnegie-Mellon University

The institutions developed and the policies proposed by governments are expected to facilitate man's struggle for economic improvement. The link between these expectations and realizations, however, remains tenuous and uncertain. There is little doubt that the state can effectively condition the citizens' economic welfare, but the institutions and policies of governments may either encourage or obstruct man's search for economic improvement.

The examination of the role of the state in economic development and the clarification of the economic effects of a wide range of government policies is an ancient and central theme of economic inquiry. It was thrust on our profession in Adam Smith's <u>Wealth of Nations</u>. In an era of rapidly expanding government, the role of government requires more extensive analysis. The sixth volume of the Carnegie-Rochester Conference Series on Public Policy explores this theme.

The volume is organized in three parts. The first examines the increasing influence of international organizations on economic policymaking in individual countries and particularly in western and Latin American countries. These organizations introduce new constraints affecting policies and shaping the economic prospects of many countries. The resulting changes in opportunities and constraints are very likely to exert a pervasive influence.

In the second part of the volume, two papers address specific problems in the most developed Latin American countries, Brazil and Mexico. One investigates the changing patterns of government policies in Brazil and the consequences of the policies pursued in the past 15 years. The other covers an important institutional problem, the role of specific property arrangements in agriculture. The consequences of the usufruct system of land tenure for output, labor, and capital intensity in agricultural production are much broader than the specific conclusions for the Mexican case, which is studied in detail. A reliable knowledge of property arrangements and conditions relating ownership and use

1

discriminates between institutional patterns fostering rising real income and those arrangements obstructing development or even producing stagnation.

The third and last part looks at some more general issues of economic development and the potential contribution of economic history to a theory of economic development. Two papers explore the question: what can we learn from economic history about the conditions for economic development?

The Emerging Role of International Organizations

The United Nations offers an excellent opportunity to explore the evolution of an institution responding to new opportunities. Rachel McCulloch (Harvard University) notes the gradual change in the United Nations during the few decades of its existence. World organizations offer opportunities to exploit political mechanisms to effect transfers of wealth. The United Nations and its associated or subsidiary institutions are increasingly viewed by some of the member states as conduits for the redistribution of wealth among nations by political fiat. "A voting majority of poor countries in the United Nations General Assembly has sought to convert the claims of the developing nations into economic rights and the desired responses of the developed nations into duties or obligations rather than matters of discretion." The political struggle to mobilize existing institutions for the desired transfer of wealth has recently centered on the battle cry for a New International Economic Order (NIEO). McCulloch discerns three distinct aspects in the "Third World's" exploitation of the "institutional weapon." "First, there are the specific proposals which have been advanced, and--perhaps more crucial--the view of economic reality upon which they rest. Second, there is an explicit rationale for massive redistribution. And, finally, there are the changes in the role and structure of the United Nations implied by the NIEO." The author suggests that the range of specific proposals, containing a modest selection of sensible recommendations, is probably less important in the long run than the explicit attempt to change the function of the United Nations. The NIEO should basically "effect an important increase in the power of the United Nations as an economic policy-making body." A majority of members of the United Nations wishes to shift the focus of the world organization and to centralize important powers of policymaking in the institution.

McCulloch examines in some detail the series of institutional changes and changes in institutional focus occurring in the past decade to assess the nature of economic policymaking potentially emerging from the United Nations. An exploration of characteristic cases reveals, in the author's judgment, some pervasive patterns in the use of United Nations resolutions for the benefit of

2

the United Nations majority. Notable are the "emphasis on redistribution, rejection of price as a mechanism of resource allocation [and a] failure to appreciate the economic function of secure property rights. . . ."

The author traces the political evolution of the debate in detail. The process begins with a gradual realignment of perceptions, a shifting emphasis within existing institutions, and the development of new arrangements that accommodate the interests of the bureaucracy. The issues under discussion become more extensive; the arguments are more developed and are pressed with increased insistence by an expanding bureaucracy which understands the long-run advantages of searching for and encouraging these developments. The success of OPEC in achieving greatly increased wealth through redistribution encouraged the developments. A period of confrontation and escalation follows. McCulloch ponders whether "the frequent repetition and elaboration of unrealistic and even outrageous demands reflect the inexperience and lack of sophistication of. . .the Third World." An alternative explanation suggests that this behavior is part of "an effective strategy for wresting economic concessions from. . . governments in the industrialized nations." McCulloch indicates that this behavior has already assured some definite gains to specific subgroups in the United Nations majority following a softening of the U.S. position from opposition to conciliation.

Important aspects of the transformation of function and institutional machinery planned by the majority are discussed in a series of special sections. These discussions expose some important problems in the interrelation between underlying institutional conceptions and political action which merit detailed examination in the future. Groups such as UNCTAD, UNIDO, the North-South Conference, and related organizations are examples. The author's extensive attention to pending issues and proposals, including recommendations for the restructuring of the United Nations, yields further clues about the dominant trend resulting from the political pressures of the majority in the United Nations. The intended transformation of world organizations would be used, it appears, "to implement policies likely to inflict substantial damage on the world economy, leaving a smaller global pie to be allocated among competing groups." The author concludes that U.S. problems would only grow worse in case "the U.S. goes along with policies which ultimately decrease the amount available for the world to share." The U.S. government is admonished to "eschew short-run policies of partial accommodation, as exemplified by the Kissinger speech at the Seventh Special Session. Instead, the U.S. ought to throw its full support behind policies likely to increase rather than decrease overall efficiency of the world economy." The political trend among world organizations appears well designed to raise levels of conflict, extend the range of intractable conflicts, and obstruct the useful development of the world's resources. The current trend penalizes energies devoted to productive expansion of human welfare and rewards political activities addressed to the manipulation of wealth transfers. It appears increasingly urgent for the U.S. to reconsider a policy which blandly accepts a trend obstructing the increase in the world's wealth through the mechanism of arbitrary transfers. It should use whatever influence it possesses to develop a reasoned alternative well designed to raise the nations' wealth and human welfare.

The second paper looks in detail at a subsidiary organization of the United Nations, the Economic Commission for Latin America (ECLA). Rolf S. Luders (Banco Hipotecario de Chile and Catholic University of Chile) examines governing conceptions, the range of policies, proposals and recommendations, and the impact of the Commission on Latin American economic policies.

The major conception and concern of ECLA was based on a specific view of the relative position of Latin American economies in the world economy. "The most important and original work done by ECLA starts out with this dichotomy. The center (the U.S., Japan, and perhaps Europe) is economically developed. . . .The periphery (Latin America, Africa, Asia) is composed of poor countries which. . .produce raw materials for the center and whose technological development is scarce." [Emphasis in the original.] The study of the interrelation between center and periphery formed the core of ECLA's approach to policy recommendations and shaped the program of industrialization via import substitution, foreign aid, technical assistance, and related proposals.

Import substitution as an instrument of economic development was used, according to the author, for two distinct purposes. One involved industrialization within an integrated economic area, potentially all Latin American economies. The other emphasized the development of industrial exports to the center countries and the rest of the world. ECLA sought to broaden the market for regional industries by encouraging the formation of regional economic units and by seeking preferential tariff treatment from the center countries. The general planning approach favored by the Commission was not acceptable to the members. Instead, they developed an extensive and detailed system of government intervention in the market. Controls over foreign trade, restrictions on foreign exchange holdings and the foreign exchange market, and the fixing of prices and wages were common.

4

There can be little doubt that Latin America experienced, on average, substantial economic progress during a major part of the postwar period. The ECLA model, based on import substitution, gradually lost its appeal, however, for the member countries. A search for new ideas and programs started. The Commission acted more as a passive adjuster to newly evolving ideas than as a leader of the search. This change in role reflected the increase in the number of professionally trained economists in Latin America outside ECLA.

The Commission's monopoly on the supply of economic programs was eroded. A major shift occurred. The emphasis on import substitution changed following the insistence by non-ECLA economists that import substitution programs have high social cost. Countries adopted policies to promote exports.

In recent years, ECLA increasingly stressed the importance of "social development" instead of "economic development." This emphasis was intended to support measures lowering the inequality of income distribution and to reinforce the belief that economic progress left the poorest groups in the country with unchanged or low relative incomes. Concern with social development led to a growing alignment with the ideas and demands for a New International Economic Order.

Luders offers a critical appraisal of the Commission's policy proposals. It is noteworthy that even before ECLA a series of persistent balance of payments problems "induced the governments to raise customs duties on imports of industrial products. These measures, in fact, started the import substitution process. The remaining policies were then adopted one by one to solve the different problems which the import substitution process brought about. . . .The Commission provided a rationalization for the. . .process."

The Commission's rationalization started from the observation of chronic balance of payments difficulties in the region. The Commission rejected any monetary explanation of endemic balance of payments problems and centered its explanation on real aspects of the interrelation between "center" and "periphery." Chronic deficits were said to result from the movement of the terms of trade brought about by technological change. "The essence of the argument is that the gains from technological progress in the production of basic raw materials and foodstuffs are passed on to the consumers via a reduction in the price of the product, while the same gains in the production of industrial goods are translated into higher incomes for the producers of these goods." Luders then examines in detail the various arguments advanced by the Commission "for this curious behavior of the gains from technological development." Luders finds it unfortunate that ECLA "induced, or reinforced,

5

wrong economic policies in many Latin American countries." The reader will find a detailed critique of ECLA's governing policy conception and the analysis developed to support the policy programs. The translation of ECLA programs into policymaking by the member countries probably raised the social cost of the import substitution program.

Luders offers an alternative to the commercial policies proposed by ECLA. The alternative emphasizes lower levels of protection against imports, promotion of nontraditional exports, and greater integration of national economies. These recommendations are compared to the policies encouraged by ECLA.

The paper concludes with an examination of the Commission's impact on public policy in Latin America. Luders judges that the Commission exerted major influence by stimulating interest in the study of economics. The Commission's main impact on policy occurred during the first two decades of its existence when its principal role was to supply ex post rationalizations reinforcing policies of member countries and conveying a sense of coherence. The Commission's impact depended on the member countries' economic conditions and policy responses. When the demand for ECLA-type explanations faded, the Commission's influence waned. Changing conditions, growing interest in export promotion, and competition from new international organizations eroded the position of ECLA. But, the established bureaucracy remains. It is quite understandable that the "Commission is now in search of a new set of policy recommendations which might regain for ECLA some of the past preeminence."

National Policies

Brazil and Mexico were selected for a study of the influence of national policies or institutions on an economy's performance. Carlos Geraldo Langoni and Edy Luiz Kogut (Fundacão Getulio Vargas, Rio de Janeiro) explore the Brazilian experiment. The authors start by surveying Brazilian developments during the period 1964-1975 with particular attention given to the policies "to control inflation and to open the economy." A brief review of the behavior of the Brazilian economy acquaints the reader with the broad facts. The rate of real growth for gross domestic product averaged 7.5 percent during the period considered and ranged between a minimum of 2.7 percent (1965) and a maximum of 11.4 percent (1973). Inflation measured only 7 percent per annum in 1957, mounted to 91.9 percent in 1964, fell to 15.1 percent in 1973, and accelerated an estimated 46 percent for 1976. It appears that the broad sweep of inflation was driven by the long-run patterns of monetary growth. The latter was dominated by the behavior of the monetary base. The proportion of imports relative to gross product fell from about 13 percent immediately after the war to 8 percent in 1958-1961. It fell even further to about 6 percent over the years 1962-1967. But a "change in the development strategy directed toward a substantial opening of the economy" raised the import proportion to 12 percent by 1974.

The factual background demonstrates the importance of inflation and exports. The middle section of the paper discusses the policies for coping with inflation and the promotion of exports. As Larry Sjaastad (Chicago) notes in his comments on the papers by Langoni and Kogut and Luders, the Brazilian experience with growth, inflation, and exports probably did "more to discredit ECLA than all the attacks of academic economists over a period of nearly two decades."

The government's budgetary policies played a central role in Brazilian inflation prior to 1964. "Until 1964, the government deficit was the largest source of monetary expansion. In fact, early in the 1960s, when inflation rates accelerated, the government deficit increased from 2.8 percent of GDP in 1960 to 4.2 percent of GDP in 1963." After 1964, government deficits declined in importance as a source of the expansion in the monetary base. Langoni and Kogut emphasize that "there is no doubt that the government deficits were extremely important in the 1962-64 period when inflation reached its peak."

The Brazilian approach to inflation control concentrated on the budget. A variety of measures lowered the deficit and the Central Bank's rate of monetization of public expenditures. The determined assault on the budget deficit also contributed to moderate inflationary expectations. Brazil also instituted some price controls, as most governments do in inflationary circumstances. The authors find, however, no "clear evidence of the net contribution of price controls to curbing inflation."

Attention is given to the extensive experience with indexation of financial assets and the resulting effect on credit markets. Two indexation procedures, ex post and ex ante indexation, are distinguished. These differences affect relative demands for the assets involved in periods of accelerating or decelerating inflation. Indexation also produced, in conjunction with price controls, substantial distortions. Some of the problems attributed to indexation are properly attributable to the specific implementation and the operation of price controls in an indexed economy.

Major changes in policy affected Brazil's foreign trade. "From the end of World War II to 1964, Brazil followed a typically inward-looking model of economic growth based on the substitution of manufactured imports." Policy was reversed subsequently, based on the belief that an opening of the economy with expanding exports would accelerate Brazilian development. The policies fostering import substitutions were based on several fallacies that ECLA promoted. First, import substitution was expected to alleviate balance of payments difficulties. Actual experiences falsified these expectations. Second, Brazil as a primary producer was said to be unable to develop new exports or expand old lines of exports. Again, experience contradicted these beliefs. ECLA taught that prices of primary products should fall. There was no long-term trend lowering the prices of Brazil's primary products. Contrary to ECLA, Brazilian agriculture responded to economic incentives, so increases in demand raised price and quantity produced. In these and other respects, the Brazilian experience ran counter to ECLA doctrines. The authors argue that Brazilian exchange rate policy deserves major attention; it was "a key factor in explaining the growth of exports of basic products."

The new acceleration of inflation since 1973 suggests the emergence of a new set of problems confronting the Brazilian economy. Langoni and Kogut discuss prevailing problems. These long-run problems "include the increasing participation of the state in the economy and the controversial question of the inequality in the distribution of income. Short-run problems are the balance of payments disequilibrium and the acceleration of inflation." Increased involvement of the state in the economy occurred independently of political regime. This involvement has, so far, not discouraged private investment, but the authors wonder how long the process of government growth can continue without obstructing the private sector of the economy. The growing complexity of economic legislation and institutional arrangements fostered by the government sector raise costs and increase uncertainty for the private sector.

The evolution of income distribution is an explosive political issue in Brazil, as elsewhere. All groups appear to have benefited from economic growth, but the higher income groups apparently gained proportionately more. The increasing inequality occurred mostly in the urban centers with the highest rate of growth. Examination shows the income distribution does not reveal a frozen social structure. The association of skewness with rapid real growth suggests a longer-run adjustment in a "disequilibrium process."

New balance of payments deficits and accelerating inflation confronted the monetary authorities with old problems in a new context. The new surge of inflation seems less powered by budget deficits than the earlier inflation. A large accumulation of foreign reserves resulting from capital inflows expanded the monetary base. Implementation of an anti-inflationary monetary policy was apparently obstructed by maintenance of an interest target policy which prevents suitable action to control the monetary base, so inflationary potential rose even before the oil crisis. After 1974, domestic credit expansion replaced foreign reserves as the driving source of the monetary base. The advances made by the Bank of Brazil to the private sector rose spectacularly, and were accompanied by a massive increase in the balance of payments deficit.

Effective policies to lower inflation and eliminate the deficit had not been undertaken at the time the paper was written. The authors express some concern that the last round of balance of payments difficulties may evolve into a repetition of ECLA-type policies tried in the 1950s and early 1960s with little benefit for Brazilian economic development.

The second paper on the role of national policies studies an institutional problem of fundamental importance. The role of property rights and the nature of incentives affecting agents and determining their effort is often neglected in the literature on economic development. Arthur De Vany (Texas A&M) considers a narrow and well-defined aspect of the general problem of property rights by examining the impact of land tenure in Mexico on the use of available resources and agricultural output.

Mexican agriculture is organized in two principal sectors, a private sector and an ejido sector. In the latter sector, land is made available by the government to landless laborers. The land is obtained by expropriation from the private sector. The land allotted to the laborers in the ejido system remains the property of the state. The laborer acquires only the right to use the land for a limited period.

The tools developed in standard two-sector analysis are used to explore the implications of the ejido system. Private ownership induces the owner to maximize profits on his land. The incentives under the ejido system induce an adjustment of the number of land users (and thus the size of an average farm) equilibrating real wage bill and product on the ejido.

De Vany's analysis yields some far-reaching implications. The interaction between the two sectors determines an inefficient solution. Neither marginal product of labor nor the marginal product of land tends to be equalized between the sectors. "The source of inefficiency is the labor allocation mechanism under

9

the incentive provided by the usufruct form of land tenure. Under this system, so long as there is free entry, labor enters the ejido sector until its average product therein equals its marginal product in the private sector." An increase in the amount of land allotted to the ejido system raises the volume of labor in this system, raises real wages in both sectors, and lowers land rent in the private sector. The ejido system thus sacrifices efficiency in resource utilization in order to achieve a redistribution of income.

The analysis requires a careful distinction between the effects of an existing land reform program and the effects of changes in the amount of land in the reform sector. These distinctions produce the following result. "Relative to the efficiency locus, the land reform locus is inefficient, and is characterized by too low a land/labor ratio in the ejido sector, too high a land/labor ratio in the private sector, lower land rents, higher wage rates, and less output relative to the efficient outcome. From a starting point at which some amount of land is in ejidos, a further allocation of land to the ejido will raise the land/labor ratio in both. . .sectors, raise the wage rate, and lower land rents, but may increase or decrease the amount of output."

In his comment on the paper, David Henderson (Rochester) argues that the analysis stops too soon. Once the farmer obtains the land, he has an incentive to reduce the labor he supplies. He can do this unless enforcement costs are low and the state insists on performance.

De Vany surveys earlier empirical work on the problem. It confirms the principal implication--a relatively higher land/labor ratio on private farms and the approximate equality between average product in the ejido and the marginal product on private farms. An extension of the model in order to include real capital reveals another source of inefficiency. The marginal product of capital also differs in the two sectors.

The implications of the analysis bear on standard assertions about the efficiency of agriculture in the "traditional sector" of less developed countries. Agriculture in less developed countries is said to have a dual structure. Efficient private farms and small inefficient family farms coexist. The marginal product of labor on the family farms is said to be near zero; there is "surplus labor" in agriculture.

De Vany indicates that the tenancy rights of the traditional sector should not be overlooked. If families in the traditional sector operate their holdings on a usufruct basis, alternative wage opportunities tend to be equated with the average product on the farm. The marginal product of labor in maximizing households is driven close to zero. If these families "owned their land outright, they would never drive the marginal product of labor below the wage, even if they were to pool income to maximize average income per family member. It is clearly important, therefore, to examine the form of land tenancy rights. . . before drawing any conclusions about the efficiency of the traditional agricultural sector."

Some Lessons of Economic History

Two economic historians contributed papers that differ markedly in perception and emphasis. Both attend to important aspects of economic growth and development. Douglass North (University of Washington) surveys a vast landscape of historical experience. Paul A. David (Stanford) attempts to separate the roles of invention and accumulation in U.S. growth during the nineteenth century. Edward F. Denison (The Brookings Institution) and John W. Kendrick (George Washington) comment on the two papers.

The broad sweep of history should convey the operation of dominant institutional arrangements shaping the structure of incentives affecting economic agents at different times and places. North directs our attention to the variations in incentives to undertake productive activity. Such variations are usually associated with major institutional or organizational changes in a society. The paper explores therefore "some major turning points in institutional organization in the history of the Western world." Some implications of this approach for the study of economic growth are also considered.

The Neolithic revolution leading to the development of settled agriculture is the first of the major turning points examined. North stresses that the rapid development after this revolution proceeded at a rate strikingly different from the minuscule progress over millions of years. The explanation of this "inflectional change" in human progress poses an intellectual challenge not satisfactorily answered, in the author's judgment, by the existing anthropological and archaeological literature. An explanation is sought in population growth and diminishing returns. North adduces that population was probably growing and gradually lowered the returns from hunting and gathering. Cultivation of plants and breeding of livestock appeared increasingly attractive.

The change in the relative attractiveness of different activities induced the development of new property rights. Deliberate cultivation was associated with exclusionary property rights minimizing the externalities otherwise imposed by common property. The incentive to cultivate would not survive in the absence of an exclusive property right to the return from the efforts and

11

resources invested. "The development of a set of property rights around animals and plants involves some form of organized defense." Moreover, the evolution of irrigation required social coordination and organizational structure.

Associated with these developments, extensive division of labor emerges with highly specialized crafts and skills all requiring further adaptations in the form and structure of property rights. Wider trading areas and the formation of states manned by specialists in specifying and enforcing rules of the game followed. The nature of the property rights emerging in this process is still disputed, and North recognizes that "relatively little is known about the structure of property rights in earlier times." But, North suggests that a new approach to earliest history should "focus on the creative role that government played in innovating the basic rules of the game which provided incentive for economic expansion."

The cycle of civilizations observed over the millenia is explainable, according to North, with the aid of two broad themes: the "barbarians at the gate" and population growth combined with diminishing returns. Both events mobilized social pressures, modified property rights, and, consequently, changed economic incentives. These themes North applies with particular force to the story of the Roman Empire.

The medieval experience begins with a puzzle for North's argument. There is a decline in the political-economic unit in the area once occupied by the Romans. But, the basic theme resumes in the post-medieval years. Population growth produced "two diametrically opposed pressures for institutional change." Factor endowments were "increasingly differentiated" and potential gains from trade rose correspondingly. The realization of such potential gains required institutional adjustments lowering transaction costs and risks. Population growth also lowered returns in agriculture and brought induced pressures on existing land tenure systems. Changes in the structure of property rights were slow and delayed. Differences in the rate of change, however, are consistent with differences in development, as in England and Spain.

Changes in the technology of warfare affected the relative survival probability of political-economic units of different sizes and, thus, changed the size of political units. Technology, population pressures on land, and other factors North cites induced gradual institutional change. In England and the Netherlands, the changes encouraged economic growth. In Spain, they produced stagnation and economic decline.

The Industrial Revolution opened a new and remarkable phase of human history. Innovation accelerated. North speculates "that the capturability of returns to innovation rose" to a large extent as a consequence of major political developments. The accumulation of scientific knowledge abetted the development, but poses another problem for North. There seems to be no adequate explanation for the expanding investment in this "pure public good."

North sees history as a sequence of crises engendered by changes in population and technology, producing economic changes and requiring institutional changes. The author conjectures that "most societies. . .never developed a structure of property rights that encouraged economic growth." Those societies with an initial development experienced changes in institutions leading to the replacement of institutions and to eventual decline. North concludes his sweeping survey with some paragraphs that summarize the major gaps in our knowledge and pose a challenge for economists and historians.

Paul David's paper concentrates our vision both in time and method of procedure. The author examines the role of invention and accumulation in the growth of the U.S. economy during the nineteenth century. Some broad facts of U.S. history set the frame for David's account. The growth rate of long-term per capita output accelerated from the first to the second half of the nineteenth century. This acceleration lowered the time required for doubling the level of real output from 60 to 40 years. The change cannot be attributed to the trend behavior in total factor productivity.

David asks, "How and why did this unspectacular but eminently successful transition to a modern rate of economic progress come about?" An answer is developed with the aid of the neoclassic production function. Production is assumed to be governed by the following function.

$$(1) \quad Y = [a(E_L L)^{1-1/\sigma} + \beta(E_K K)^{1-1/\sigma}]^{\frac{\sigma(1-\theta_R)}{\sigma-1}} [E_R R]^{\theta_R},$$

where total output (Y) depends on labor (L), real capital (K), and non-reproducible resources (R); σ designates the substitution elasticity between labor and capital; a and β are distributional coefficients. Technological progress is manifest by changing the efficiency of the three primary factors of production, L, K, and R. The "Progress of Invention" appears as a pure factor-augmenting change. The growth of inputs measured in efficiency units $(E_L L, E_K K, E_R R)$ differs in general from their growth rate in natural units.

The class of production functions defined by (1) yields the following relation used in standard accounting for growth patterns.

$$(2) \qquad \overset{*}{Y} = (\theta_L \overset{*}{E}_L + \theta_K \overset{*}{E}_K + E_R \overset{*}{E}_R) + \theta_L \overset{*}{L} + \theta_K \overset{*}{K} + \theta_R \overset{*}{R},$$

where asterisks denote proportionate growth rates and θ_L and θ_K are elasticities corresponding to the elasticity θ_R. For purposes of a manageable analysis, the author imposes a simplifying assumption generalizing the condition of Harrod neutrality. This implies that the first term in (2) is reduced to the expression $\theta_L \overset{*}{L}$. The rate of total factor productivity growth can thus be interpreted to reflect the effect of labor augmentation. With constant returns to scale a further transformation yields

$$(3) \qquad \overset{*}{Y} = \overset{*}{L} + \overset{*}{E}_L + \frac{\theta_R}{\theta_L}(\overset{*}{R} - \overset{*}{Y}) + \frac{\theta_K}{\theta_L}(\overset{*}{K} - \overset{*}{Y}).$$

David next decomposes the growth rate into two components, the natural rate of growth G and the contribution from the rate of traverse between equilibrium paths. The rate of traverse is a disequilibrium phenomenon associated with a motion between steady states and reflected by changing patterns of the economy's capital intensity. The resulting expression is

$$(4) \qquad \overset{*}{Y} = G + \frac{\theta_K}{\theta_L} \overset{*}{v} \qquad v = \frac{K}{Y}$$

and $\quad G = (\overset{*}{L} + \overset{*}{E}_L)\left\{\dfrac{\theta_L}{1-\theta_K}\right\} + \overset{*}{R}\left\{\dfrac{\theta_R}{1-\theta_K}\right\}.$

The decomposition of measured rates of change into the components of $\overset{*}{Y}$ and G is used to study four major periods (1800-1835, 1835-1855, 1855-1890, 1890-1905). A pattern emerges. The contribution of the "traversing motion" was negligible in the first and last period but dominant in the period 1835-1890. The movement toward a higher capital/output ratio dominated the growth of labor productivity and "constituted the preponderant source of the quickening rise of per capita real product during the 55-year phase of development."

A "classical interpretation" of the traverse is attempted first using the framework of the Harrod-Domar equation relating the capital/output ratio to the rate of gross real savings. The equation describes "steady state" conditions and holds approximately before and after the period of the Grand Traverse. With the gross savings rate interpreted as the dynamic driving force, the equation implies that the capital/output ratio adjusts over time to the new conditions determined by the underlying savings patterns.

David explores the Thrift hypothesis of the Grand Traverse with skill and imagination. The data confirm an increase in the gross savings ratio during the century. Further examination is made using computations of the adjustment path of the capital/output ratio induced by the shock of shifting savings patterns. These computations show a remarkable coincidence between computed and observed capital/output ratios.

A strong confirmation of the Thrift hypothesis would strengthen an old argument that policies and institutions encouraging the flow of savings were the crucial conditions for the country's economic development. The author submits that this classic tale is not the only, and possibly not the best, explanation of the events observed during the last century. He offers an alternative account--the Progress of Invention hypothesis--centered on the nature of nonneutral technological change which he believes to be more relevant than the Thrift hypothesis.

The problem, as David presents it, is to find a reliable explanation of the increasing rate of real capital formation and the increasing capital intensity observed for many decades of the nineteenth century. This phenomenon, according to David, is the Grand Traverse from one steady state to a new steady state with higher capital intensity. The Thrift hypothesis assigns the causal force to exogenous shifts in a vertical supply curve of savings along a downward sloping investment demand curve. The Progress of Invention alternative emphasizes technologically induced shifts of the investment curve and implies that real returns on real nonhuman assets increased gradually. Real returns fell during the century, suggesting that the savings supply curve shifted out. The increase in saving partly offset the effect on real returns of an increased demand for investment.

In David's analysis, the shift in savings supply is closely associated with a decline in the relative price of fixed investment goods that accompanied the relative expansion in demand for these goods. David conjectures that the co-movements reveal a portfolio reallocation induced by changes in the relative prices of assets resulting from specific technological changes. About half of the secular decline in the real rate of return can be explained by the effect of technological changes on relative prices. The other half is tentatively explained in terms of some aspects of financial intermediation.

The case for the alternative Progress of Invention hypothesis is argued with subtlety and with revealing detail. David notes, first, that the production function implies an investment function with an absolute elasticity with respect to real returns less than unity. Second, some arguments support the nonneutral character of technical progress and particularly the pattern of capital deepening. The third, and most novel, aspect of David's argument pertains to the justification of a highly interest-elastic savings supply. This argument starts by recognizing that the standard definitions of savings and investment omit important channels of capital formation such as improvement of land and formation of human capital in a broad sense. Estimates of a net saving ratio that includes accumulation of this kind indicate that this ratio remained approximately unchanged from the beginning to the end of the century. The expansion of standard savings is interpreted as an interest-elastic reallocation process "largely instigated by technological change which, at least for a time, had the effect of raising the relative rate of return on tangible nonhuman forms of capital."

The probing conjectures and searching examinations of a "Schumpterian tale" bring David to a suggestive conclusion. "Unless domestic and foreign financial intermediaries in the public and private spheres facilitate the reallocation of a country's savings and the reshuffling of asset portfolios over time, the realized rate of return on its investments will fall farther and farther below the potential rate. This is nothing more than a familiarly classical diminishing returns phenomenon. Technological change may continually create new frontier regions which hold out the hope for sustained economic progress, but if resources become trapped in the long-exploited territories, persisting accumulation there will inexorably result in capital saturation and in the onset of the stationary state--if things go at all well."

ECONOMIC POLICY IN THE UNITED NATIONS:
A NEW INTERNATIONAL ECONOMIC ORDER?*

Rachel McCulloch

Harvard University

I. INTRODUCTION

A. A New International Economic Order?

Citizens of the advanced countries have been perplexed and dismayed by the recent mood in the United Nations. With increasing vehemence, representatives of the Third World have expressed their dissatisfaction with the pace of economic development in the poorer regions of the globe. These leaders have castigated the U.S. and other wealthy countries for their indifference to the needs and aspirations of the poor nations. Indeed, the rich countries stand accused of actively perpetuating poverty through their neocolonial economic policies.

A voting majority of poor countries in the United Nations General Assembly has sought to convert the claims of the developing nations into economic rights and the desired responses of the developed nations into duties or obligations rather than matters of discretion. As yet, the developing countries have gained control of the international machinery for publicizing and legitimizing their demands, but not of the means for compelling the developed countries to provide the tangible resources needed to carry out these programs. However, the rhetoric emanating recently from United Nations forums darkly threatens the use of new economic weapons, threats which have gained credibility in the years since the stunning economic assault on the industrialized nations by the Organization of Petroleum Exporting Countries (OPEC). A more subtle but perhaps ultimately more effective form of pressure relies on appeals to the guilt feelings of the rich by implying that their present economic status could only have been attained through past and present exploitation of the world's poor.

The often acrimonious debate between rich and poor nations has centered on Third World demands for establishment of a "New International Economic Order" (NIEO). This vaguely defined objective entails adoption of a number of economic and social proposals intended to redistribute world wealth in favor of the countries termed poor or developing. Ironically, neither designation of the

_____

*This is a revised version of the paper presented at the Conference. The extensive comments and criticisms of the Conference participants are gratefully acknowledged. I am also indebted to Jorge Dominguez, Stephen Krasner, J. Huston McCulloch, and Joseph S. Nye for their comments on the earlier version, and to Barbara Norwood and Karl Sauvant for helpful conversations.

would-be beneficiaries of these redistribution schemes is particularly appropriate. The bloc of self-styled "poor" nations includes countries with per capita incomes higher than those of a fair number of industrialized nations. Likewise, the label of "developing," accurate for some, constitutes mere wishful thinking for others better described by the older term "backward regions."

NIEO became an official part of United Nations vocabulary in May 1974, when the Sixth Special Session of the General Assembly adopted a "Declaration on the Establishment of a New International Economic Order"[1] over the objections of developed country representatives. This was followed in December 1974 by General Assembly approval of the "Charter of Economic Rights and Duties of States"[2] which spelled out in greater detail a number of principles intended to promote the establishment of the new international economic order. For the developed countries, the Charter was unacceptable in both tone and substance. Particularly objectionable were provisions affirming each state's "full permanent sovereignty" over its natural resources and economic activities, specifically including the right to nationalize foreign property under terms set by domestic rather than international law. Furthermore, while the Charter reserved to primary commodity exporting states the "right" to associate in producers' organizations, consuming nations were enjoined from common retaliatory action under the "duty" to respect that right by refraining from applying economic and political measures to limit it.

At least three distinct aspects of the NIEO deserve attention. First, there are the specific proposals which have been advanced, and--perhaps more crucial--the view of economic reality upon which they rest. Second, there is an explicit rationale for massive redistribution. And, finally, there are the changes in the role and structure of the United Nations implied by the NIEO. The specific proposals themselves contain little that is new. Most can be traced to venerable ancestors in United Nations documents dating from the early days of the organization. Some, such as the proposals regarding trade in primary commodities, predate even the founding of the United Nations. A few of the proposals are actually rather sensible and efficiency creating, such as those which call for lower barriers to trade flows. Others, such as the commodity buffer stock arrangement hotly debated at the May 1976 United Nations Conference

---

[1]General Assembly Resolution 3201 (S-VI), adopted without vote on May 1, 1974.

[2]General Assembly Resolution 3281 (XXIX), adopted on December 12, 1974 by a roll-call vote of 120 in favor to six against, with 10 abstentions.

on Trade and Development (UNCTAD IV), are potentially harmful to the world economy and perhaps even to their intended beneficiaries.

It is less the specific proposals than the way in which the overall program has been put forward that makes the NIEO unacceptable to many in the industrialized countries. The proposed measures have been justified in terms of restitution for past wrongs perpetrated under colonial, quasi-colonial, and neocolonial regimes. By rooting their reform proposals in this rationale, the advocates of the NIEO have called forth a flurry of denunciations from articulate neoconservatives like P.T. Bauer, Daniel Patrick Moynihan, and Irving Kristol.[3] These critics argue that, far from impoverishing their colonial subjects, the industrialized countries have actually been the source of much of the wealth currently to be found in Third World nations. History offers considerable support for this position; colonial ties served as the potent vehicle for international transfers of knowledge and capital. Yet the argument goes too far; the colonizers quite rationally sought out those areas which offered greatest natural advantage in terms of resource endowment or location. The landlocked countries, the regions of inhospitable climate, and the resource-poor lands are not poor merely because they missed the Midas touch of the colonial powers. However, the question of responsibility is a distracting one. Shrill demands for restitution have diverted the attention of critics from what may be a far more important issue in terms of long-range significance–the future of the United Nations as an economic policymaking body.[4]

The particular proposals included under the NIEO umbrella have shifted significantly over the past three years. However, a basic aspect of the NIEO as a whole is that it would effect an important increase in the power of the United Nations as an economic policymaking body. Interestingly, even those who have rejected many of the specific NIEO proposals have been more receptive to the general objective of investing the United Nations with greater power to make and carry out worldwide economic policy. For example, this is precisely the theme of the May 1975 report of the group of experts headed by Richard Gardner on structural reform in the United Nations.[5] In focusing on an array of specific proposals, friends and critics alike have failed to appreciate that the

---

[3]See Moynihan (1975), Kristol (1975), and Bauer (1976).

[4]Moynihan did raise this question in his much-quoted Commentary (1975) article. However, he later lost interest in the subject, having immersed himself in the broader (but related) question of the future of democracy.

[5]United Nations, A New United Nations Structure for Global Economic Co-operation (1975).

NIEO is fundamentally an attempt by the developing nations to move the locus of international economic policymaking into the United Nations, which until now has been able to play only a hortative role in determining changes in the international system. This raises a basic question. If the United Nations begins to exert a serious influence on world economic policy, what kind of policy is likely to be forthcoming?

This issue is examined from a number of perspectives in the sections which follow. Below, an example is used to provide a tentative characterization of the United Nations as an economic policymaking body. Section II reviews the recent economic and political developments leading up to the current confrontation in the United Nations. Section III describes the evolution and structure of the United Nations as an economic policymaking body. Section IV summarizes the substantive economic issues currently before the United Nations and attempts an assessment of the major proposals now under consideration.

B. The Economics of Restitution

In characterizing the probable consequences of an important further expansion in the capacity of the United Nations to undertake international economic policymaking, it is illuminating to begin with a case somewhat removed from the NIEO. In November 1975, just after the Seventh Special Session, the General Assembly passed Resolution 3391 (XXX), entitled "Restitution of works of art to countries victims of expropriation."[6] The resolution was passed by a majority of 96 to none, with 16 abstentions. It calls on members "to make restitution of works of art, monuments, museum pieces, manuscripts, and documents, which are part of a nation's cultural heritage, to their countries of origin." Recognizing a special obligation incumbent upon countries which have acquired valuable works of art as a result of colonial rule or military occupation, the resolution affirms that "prompt restitution of such objects, without charge, was calculated to strengthen international cooperation inasmuch as it constituted reparation for damage done." A similar resolution adopted in 1973 was largely ignored.[7] For this reason, the 25 sponsoring nations decided that the General Assembly should reiterate its appeal.

In introducing the resolution on behalf of the sponsoring nations, Zaire said that restitution of works of art should be understood in terms of the role they could play in awakening each people to its own identity and creative genius. Egypt, a co-sponsor, urged prompt restitution of works of art removed

---

[6]See UN Monthly Chronicle, December 1975.

[7]General Assembly Resolution 3187 (XXVIII).

during colonial administrations. Greece urged the termination of the practice of removing works of art from any country under any pretext.[8] Poland and the Byelorussian S.S.R. recalled the destruction of their cultural heritage by Nazi invaders. Algeria stated that it had been plundered on the eve of independence.

On the whole, the tone of the resolution and the implied view of economic transactions give a surprisingly accurate picture of United Nations policy on broader economic issues. In terms of its economic content, the resolution has four noteworthy features. (a) Property relationships. The resolution contains an implicit assumption that a broad class of present property relationships necessarily reflects past exploitation. No attempt is made to distinguish acquisitions made through force or theft from routine legitimate purchases, or even removal to protect treasures from destruction in time of war or natural disaster. There is an automatic presumption that restitution or reparation is due. Since the property rights in question are viewed as illegitimate, they can be arbitrarily reassigned. Furthermore, private property rights are now seen to exclude the right to transfer ownership to foreigners. (b) Intent. The primary aim of the resolution is to promote a redistribution of wealth between developed countries and developing countries. (c) Price. In the resolution, price serves a distributive rather than an allocative function. The "just price" for this transaction is set at zero, a determination based on the relative wealth of the transactors. (d) Economic efficiency. By casting into doubt the status of future transactions, the resolution whittles away the possible mutual gains from future exchange. A developing country may well wish to trade a few treasures for a few tractors. The would-be partner to such a transaction is deterred at least marginally by this devaluation of the security of property relations. As with many United Nations proposals, the attempt to get a bigger piece of the pie leads to a shrinking pie.

The emphasis on redistribution, rejection of price as a mechanism of resource allocation, failure to appreciate the economic function of secure property rights, and other similar features have been interpreted by some critics as evidence of a coherent socialist philosophy at work within the United Nations.[9] However, this characterization appears to be valid only in the very limited sense that nearly all religious and philosophical systems must be regarded as socialistic. The functions performed by property rights, prices, and markets

---

[8]This would include, one must assume, saving the Parthenon friezes from being burned for lime.

[9]See, for example, Moynihan (1975).

are not well understood even by those who uphold the principle of the free market. The failure of United Nations delegates to challenge myths about the capitalist system appears to mirror the general lack of sophistication on this subject in other intellectual discourse.[10]

Apart from its characteristic economic underpinnings, the resolution also serves as an example of current United Nations effectiveness as a policy-making body. The measure was passed by an overwhelming majority of countries, 96-0. As in many other cases, the majority comprised the developing nation members along with some sympathetic Second World countries; the abstainers were all industrialized nations. However, despite the overwhelming majority approval (on two separate occasions), the resolution has had no effect. The General Assembly, sometimes given the benign label "Town Meeting of the World," has no power to enforce its policy recommendations except to the extent that resolutions deal with the operation of the United Nations itself. The current situation in which poor nations have a vast majority of the votes and rich nations pay the bulk of the total cost of the operation affords little or no possibility for the United Nations to force an objectionable policy upon the developed countries. The NIEO would enhance the ability of the majority to implement policies without changing the basic character of the policies chosen.

II. POLITICAL EVOLUTION OF THE DEBATE

A. Realignment of Perceptions

Few of the specific proposals advanced as part of the NIEO can be called new. What is new about NIEO is that these proposals are now receiving the serious consideration of the industrialized countries, without whose active cooperation little reordering of the international economy is likely to come about. Heightened attention to the expressed needs and desires of the developing nations followed closely on the heels of the 1973 Arab oil embargo and the subsequent success of OPEC in achieving spectacular increases in the price of oil. These events have had far-reaching repercussions.

First, the OPEC venture altered drastically the perceptions of Third World countries concerning their own economic prospects. In marked contrast to the hardship and national sacrifice stressed in traditional development success stories, the OPEC members had benefited from a process entailing rapid results and minimal effort--indeed an irresistible combination. The possibility of achieving instantly the desired results of economic development through a

---

[10]For a sophisticated and tough-minded presentation of the case for capitalism, see Brunner (1976).

redistribution of existing wealth, rather than through the far slower process of creating new wealth, presented a fresh and alluring vision of the future. The OPEC route to prosperity also had a second virtue which no doubt strengthened its appeal in the eyes of Third World leaders. Unlike traditional development strategies, prosperity brought about largely through higher export prices requires little internal economic transformation and, thus, far less risk of political instability and challenges to current leadership.

OPEC's successes also conveyed an eloquent message to the industrialized countries. The OPEC members had managed to engineer a vast improvement in their joint fortunes without the assistance or consent of their "benefactors." This outcome had a predictable impact upon the perceived balance of economic power between the industrialized bloc and the Third World. While perhaps only a minority in the developed countries continue to view OPEC as the first in a continuing sequence of successful producer cartels controlling world flows of raw materials, many more have acknowledged the latent collective power of the supplier nations to impose serious if temporary dislocations on the international system.

Without OPEC's dramatic show of force, it seems unlikely that the NIEO could have moved so swiftly to the forefront of world affairs. However, much of the tone and substance of the current confrontation between the industrialized countries of the "North" and the developing nations of the "South" had already been set by the time of the Arab oil embargo. The confrontation of the rich nations by the poor nations, long implicit in international economic relations, became highly visible at the Summit Conference of Non-Aligned Nations held in Algiers in September 1973. Only the fourth international meeting of the nonaligned since the 1955 call by Tito, Nehru, and others for a "third position" in the cold war, the conference was far larger than its predecessors. Participants included leaders of 76 nonaligned states, as well as observers representing at least a dozen other countries and national liberation movements. Convened by Algerian President Boumedienc with the express purpose of formulating a common economic position for its members, the conference marked a shift of the nonaligned movement from political to economic issues as its primary organizing principle.

The theme of the conference was expressed by banners proclaiming, "Poor of the world, unite!" A draft declaration prepared by the Algerians urged the world's majority to rid themselves of the colonial yoke, to achieve real independence by eliminating foreign monopolies and assuming control of natural resources.[11] Conference participants stressed the gains to the Third World from solidarity in confrontations with the industrialized nations. An economic declaration issued on the last day emphasized two specific economic goals: improved terms of trade for commodity exporters and full national control over natural resources. The declaration urged member nations to form producer associations for major products "to halt the degradation of their terms of trade, to eliminate harmful activities by multinational companies, and to reinforce their negotiating power."[12]

While economics dominated the agenda at Algiers, the Arab states introduced a number of political issues as well. Highest on the list was unified action against Israel, but Asian and Latin American representatives, mainly interested in common economic action, declined to support Arab proposals for economic sanctions.[13] And, although the conference took place just a short time prior to the Arab oil embargo, the use of oil or other commodities as political weapons was not discussed. However, the success of OPEC in achieving steady increases in the producers' share of oil profits was cited as an example of the economic benefits to be derived from common action through commodity producers' associations.

Neither the issue of terms of trade nor that of full control over natural resources by the developing nations was new. The alleged deterioration of the terms of trade experienced by raw material producers was stressed by followers of Dr. Raúl Prebisch, first Secretary-General of UNCTAD. Sovereignty over natural resources and the accompanying right to nationalize foreign holdings and determine compensation under national rather than international law had been the subject of General Assembly debates since 1962. Even the strategy of common economic action had long been favored by the so-called Group of 77, the semi-official caucus of developing nations in UNCTAD. The real significance of the Algiers conference lies in the emergence of a clear North-South polarity, a conscious political decision to pit the underdeveloped world against the industrialized world, whether capitalist or communist.[14]

---

[11]New York Times, September 3, 1973.

[12]New York Times, September 11, 1973.

[13]New York Times, September 10, 1973.

[14]However, the substance of the nonaligned economic position clearly predates Algiers. See Jankowitsch and Sauvant (1976).

B. Development of the Issues

The Algiers conference of nonaligned nations marked the beginning of a two-year episode of intensified North-South confrontation over economic issues, both within the United Nations and in other international forums. However, the underlying areas of conflict had been established much earlier in such documents as the General Assembly's 1961 resolution designating a United Nations Development Decade.[15] That document provides an interesting comparison with more recent resolutions bearing on the same basic issue of international economic cooperation for development. The 1961 resolution reviewed in positive terms the progress already made through the efforts of both developed and developing countries but noted a growing gap between per capita incomes in the rich and poor nations. The resolution called for intensified efforts on the part of both; an overall objective of a minimum annual rate of growth of aggregate national income of 5 percent was set. The specific recommendations included policies to assure primary commodity exporters the opportunity to sell more of their products at "stable and remunerative prices," as a means of providing greater opportunity for self-financing of economic development. Likewise, the resolution called for policies to "ensure to the developing countries an equitable share of earnings from the extraction and marketing of their natural resources by foreign capital, in accordance with generally accepted reasonable earnings on invested capital." An accompanying resolution called for substantial increases in the flow of international assistance, to "reach as soon as possible approximately 1 percent of the combined national incomes of the economically advanced countries."

An interesting feature of the resolutions passed in conjunction with the United Nations Development Decade is the absence of certain important rhetorical elements present in most recent United Nations documents. The poverty of the Third World is nowhere attributed to past or present colonial or neocolonial exploitation by the industrialized countries. There is no call to "redress existing injustices." Rather, the resolutions affirm past progress while urging both rich and poor nations to intensify their efforts. Likewise, calls for international measures to supplant markets are also absent. The market appears in the resolutions as a positive force for development, impeded in its benign function by tariffs and other trade barriers. Many of the specific recommendations made in the resolutions constitute movements toward freer trade. Especially notable in this connection is the resolution on "International

---

[15] General Assembly Resolution 1715 (XVI), December 19, 1961. Also see Resolutions 1706-1720 adopted the same day.

trade as the primary instrument of economic development."[16]

The Development Decade saw major institutional evolution within the United Nations as the organization responded to pressures from the new majority of developing nations.[17] The mammoth United Nations Conference on Trade and Development held in Geneva in 1964 shifted world attention at least transiently to the needs and objectives of the Third World. But substantive accomplishments were few, while rising aspirations on the part of Third World leaders increased the gulf between aims and achievements. In 1970, the General Assembly passed a resolution proclaiming a second United Nations Development Decade.[18] The preamble to that document, while duly noting past efforts, expresses frustration with achievements to date. Furthermore, the growing per capita income gap between rich and poor is underlined in tones of reproach: "While a part of the world lives in great comfort or even affluence, much of the larger part suffers from abject poverty. . . ." The preamble goes on to state that the success of international development programs rests in large part on elimination of colonialism.

In terms of development objectives, the resolution on the second Development Decade goes into greater detail than its predecessors. Growth targets are set not only for national income as a whole, but for annual expansion of agriculture, manufacturing output, domestic saving, imports, and exports. In terms of policy recommendations, the section on international trade represents a move away from the strong free trade orientation of nine years before. The document proposes "a set of general principles on pricing policy" for primary commodities. Also notable in the resolution is a call for serious consideration of the establishment of a link between allocation of new Special Drawing Rights (SDR) and the provision of international development finance. This proposal reflects an increasing emphasis on the part of developing countries on resource flows which are automatic, unconditional, and untied.

By the time of the third United Nations Conference on Trade and Development in 1972, an air of increasing militancy was evident in the Group of 77, by then including nearly one hundred less developed countries (LDC). Strong dissatisfaction was expressed with U.S. delays in implementing the Generalized System of Preferences. The LDC view of the industrialized world-- and of the U.S. in particular--as its willing partner in efforts to promote economic development had been seriously eroded. That erosion resulted from

---

[16]General Assembly Resolution 1707 (XVI), December 19, 1961.

[17]See section III for a detailed account.

[18]General Assembly Resolution 2626 (XXV), October 24, 1970.

both unrealistic expectations in the Third World and the primary preoccupation of developed country policymakers with their own national concerns. The combined effect was to strengthen the emerging position that development could only be achieved if the developing countries themselves gained a more significant role in international institutions, a process which had already begun in the United Nations during the previous decade. The stage was now set for a major LDC challenge to the economic and political power of the industrialized world. Rather than continuing to argue over the size of their slice of the world economic pie, the developing nations now looked for control of the knife.[19]

C. Confrontation and Escalation

Press coverage of the Fourth Summit Conference of Non-Aligned Countries at Algiers emphasized an apparent lack of unity of purpose among the members represented. Much attention was given to doubts expressed by some conferees themselves concerning the feasibility of carrying out common action for economic or political ends.[20] However, the capacity of the non-aligned to take unified action to achieve joint objectives was swiftly reassessed by the industrialized world just weeks later when the Arab oil embargo began. The subsequent quadrupling of the world price of oil convinced the richer nations that it might be timely to give developing country grievances a fresh hearing. While the primary concern of the industrialized countries was to negotiate a reduction in the price of oil from its unprecedented new level, the producing nations demanded that the agenda of any conference to discuss oil prices include other commodities as well.

Meanwhile, other raw material producers emulated the tactic of joint action so successfully exploited by OPEC. In the favorable climate of strong demand fueled by rapid economic growth in the developed nations, new producers' organizations bargained aggressively to get higher prices for their raw material exports. While none of these efforts was as spectacularly successful as the OPEC coup, some developed country observers noted the successes and argued that it was only a matter of time until effective cartels would exercise control over the markets for most primary products.[21]

In early 1974, the General Assembly unanimously decided to hold a Sixth Special Session to discuss raw materials and development, even though a

---

[19]See Gregg (1972).

[20]New York Times, September 4-12, 1973.

[21]Bergsten (1974a, 1974b) was the leading proponent of this view.

special session on development[22] and economic cooperation was already scheduled for 1975. The Sixth Special Session, held in April and May 1974, thus became the first to be devoted principally to economic issues. The "Declaration on the Establishment of a New International Economic Order,"[23] adopted without a vote at that session over the objections of the U.S., Germany, France, Japan, and the U.K., brought into the United Nations many of the attitudes and aims which had been expressed a few months earlier at Algiers. For the developed countries, the most significant sections of the Declaration were those affirming "full permanent sovereignty of every State over its natural resources and all economic activities," including the right to nationalize foreign-owned property under domestic law; the right to "restitution and full compensation for the exploitation and depletion" of resources; and the right to regulate and supervise activities of multinational corporations in the national interest. The Charter of Economic Rights and Duties of States,[24] adopted over the objections of the U.S. and other developed countries by the General Assembly in its regular session a few months later, added fuel to the fire by reserving to developing nations the right to form commodity exporters' associations in order to pursue common economic and political ends while appending the duty of consuming nations to refrain from measures which would limit the effectiveness of producers' groups.

The Conference of Developing Countries on Raw Materials, held in Dakar in February 1975, reaffirmed the principles of Algiers and added a call for establishment of an indexation mechanism to "maintain and strengthen the purchasing power" of commodity exporting nations.[25] Also emphasized in the Dakar Action Program on raw materials were measures to increase processing of raw materials in developing countries, to improve the competitive position of natural products versus synthetics, and to promote diversification of the economies of developing nations. Furthermore, the conference "invited" industrialized nations to agree to a moratorium on debt contracted by the developing nations until their development objectives had been achieved, as well as rescheduling or outright cancellation of debts contracted on "unfavorable terms."

---

[22]IMF Survey, September 29, 1975.

[23]General Assembly Resolution 3201 (S-VI).

[24]General Assembly Resolution 3281 (XXIX).

[25]The Action Program and resolutions on economic matters of the Dakar conference are reproduced from UNCTAD (1975a) in International Legal Materials, March/April 1975.

The Second General Conference of the United Nations Industrial Development Organization (UNIDO) held in Lima the following month produced the "Lima Declaration"[26] reaffirming most of the Dakar proposals and setting a specific and ambitious target for industrialization of the developing nations. Noting that the developing nations constitute about 60 percent of world population while production of manufactured goods in those countries makes up only about 7 percent of the world total, the Lima Declaration called for an increase in that share to 25 percent by the year 2000. This announced goal caused chagrin in western Europe and the U.S. as industrialists there envisioned manufacturing capacity idled by competition from Third World exports.[27] These reactions largely failed to take into account the expansion of developing country purchasing power which would inevitably accompany such a dramatic growth of industrial output–the degree to which developed country production of manufactures would be displaced rather than augmented could be quite small.

Did the frequent repetition and elaboration of unrealistic and even outrageous demands reflect the inexperience and lack of sophistication of the new leaders of the Third World coalition? Or were they part of an effective strategy for wresting economic concessions from indifferent or hostile governments in the industrialized nations? Some years hence, the autobiographies and posthumously published diaries of elder statesmen el-Qaddafi, Bouteflika, and Echeverria may yield some insights into the significance of this interesting historical period. However, in terms of results, the techniques appear to have been at least somewhat effective.

In early 1975, members of the European Economic Community (EEC) endorsed the Lomé Convention with 46 African, Caribbean, and Pacific developing nations. Among the far-reaching provisions of this package was an export earnings stabilization scheme for primary commodity producers.[28] Then, in the spring and summer of 1975, a series of speeches by Secretary of State Kissinger signalled a thaw in American policy toward the Third World. In particular, the speeches indicated U.S. willingness to consider commodity agreements on a "commodity-by-commodity" basis.[29] Although the concessions fell far short of LDC demands, representatives of developing nations privately

---

[26] Reprinted in UN Monthly Chronicle, May 1975.

[27] See Janssen (1976), in which he reports on European reaction to UNIDO's announced target.

[28] For details, see Bywater (1975).

[29] On the change in the U.S. position, see Frank (1975).

indicated their willingness to back down on some issues in exchange for positive moves on the part of the U.S. As the Seventh Special Session of the General Assembly approached, the State Department spent a frenzied summer formulating specific proposals which could gain the approval of both the developing nations and free market-oriented Treasury officials. Secretary Kissinger's speech, delivered at the Seventh Special Session by U.S. Ambassador Moynihan, was less important for the comprehensive package of economic proposals it contained than as the first clear signal that the U.S. was willing to make some concrete concessions to Third World demands.

III. ECONOMICS IN THE UNITED NATIONS

A. Transformation of United Nations Membership and Focus

The developing countries are now seeking an important increase in the power of the United Nations to determine economic policy for the international community—a change which would enhance their collective leverage in the world economic system. This objective implies a major transformation of the United Nations from its present status. However, the role of economics in the United Nations today is already significantly different from that envisioned by the founders.

The United Nations of 1945 was primarily an organization to secure world peace; political rather than economic issues were to be its central concern. Nevertheless, the provisions of the Charter reflected the conviction that preservation of world peace necessarily entails responsibility for world economic and social problems. Events leading to World War II had vividly underlined the contribution to political instability made by economic discontent. Thus, from the very beginning, the United Nations was supplied with a mandate for action to promote economic and social progress. However, the reality of today differs from the conception of the founders in important respects. Economic and social activities have expanded to dominate the total operating budget of the United Nations--at least four-fifths of the $1.5 billion now spent annually by the United Nations system goes to support economic and social programs.[30] Furthermore, the economic and social activities undertaken are almost entirely redistributive in character, their primary and nearly exclusive focus being the countries of the Third World. Finally, the divergence of political and economic influence within the United Nations membership has greatly undermined its effectiveness in economic and social undertakings.

---

[30]This statistic is cited in the introduction to United Nations, A New United Nations Structure for Global Economic Co-operation (1975).

Like the current drive for an NIEO, the rapid changes which have already transformed the United Nations' role in economic activities are a reflection of dramatic changes in the membership of the organization. In 1945, less developed countries exerted little independent political influence within the United Nations; today they constitute an overwhelming majority of the membership.[31] Of the newer members, most have small populations and underdeveloped economies. Insulated by their geographic remoteness and economic backwardness from the main currents of world politics, these countries have viewed participation in the United Nations primarily as a means of generating the external resource flows required to finance their internal economic transformation.

All members of the United Nations are members of the General Assembly. Each sovereign state casts one vote.[32] The number of less developed country members in the United Nations need not by itself have generated an automatic majority vote on every issue. However, remarkable solidarity has been maintained through the persistent efforts of the leaders of two largely overlapping groupings, the "nonaligned nations," in number about 110, and the Group of 77 less developed countries, also numbering over 100.[33] A group position on each issue is hammered out in private meetings; members then adhere strictly to the official position in all public and semipublic meetings. Efforts by the U.S. to appeal to particular constituents within the group, such as the "most seriously affected" (poorest) nations, have so far yielded little but frustration. Tentative private expressions of interest are rapidly followed by a public stonewall as group pressure is applied to the straying parties.

The actual powers of the General Assembly are few. The Assembly can make recommendations on any matter except those on the agenda of the Security Council, but apart from ones which concern the internal affairs of the organization, the resolutions of the General Assembly carry no legal force; they are binding neither on the member states nor on the citizens of those states.[34] The General Assembly thus functions mainly as a forum in which member states can express their views and formulate general principles for the activities of the organization.

---

[31]See Kotschnig (1968).

[32]On the majoritarian voting system, see Claude (1971, ch. 7).

[33]The Group of 77, originally 75, first came to prominence as an economic bloc of developing nations at UNCTAD I in 1964. The nonaligned originated in 1955 as a political "third position" and only evolved into an economic Third World bloc in 1973. In a 1976 Harvard Law School speech, Professor Clyde Ferguson called the merger of these two blocs the most significant event of the Sixth Special Session.

[34]See Goodrich (1974, ch. 2) on the powers of the General Assembly.

The obvious disparity between voting power in the General Assembly and financial obligations to the United Nations has tended to undermine the role of the General Assembly in matters of economic policy. The developed nations and particularly the U.S. have responded to the automatic developing country majority by deflecting substantive decision making to such preferred forums as the World Bank and the International Monetary Fund (IMF), in which members "vote money," i.e., votes are proportional to financial commitments. The U.S. has also endeavored to diminish the influence of the United Nations by creating special-purpose organizations to meet the requirements of new programs. Dr. Kissinger's speech prepared for the Seventh Special Session in September 1975 called for the creation of a host of new intergovernmental bodies to implement U.S. proposals, rather than suggesting that these efforts be channeled through existing United Nations machinery.

"Forum shopping" sometimes serves a useful function; successful negotiations can depend not only on the basic issues but on the composition of delegations as well. But, as with attempts to create cleavages among the 77 through appeal to special interest groups, the success of the forum shopping strategy has been limited by the solidarity maintained by the developing group. The positions enunciated by developing country representatives at the non-United Nations Conference on International Economic Cooperation (CIEC) in Paris are identical to the developing country positions held in New York. Furthermore, the militant and newly rich OPEC countries are now demanding and obtaining a larger role in these organizations.[35] Thus, the developed countries may no longer be able to shut out the unwelcome views of their economic adversaries, even in the clubs previously kept exclusive by high membership fees.

B. Economic Machinery of the United Nations

In designing an appropriate structure for international economic cooperation, the framers of the United Nations Charter were circumscribed in their task by the prior existence of a number of specialized intergovernmental agencies.[36] These included the International Labor Organization, the United Nations Relief and Rehabilitation Administration, the United Nations Food and Agriculture Organization, the International Monetary Fund, and the International Bank for Reconstruction and Development. The domain and

---

[35] New York Times, August 31, 1975.

[36] Goodrich (1974, ch. 10).

32

autonomy of each special-purpose body was protected by the commitments of various governments and interest groups. Recognizing that much of the future pattern of intergovernmental cooperation had already been set by this existing network of specialized agencies, the authors of the Charter adopted a "functional"[37] approach to economic issues, with powers and responsibilities widely dispersed within a decentralized system.

The Charter called for the creation of six principal organs: the General Assembly, the Security Council, the Economic and Social Council, the Trusteeship Council, the International Court of Justice, and the Secretariat. The Economic and Social Council (ECOSOC) was intended to serve as the economic counterpart of the Security Council and as the focus for the coordination of economic programs and projects undertaken throughout the United Nations system. In performing this function, ECOSOC confronted at least three major obstacles. First, the task of coordinating the activities of an increasing number of autonomous and semiautonomous bodies--by 1974, these included 14 specialized agencies plus numerous special programs, interagency bodies, and subsidiaries of ECOSOC itself--was of a scale and complexity far beyond what could be successfully undertaken with ECOSOC's modest powers and resources. Furthermore, in contrast to the Security Council, which had been invested under the Charter with primary responsibility for the maintenance of international peace and security, ECOSOC's authority in the economic sphere was subordinated to that of the General Assembly.

Problems raised by this lack of primacy in the economic area were further compounded by the new members' dissatisfaction with ECOSOC's composition. Originally constituted as a group of 18 member states, ECOSOC was considered unrepresentative of the changed membership and dominated in its operations by traditional Western theories of economic development. The efforts of the newer members to gain more effective representation of their economic interests resulted in two expansions of ECOSOC. However, tripling the number of states represented did not increase its effectiveness in achieving the objectives of the members. Rather, the membership expansion has had the effect of "making the Council increasingly a replica of the Assembly itself and as a consequence bringing into question the need of its existence."[38]

The Charter provision for bringing existing and newly created autonomous specialized agencies into relationship with the United Nations allows each agency

---

[37]For an evaluation of functionalism as an approach to peace-keeping, see Claude (1971, ch. 17).

[38]Goodrich (1974, p. 66).

to retain its own membership structure, financial arrangements, and operational character. While this relationship has the advantage of great flexibility, it also seems in practice to lead to an excessive proliferation of international bureaucracy; with many groups working to achieve the same general purpose, competitive empire building can absorb a considerable fraction of total effort and resources. Of the 14 specialized agencies, the most important in terms of total resources are the International Monetary Fund (IMF) and the International Bank for Reconstruction and Development (World Bank). With votes allocated in proportion to financial commitments, the IMF and World Bank have avoided the policy paralysis characteristic of the United Nations, where the majority which approves new programs lacks the capacity to provide the resources required to make them effective. However, both agencies have been under continued pressure from Third World members to increase the amount of credit available to poorer countries and, more generally, to increase the role of these countries in the policymaking process.[39]

C. UNCTAD, UNIDO, and UNDP

Within the United Nations itself, dissatisfaction on the part of the newer members with the pace of economic and social progress in general and with the existing machinery in particular has led to a rapid proliferation of the number of separate bodies attempting to act in each substantive area. The earliest important result of this process was the creation of the United Nations Conference on Trade and Development (UNCTAD), in effect a poor nations' pressure group at the United Nations.[40] During the late 1950s and early 1960s, "the dreams of rapid economic development to follow in the wake of independence were rudely shattered."[41] Falling prices for some primary commodities and disappointing levels of foreign aid flows contributed to the pressure from the LDC group for fundamental changes in world trading patterns. Under the charismatic leadership of Dr. Raúl Prebisch of Argentina, pressure mounted for a new body specifically representative of and responsive to the needs of the developing nations. A 1961 General Assembly resolution proclaimed an official "United Nations Development Decade."[42] Shortly

---

[39]The IMF has recently taken important steps in this direction: a general increase in the availability of credit; liberalization of the compensatory finance facility; and establishment of a trust fund to provide poor countries with increased credit at low rates of interest (to be financed by sale of gold).

[40]On this role of UNCTAD within the United Nations, see Nye (1974).

[41]Gardner (1968, p. 100).

[42]General Assembly Resolution 2626 (XXV).

thereafter, ECOSOC began to formulate plans for a United Nations Conference on Trade and Development to be held in Geneva in 1964. Action by the General Assembly later in the same year gave UNCTAD the status of a permanent organ of the United Nations.

UNCTAD's major role has been as a forum for discussion and analysis of issues related to economic development, largely but not exclusively those aspects of development linked to patterns of world trade. As in the cases of the General Assembly and ECOSOC, UNCTAD decisions and recommendations, except those dealing with the internal affairs of the body, are not binding on the member states. Rather, the aim of UNCTAD has been to change world opinion regarding the key issues of trade and development. One case in which this process has been relatively successful in influencing national policy is that of tariff preferences for less developed countries. Under the leadership of Prebisch, UNCTAD urged that manufactured exports of developing countries be given preferential treatment in developed countries' markets. A decade later, such preferential schemes have been enacted by most industrial countries.[43] Even the U.S., initially opposed to this violation of the "most-favored-nation" principle of nondiscrimination, has now extended tariff preferences on a wide class of imports from developing countries. However, UNCTAD has experienced considerably less success in reshaping developed country attitudes toward commodity agreements and levels of foreign aid commitments, two other issues which have been focal points of lobbying activity.

The United Nations Industrial Development Organization (UNIDO), a second body specifically designed to serve the needs of the developing countries, was created by the General Assembly in 1965.[44] Modeled after the example of UNCTAD,[45] UNIDO was established to promote industrial development and to accelerate the process of industrialization in the developing countries. UNIDO maintained a relatively inconspicuous public profile until its Second General Conference, held in Lima, Peru during March 1975. That conference made headlines by calling for an increase in the developing countries' share of world industrial production from its fairly constant level of about 7 percent during the previous decade to 25 percent by the year 2000. Even more newsworthy were statements affirming "the inalienable right of every State to exercise sovereignty over its terrestrial and marine resources. . .[which] specifically

---

[43] On UNCTAD efforts to promote the Generalized System of Preferences, see Wall (1971). Provisions of the various national schemes are reviewed in IMF Survey, June 23, 1975.

[44] The functions and structure of UNIDO are spelled out in General Assembly Resolution 2152 (XXI), November 17, 1966. On the background of UNIDO, see also UN Monthly Chronicle, February 1975.

[45] See Elmandjra (1973, p. 56).

includes the right to nationalize in accordance with <u>national</u> laws."[46] As the conferees no doubt intended, the specter of widespread nationalization of foreign investments without recourse to international law caused shock waves throughout the developed world. (By this time, expropriation with unsatisfactory terms of compensation was already a well-established practice in many parts of the developing world. The purpose of international resolutions like the Lima Declaration is to lend legitimacy to the status quo.) The Lima Conference also formulated a plan to convert UNIDO into a specialized agency, "as a means of increasing its authority, autonomy and resources."[47]

The United Nations Development Program (UNDP) was formed in 1965 by the merger of two previously existing bodies, the Expanded Program of Technical Assistance and the Special Fund.[48] Its primary activity is the provision of technical assistance to developing nations. Unlike UNCTAD and UNIDO, UNDP has no membership but only "participating" governments and specialized agencies. Its Governing Council is constituted so as to give approximately equal voice to financial contributors and aid recipients.[49] UNDP activities are financed entirely by voluntary contributions. Predicting a "liquidity crisis" in 1976, the incoming UNDP Administrator recently urged all participating governments to pay their pledges early and to make additional voluntary contributions. In a somewhat different reaction to impending financial stringency, the Governing Council asked the Administrator to "reduce the top-heaviness of the UNDP management structure at headquarters, limit staff promotions to the most deserving cases, upgrade posts only on a highly selective basis and stabilize the numbers of positions" in the organization.[50] These contrasting responses to a situation of limited resources provide a nice illustration of the desirable check on empire-building tendencies imposed by a policymaking body which must pay for its policies.

---

[46] UN Monthly Chronicle, April 1975.

[47] UN Monthly Chronicle, February 1976.

[48] See Elmandjra (1973, p. 59) on the background and structure of UNDP.

[49] Claude (1971, p. 132).

[50] UN Monthly Chronicle, February 1976.

D. Proposed Structural Reforms

The December 1974 General Assembly resolution[51] calling for a special session devoted to development and international economic cooperation also authorized the Secretary-General to appoint a small group of experts, nominated by governments and selected on a broad geographical basis, to prepare recommendations for structural changes in the United Nations system to improve its effectiveness in dealing with problems of international economic cooperation. The experts' report,[52] completed in May 1975, proposes a number of important structural reforms. The proposed reforms are designed to improve coordination and reduce fragmentation of effort within the system, to increase the transfer of resources to the developing countries, to improve methods of reaching international agreement, and to give developing countries a larger voice in international economic decision making.

The most important proposed change is the creation of a new post of Director-General for Development and International Economic Cooperation. This new official would be second in rank only to the Secretary-General, and would provide leadership to the entire United Nations system in economic matters. A key part of the proposal is that whenever the Secretary-General is a national of a developed country, the Director-General would be from a developing country. Also proposed were two deputies for the new Director-General. The first, who would come from a developing country, would head a streamlined ECOSOC. A second deputy from a developed country would be in charge of the proposed United Nations Development Authority consolidating all special-purpose United Nations funds for pre-investment activity.

The report explicitly recognizes that no structural changes can take the place of the "political will" of the member states in carrying out their obligations under the United Nations Charter. Less explicitly, the experts recognize that the willingness of the developed countries to channel resources to developing countries through the United Nations system depends on the confidence that these countries feel in the decision-making apparatus of the organization. For this reason, considerable emphasis was placed on developing new consultative procedures for promoting agreement on controversial issues. As envisioned by the experts, each issue would be tackled by a small negotiating group, representing all positions, which would attempt to reach a mutually acceptable solution. The resulting decision would then go before the General Assembly in the form of a resolution and presumably receive unanimous

---

[51]General Assembly Resolution 3343 (XXIX), December 17, 1974.

[52]United Nations, A New United Nations Structure for Global Economic Co-operation (1975).

endorsement by the full membership. Such a process, if successful, would enhance the authority of the General Assembly by encouraging a greater degree of voluntary implementation of decisions by the member states. Whether or not serious conflicts are actually susceptible of resolution through consultative procedures, the proposed method could hardly be less effective in achieving consensus and action than the present sequence of confrontation, resolution, and nonimplementation.

Other noteworthy proposals of the experts would increase the voting rights of the developing countries in the IMF and the World Bank, phase out UNCTAD and its machinery following the establishment of a comprehensive new international trade organization, and improve the quality of United Nations personnel through creation of a Staff College providing common training to officials from the various agencies.

IV. ISSUES AND PROSPECTS

A. Issues at the Seventh Special Session

Unlike the United Nations documents generated during the two-year period preceding the Seventh Special Session, Resolution 3362 (S-VII) was adopted by the General Assembly only after prolonged and serious negotiations involving representatives of all interested parties. While the resolution bears a close resemblance to the working paper prepared in advance by the Group of 77, the effects of objections from the industrialized nations and the impact of the Kissinger speech are clearly visible in the tone and substance of the final document.[53] Although the U.S. and some other developed countries entered formal reservations to certain sections, the content of the resolution is to a large extent representative of the current status of North-South negotiations within the United Nations. The sections below review the major issues and proposals now under consideration. The issues are grouped under the seven main headings used in the resolution.

1. International Trade

As in the 1960s, international trade heads the list of LDC concerns in negotiations with the industrialized nations. In this area, the proposals reflect certain basic preconceptions concerning trade between developed and developing nations. Foremost is the venerable conviction that primary commodity exporters face an inevitable long-run deterioration in their terms of trade.

---

[53]These documents are all reproduced in International Legal Materials, November 1975.

Implicitly, this is translated into the belief that commodity producers will over time receive dwindling real benefits from their raw material exports. The empirical evidence is mixed. Results depend critically on weights given to different commodities, on the period considered, and on whether commodity or factoral terms of trade are examined.[54] A secondary concern of commodity producers is the volatility of their export prices, a result of low demand and supply elasticities for these goods.

The second important preconception concerning trade is that the present world structure of barriers to trade and the process for producing changes in those barriers are skewed against the interests of LDC exporters. Here two issues are raised. First, "cascaded" tariff structures yield high effective protection rates on processing activities in the developed countries, discouraging the processing of raw materials in the producing nations. Second, the General Agreement on Tariffs and Trade (GATT) multilateral negotiating procedures, based on reciprocal tariff reductions, offer little chance for reductions of tariffs on the products of greatest interest to LDC manufacturers, generally those which can benefit from abundant unskilled labor. In addition, it is exactly these industries which are also protected by the nontariff barriers and "escape clause" actions of developed countries. The developing nations correctly regard this developed country practice as retarding the growth of their exports of the very goods in which their present factor endowments give them a comparative advantage.

Commodity exports currently generate about three-quarters of total LDC export earnings; for many countries, exports of a single commodity make up the bulk of total earnings. The specific proposals with regard to exports of commodities have two objectives: to raise and stabilize export earnings and to increase the degree of processing in the countries of production. The most controversial of the proposals currently under consideration is indexation of raw material prices. Although indexation is generally regarded by experts as impossible to enforce, it still enjoys strong support within the Group of 77. However, the U.S. remains adamantly opposed to this measure.[55] Furthermore, the poorest developing nations, which are importers rather than exporters of food and other commodities, would be adversely affected by indexation. Other proposals presently under consideration or already implemented are buffer stock arrangements, compensatory financing, and long-term producer-consumer

---

[54] An expert group convened by the Secretary-General in 1975 and headed by Professor Hendrik S. Houthakker found no clear evidence of a long-term deterioration in the net barter terms of trade of developing countries. Some of the experts later withdrew their support of the group's conclusions.

[55] This was one of the specific reservations from U.S. approval of the Seventh Special Session resolution.

commitments. These are all elements of the UNCTAD Integrated Program for Commodities.[56]

Buffering arrangements entail buying and selling on the part of a central agency in order to maintain price within a specified range. The resources required to carry on such an operation depend crucially on how the range is determined. The lowest expected costs are for a buffering arrangement which merely smooths out price fluctuations around a long-term trend.[57] If the buffering arrangement is intended to raise as well as to stabilize price, the expected cost rises accordingly. To reduce cost of operation, buffering may be combined with export or production quotas for participating producers; however, such controls are typically difficult or impossible to enforce. Furthermore, the cost of maintaining price within a given range is likely to rise over time, as high prices stimulate substitution by consumers while attracting new producers. Consequently, unsuccessful buffering arrangements may be destabilizing; breakdown is likely to be followed by a period of depressed prices and extreme fluctuations until supply and demand adjust to changed market conditions.

The only buffer stock arrangement presently in operation is that for tin, which has succeeded to the extent of moderating minor price fluctuations but which has lacked the resources required to resist major price changes.[58] Under the UNCTAD Integrated Program, buffer stocks would be maintained for as many as 18 primary commodities; the costs would be shared by consumers and producers.

Markets for most primary commodities are "buffered" to some extent by private transactions by firms or individuals who expect to profit by buying when prices are low and selling when prices are high.[59] Buffering also results from decisions regarding the timing of inventory accumulations on the part of manufacturers requiring raw material inputs. The existence of private buffering activities limited by interest rates and storage costs implies that the expected return to national or international buffer stock arrangements will be below the private return on capital. However, the extent of private buffering may be

---

[56]For details of the Integrated Program, see UNCTAD (1975b). For an assessment, see McCulloch (1975).

[57]It should be noted that, even for a purely stabilizing buffer, there is a nonzero probability that cost will exceed any fixed sum.

[58]The Tin Agreement has also been the only user of financing available through the Buffer Stock Facility of the IMF. Eligibility requires that both producer and consumer nations be participants in the buffer arrangement.

[59]There is an ongoing debate as to whether private profit-seeking transactions may be destabilizing. A recent article by Cooper and Lawrence (1975) stresses the contribution of speculative purchases to the commodity price boom of 1973-74.

depressed below the socially optimal level as a result of anticipated government intervention when prices are unusually high. Such intervention prevents private transactors from realizing the full economic value of speculatively held stocks.

U.S. officials have remained cool toward proposals for buffer stock arrangements.[60] The Kissinger speech emphasized the alternative approach of earnings stabilization through compensatory financing, which would reduce the disruptive consequences of price fluctuations without direct intervention in commodity markets. This is implemented by loans or grants which compensate for shortfalls of export earnings below their trend level. Export earnings stabilization may be provided on a commodity-by-commodity basis or for total earnings by country. Dissatisfaction with compensatory financing arrangements is likely to center on interest rates and schedule of repayment; depending on terms, the funds received through such a facility may constitute close substitutes for commercial borrowing, soft loans, or outright grants.

Two major systems of compensatory financing are already in operation. The first is the IMF facility, expanded in January 1976 along the lines suggested in the Kissinger speech. The IMF arrangement provides for stabilization of members' overall export earnings. In contrast, the Stabex plan adopted by the EEC as part of the Lomé Convention in 1975 stabilizes earnings on a commodity-by-commodity basis. Forty-six developing nations are covered by the program; for the poorest of these, payments received constitute aid grants.[61]

Long-term agreements between producers and consumers are typically an important feature of the private markets for primary commodities. The weakness of this measure for reducing uncertainty lies in the problem of enforcing the contracts. UNCTAD proposals would expand the extent of such agreements by tying together agreements for a broad group of commodities on an all-or-none basis.

Expansion of raw material processing in the producing countries is another high priority issue for the Third World. In this case, the desire for higher revenues from raw material exports is reinforced by the longer run goals of industrialization and export diversification. The developing countries have correctly identified the contribution of the tariff structures of industrialized nations to the small fraction of total processing which now takes place in the producing nations. However, even if developed countries are willing to make the required changes in their tariff barriers, the desired shift in the location of

---

[60] Although Kissinger's 1975 speeches indicated a softening of this position, Treasury Department officials continue to make public pronouncements undermining the State Department stance on commodity agreements.

[61] On Stabex, see Bywater (1975).

processing may be quite slow. The current mood in most developing nations is likely to discourage substantial new foreign private investments; financing for such ventures would have to come largely from the World Bank Group or other multilateral lending agencies.

With regard to trade in manufactured goods, the major issue for the developing nations is expansion of the Generalized System of Preferences. Now that most of the industrialized countries have implemented preference schemes, LDC representatives are pressing for broader product coverage, higher ceilings on amounts qualifying for special treatment, and elimination of the ten-year cutoff written into the original schemes. Also, since the extent to which tariff preferences give developing country producers an advantage over their competitors in developed countries depends on the level of the most-favored-nation tariff, there is concern that the Multilateral Trade Negotiation now in progress will erode the preferential margin. The developing countries have therefore asked for compensation through measures such as increased product coverage. In addition, two further proposals have been made regarding nontariff barriers. First, the developing countries have requested preferential treatment with respect to nontariff barriers of the developed countries, a proposal endorsed in the Kissinger speech. The developing countries also want exemption from the countervailing duty actions of the industrialized nations; this would allow the LDC to use export subsidies as a means of promoting development goals.

The effectiveness of preferential access to markets as a means of promoting industrialization is limited by two important considerations. First, the present schemes generally exclude the very goods, such as textiles and shoes, of which developing country producers are most likely to succeed in expanding production and exports. Since developed countries already face severe domestic problems arising from the declining competitiveness of these industries, they are unwilling to force an even more rapid adjustment to changes in comparative advantage. Unless the industrialized countries can make great strides in easing the required internal adjustments, it is unlikely that the desired liberalizations of tariff and nontariff barriers will be soon forthcoming. However, even if preference schemes are expanded, the resulting increase in manufactured output and exports may be modest. Current attitudes in many developing countries are likely to dampen the enthusiasm of potential investors. As in the case of processing of primary commodities, the necessary capital for expansion of manufacturing will have to come largely through multilateral channels.

2. Transfer of Real Resources

A major demand of Third World leaders is, not surprisingly, for larger resource transfers on more attractive terms. The relevant section of the resolution passed by the Seventh Special Session opens by stating that "concessional financial resources to developing countries need to be increased substantially, their terms and conditions ameliorated and their flows made predictable, continuous and increasingly assured. . . ." Among the specific proposals are that the developed countries increase their development assistance to meet the official Second Development Decade target of 0.7 percent of GNP; that the SDR-aid link proposal be revived, along with other automatic transfer mechanisms; that funds available through multilateral lending facilities be increased; that aid be provided on softer terms and untied; and that measures be devised to decrease the burden of debt already incurred, especially for the "most seriously affected" countries.[62]

The developing countries seek to divorce aid flows from the national policy objectives of developed countries. The emphasis is on multilateral, untied flows which are automatic rather than discretionary. Given the current structure of the international monetary system, it is unlikely that the SDR-aid link will soon be implemented. Some observers have suggested an alternative source of automatic flows, namely royalty payments associated with exploitation of seabed resources.[63] This has not, however, been proposed by the Group of 77, presumably because the 77 have not been able to resolve the very important differences of interest within the membership on the issue of ocean resources.

With regard to the prospects for increased official development assistance, the trend in developed countries over the past few years has been in the opposite direction. Between 1960 and 1975, U.S. official development assistance fell from .53 percent of GNP to .20 percent. Somewhat smaller reductions over the same period occurred in France, Germany, and the U.K. While some developed countries did increase their aid as a fraction of GNP, for the First World countries as a group the figure fell from .52 to .29 percent.[64] Furthermore, it is unlikely that this trend will be reversed in the near future. Foreign aid was sold to the voters as a way of gaining friends among the developing nations; these friendships have patently failed to materialize, and the

---

[62]The Dakar conference (see section II) called for an indefinite debt moratorium or outright cancellation of existing debt. However, an LDC meeting in Manila in preparation for the May 1976 UNCTAD IV took a more moderate stand, calling for consideration of debt rescheduling; only in the case of the "most seriously affected" was outright cancellation proposed.

[63]See Gardner (1976).

[64]Howe, and the Staff of the Overseas Development Council (1975, pp. 256-58).

recent outbursts of extremist rhetoric do not augur well for larger legislative appropriations for aid. An exception is humanitarian (rather than development) aid to countries suffering the effects of major natural or man-made disasters.

3. Science and Technology

As in the case of real resources, the developing country objective in this area is increased transfers on more attractive terms. It is widely accepted in the Third World that the present system of technology transfers through government, international agency, and multinational corporation channels has two serious shortcomings. First, the technology transferred is deemed inappropriate to the needs and objectives of the host countries. In addition, the transferred technology is typically utilized in such a way as to engender host country dependence on skilled labor and other inputs which must be imported from the industrialized countries. This tends to minimize local involvement in scientifically advanced enterprises and to limit the real benefits accruing to the host country.

The proposals made under this heading center on major efforts to develop local scientific and technological capabilities and, as a shorter run measure, increased attention to the adaptation of imported technologies to host country requirements. An international code of conduct governing the transfer of technology would be developed as a means of promoting the special needs of the developing countries. The proposals in the resolution would entail a considerable expansion of the role of the United Nations in facilitating inter-national transfer of technology. In contrast, Kissinger's speech calls for the creation of several new special-purpose intergovernmental bodies, presumably outside the United Nations, to implement proposals in this area.

4. Industrialization

The General Assembly resolution endorses the Lima Declaration and Plan of Action of UNIDO[65] and urges the member states to take individual and collective action to implement them. (The U.S. entered a specific objection to this section of the resolution.) A number of concrete proposals to promote industrialization is appended. Included is the recommendation that developed countries facilitate LDC industrial growth by improving their own internal policies for shifting productive resources toward sectors less competitive with those likely to expand in the LDC as industrialization proceeds. As previously noted, the implementation of this recommendation presupposes a new solution to one of the major policy problems now faced by developed countries. The prospect for speedy action is not bright.

---

[65]Texts are reproduced in UN Monthly Chronicle, May 1975.

5. Food and Agriculture

A major long-run goal of the Third World is a rapid increase in food production in the developing countries. In past decades, the trend for at least some of these countries has been in the opposite direction. A number of countries which were once self-sufficient in food production have taken advantage of U.S. food aid to shift resources from agriculture toward industrial production. Rapid population growth has reinforced the movement toward greater dependence on food imports. To increase Third World self-sufficiency in food and fertilizers, the resolution proposes increased aid for development of agricultural capacity. As a transitional measure, expanded food aid with soft financing channeled through multilateral agencies is proposed. A world grain reserve, also endorsed in the Kissinger speech, would be established.

6. Cooperation Among Developing Countries

The proposals in this section of the resolution call for increased United Nations support and assistance to developing countries in strengthening and expanding regional and interregional cooperation. Particular areas for cooperation singled out are utilization of technology, funds, resources, and skills to promote investment; and regional trade liberalization measures.

7. Restructuring of the United Nations System

The structure of the United Nations has already been transformed in many respects in response to pressure from the Third World. The resolution endorses further basic structural reforms which would make the organization "more responsive to the requirements of the provisions of the Declaration and Programme of Action on the Establishment of New International Economic Order as well as those of the Charter of Economic Rights and Duties of States," two documents which the U.S. specifically excluded from its approval of the resolution as a whole. No detailed recommendations for restructuring are included in the resolution, but it is suggested that the Report of the Group of Experts[66] be considered along with other materials in formulating proposals.

B. Other Issues before the United Nations

The Group of 77 has maintained its solidarity in negotiations with the industrialized countries by refraining from negotiations on any issue for which a bloc position has not been formulated and endorsed by the membership. Two potentially important projects now underway within the United Nations therefore receive no explicit discussion in the resolution adopted at the Seventh Special Session. These are the development of an international code of conduct

---

[66]United Nations, A New United Nations Structure for Global Economic Co-operation (1975).

governing the activities of multinational corporations and the ongoing negotiations on the law of the sea.

1. Multinational Corporations

While LDC attitudes toward foreign direct investment range from outright hostility to utmost cordiality and highly preferential treatment, there is a strong sense among developing nations that the managers of multinational corporations are pursuing objectives which may well be in conflict with their own national policies. In many cases, a variety of abuses is alleged, from interference with the internal affairs of host countries to transfer pricing practices which lower host country tax revenues. The United Nations Center on Transnational Corporations has undertaken to develop a code which will govern relations between host countries and multinationals and is also training accountants from developing nations to help them deal more knowledgeably with foreign investors.[67] These measures could introduce additional obstacles to the flow of private foreign capital into the Third World. However, successful efforts to curtail abuses and to specify internationally approved guidelines concerning controversial practices such as nationalization of foreign property and phase-out requirements could eliminate some sources of potential misunderstanding between host countries and investors and thus actually increase private capital flows to the Third World.

In this connection, it may be possible to link the question of adequacy of tax payments with that of fair compensation when foreign property is nationalized through the use of a self-assessed tax system similar to that proposed for domestic property taxation. Under this scheme, the foreign investor would set a value on total assets located in the host country; this value would then be used both as a basis for taxation (in place of an income or profits tax) and would also be considered the "fair value" to be paid in the event of national takeover of the enterprise. An internationally enforced system along these lines could go far in decreasing mutual suspicion on the part of host countries and investors.

2. Law of the Sea

Much of the current debate over law of the sea concerns fishing rights. However, the total value of those rights is dwarfed by comparison with rights to extract oil and other minerals from the seabed. Agreement on a position regarding law of the sea has been hampered by the very large and divergent interests of such groups as the landlocked countries; the coastal economies; the "most seriously affected," which could become beneficiaries of international

---

[67]See United Nations, Research on Transnational Corporations, Preliminary Report of the Secretariat (1976).

46

royalty payments; and the oil and mineral producing nations whose export earnings could be seriously eroded by development of alternative sources.

A recent proposal by the Trilateral Commission would institute a revenue-sharing plan to provide a relatively automatic and nonpolitical source of financing for development. Under this arrangement, a fraction of the revenues generated by exploitation of seabed minerals beyond a distance of 12 miles from shore would be paid into an international institution such as the World Bank. This would augment funds available from other sources. The plan is, in effect, an aid link to exploitation of offshore mineral resources. This proposal would probably gain the support of the landlocked LDC, but might well be opposed by coastal developing nations and also by some industrialized countries, including the U.S. The sums involved are substantial. One source estimates that a 10 percent royalty rate could generate as much as $1 billion a year by 1980 and $3 billion a year by the year 2000. (In comparison, total official development assistance is now about $15 billion annually.)[68]

C. Prospects for the Future

The current drive for a New International Economic Order is intended to transform the United Nations into a more effective policymaking body for the world economy. This increased effectiveness would be used to implement policies likely to inflict substantial damage on the world economy, leaving a smaller global pie to be allocated among competing groups. In the absence of enforcement powers, the techniques being employed to gain the assent of the industrialized countries which must pay a large part of the cost of these new programs are the usual carrot and stick. A stick is used in the form of threats--weapons such as "commodity power," which can disrupt if not permanently harm the economies of industrialized countries. And the carrot-- would not a more prosperous world be better for all? Don't the industrialized countries value equality of opportunity, not only for their own populations but also for the vast majority who happen to have been born in the poorer parts of the globe?

The end of this campaign is not in sight. Some Third World intellectuals view the current phase as the beginning of a program likely to extend over 20, 30, or more years--comparable to the length of time required to allow the former colonies to achieve independence. What should the U.S. be doing? Some have argued that the U.S. should leave the United Nations. Others feel that it is important to keep the dialogue going. I do not think that decision

---

[68]See Gardner (1976).

47

has more than symbolic importance, since the current turmoil in the United Nations simply reflects real changes which have already occurred in the world community at large. However, with respect to economic policies there are three points worth making.

First, if the U.S. goes along with policies which ultimately decrease the amount available for the world to share, U.S. problems can only grow worse. This is true for specific programs, but also (and perhaps more significantly) for proposals which would increase the potency of the United Nations as an economic policymaking body without altering the kinds of policies likely to be adopted. The U.S. should eschew short-run policies of partial accommodation as exemplified by the Kissinger speech at the Seventh Special Session. Instead, the U.S. ought to throw its full support behind policies likely to increase rather than decrease overall efficiency of the world economy. Of the proposals now before the international community, I would particularly endorse elimination of cascaded tariff systems which discriminate against local processing of raw materials in their countries of origin; of high tariffs and nontariff barriers protecting labor-intensive manufacturing activities; and of developed country "anti-inflationary" export controls. It must be recognized, however, that elimination of these world efficiency reducing measures necessarily entails finding new solutions for some difficult domestic problems.

Second, it is plain that the U.S. Congress is unlikely to reverse itself and suddenly begin to increase the level of resources devoted to assisting Third World countries, especially those which remain hostile in their attitudes toward the U.S. Just as the Congress chose to exclude the members of OPEC from the Generalized System of Preferences under the Trade Act of 1974, it will wish to reward countries which are friendly to the U.S. and refrain from helping those which are hostile. But, in the past, the Congress has been singularly heavy-handed in pursuing this kind of discrimination. U.S. policymakers have given the developing countries little room in which to pursue their own economic and political objectives. The neoconservatives (and others) have argued that the industrialized countries should allow the developing nations to make their own choices, but without guaranteeing to provide them with additional resources when, as a result of those choices, their economic performance is disappointing. This is an attractive line to take, but unfortunately it cannot be carried to its logical conclusion. Most residents of developing nations have no opportunity to voice their approval or disapproval of government policies through free elections or a free press. Likewise, most have little alternative in terms of international emigration. Thus, it is illogical to hold individual citizens responsible for the policies of their "leaders." The U.S. may therefore rationally choose to provide emergency aid even when the emergency results from following a policy it has openly condemned; the case of India comes to mind. It should be emphasized that the interests of the leaders, who usually represent a bureaucratic elite in most developing countries, may be very different from those of the population as a whole. For example, it is notable that no document emanating from the Third World calls for lower barriers to international immigration—a force important in increasing economic welfare and protecting political freedoms in past centuries.

Finally, is it in fact likely that the United Nations will be transformed in the near future from a town meeting into an important economic policymaking body? It seems probable that most substantive decisions concerning the future of the international economic system will continue for some time to be made outside the United Nations, in intergovernmental bodies such as the IMF and World Bank where countries "vote money." Policies can only be as effective as the means to finance them, and a policymaking body which does not take this into account is unlikely to be effective. But it ought also to be recognized that the world is changing very rapidly. The U.S. should be looking now to the future of the international economic community, and using its considerable international power and prestige to advance policies which expand rather than shrink world wealth.

REFERENCES

1. Bauer, P.T., "Western Guilt and Third World Poverty," Commentary, 61, No. 1, (January 1976), 31-38.

2. Bergsten, C.F., "Commodity Power is Here to Stay," The Brookings Bulletin, Washington, D.C.: The Brookings Institution, 11, No. 2, (Spring 1974), 6-8(a).

3. _____, "The New Era in World Commodity Markets," Challenge, 17, No. 4, (September/October 1974), 34-42 (b).

4. Brunner, K., "The New International Economic Order: A Chapter in a Protracted Confrontation," University of Rochester Center for Research in Government Policy and Business, mimeo, April 1976.

5. Bywater, M., "The Lomé Convention," European Community, No. 184, (March 1975), 5-9.

6. Claude, I.L., Jr. Swords into Plowshares. New York: Random House, 1971.

7. Cooper, R.N., and Lawrence, R.Z., "The 1972-75 Commodity Boom," Brookings Papers on Economic Activity, Washington, D.C.: The Brookings Institution, (1975:3), 671-723.

8. Elmandjra, M. The United Nations: An Analysis. London: Faber and Faber, 1973.

9. Frank, R.S., "Economic Report: U.S. takes steps to meet demands of Third World nations," National Journal Reports, 7, No. 43, (October 25, 1975), 1480-89.

10. Gardner, R.N., "The United Nations Conference on Trade and Development," in The Global Partnership, (ed. R.N. Gardner and M.F. Millikan), New York: Praeger, 1968.

11. _____, "Offshore Oil and the Law of the Seas," New York Times, March 14, 1976.

12. Goodrich, L.M. The United Nations in a Changing World. New York: Columbia University Press, 1974.

13. Gregg, R.W., "UN Economic, Social, and Technical Activities," in The United Nations: Past, Present, and Future, (ed. J. Barros), New York: Macmillan, 1972.

14. Howe, J.W., and the Staff of the Overseas Development Council. The U.S. and World Development, Agenda for Action 1975. New York: Praeger, 1975.

15. IMF Survey, various issues.

16. International Legal Materials, Washington, D.C.: American Society of International Law, various issues.

17. Jankowitsch, O., and Sauvant, K.P., "The Evolution of the Non-Aligned Movement into a Pressure Group for the Establishment of the New International Economic Order," presented at the XVII Annual Convention of the International Studies Association, Toronto, February 1976.

18. Janssen, R.F., "Bridging the Chasm to the Third World," Wall Street Journal, February 13, 1976.

19. Kotschnig, W.M., "The United Nations as an Instrument of Economic and Social Development," in The Global Partnership, (eds. R.N. Gardner and M.F. Millikan), New York: Praeger, 1968.

20. Kristol, I., "The 'New Cold War'," Wall Street Journal, July 17, 1975.

21. McCulloch, R., "Commodity Power and the International Community," H.I.E.R. discussion paper No. 440, Cambridge, Mass.: Harvard University, 1975.

22. Moynihan, D.P., "The United States in Opposition," Commentary, 59, No. 3, (March 1975), 31-44.

23. Nye, J.S., "UNCTAD: Poor Nations' Pressure Group," in The Anatomy of Influence, (R.W. Cox and H.K. Jacobson, et al.), New Haven: Yale University Press, 1974.

24. UN Monthly Chronicle, various issues.

25. UNCTAD, "Conference of Developing Countries on Raw Materials: Action Programme and Resolutions on Raw Materials and Other Primary Commodities," TD/B/C. 1/L.45, February 17, 1975, reprinted in part in International Legal Materials, Washington, D.C.: American Society of International Law, (March/April 1975), 520-42 (a).

26. _____, "An Integrated Programme for Commodities: Specific Proposals for Decision and Action," report by the Secretary-General of UNCTAD, TD/B/C.1/193, October 28, 1975 (b).

27. United Nations. A New United Nations Structure for Global Economic Co-operation. Report of the Group of Experts on the Structure of the United Nations System, United Nations Document E/AC.62/9, New York: United Nations, 1976.

28. _____. Research on Transnational Corporations, Preliminary Report of the Secretariat, United Nations Document E/C.10/12, New York: United Nations, January 28, 1976.

29. Wall, D., "Problems with Preferences," International Affairs, 47, No. 1, (January 1971), 87-99.

THE ECONOMIC COMMISSION FOR LATIN AMERICA:
ITS POLICIES AND THEIR IMPACT

Rolf S. Luders
Banco Hipotecario de Chile
and
Catholic University of Chile

I. <u>INTRODUCTION</u>

The organizers of the Conference requested me to prepare an analysis of the policy recommendations of the Economic Commission for Latin America (ECLA) and allowed me considerable flexibility to define my work within that broad mandate.

During its almost 30 years of prolific history, the Economic Commission for Latin America has done substantial work in many areas. Some has been concerned with the broad question of achieving the highest possible rate of growth for the region as a whole. Other work was related to the equally broad subject of social development. Moreover, a high proportion of the effort has been devoted to more specific subjects such as agricultural development, industrial development, transportation problems, planning techniques, specific commercial policy proposals, and others.

This paper gives a description and critical analysis of the Commission's proposal on import substitution. In my opinion, this proposal is the cornerstone of the development model that ECLA adopted during most of its initial two decades of existence, and to which it is possible to attribute a large share of its policy influence in the region.

However, the discussion of that proposal alone would give those readers not familiar with the scope of ECLA a completely distorted view of its work. The first two brief parts of the paper, therefore, outline very succinctly those other main ideas of the Commission which I consider important, both those developed in the past and those on which it is working today. The reader should be aware, nonetheless, that it is impossible to provide a fair representation of all the work done by the Commission in such a limited space. Finally, in the last section, I try to evaluate, as objectively as possible, the influence of the Commission's proposals on the policies actually followed by the countries of the region.

What follows is based almost exclusively on the Commission's own writings, although my own perceptions of the economic problems of Latin America must certainly have influenced the selection of topics as well as the opinions expressed, especially in the last section. No additional empirical work was attempted. A list of the Commission's writings consulted for this work is in an Appendix.[*] The fact that ECLA published again during 1973 those papers it considered most relevant of the work of its first 25 years of existence helped me to select, as fairly as possible, its most important ideas among the many contained in all of its writings. Dr. Enrique Iglesias, the Commission's present Executive Secretary, was very kind to provide me with the necessary material.

A word of caution is required. The Commission has been criticized for being dogmatic in its ideas and not changing them when it became evident that they were wrong or when conditions have varied enough to make a given model or policy condition obsolete. Without intending to, this paper might reinforce this concept by emphasizing ECLA's import substitution proposal. The fact is that the Commission, to a large extent because of the important work of Dr. Raúl Prebisch and a handful of close advisers, adopted a certain approach (center-periphery) to the analysis of the region's economic development problems and applied it to the questions of international trade and internal resource allocation. Although the resulting initial model, grounded in the idea of import substitution through protection, evolved through further research and in response to changing conditions, the basic approach has not been abandoned and is still considered valid by the Commission. I did not select the import substitution proposal because the Commission still emphasizes that aspect of the development process, but because it has been, in my opinion, the most influential idea of the Commission as well as the most powerful application of the Commission's basic approach. At the same time, it also illustrates the main weakness of that approach.

---

[*] Editors' note. Copies of this Appendix are available on request from the editors.

II. THE COMMISSION'S MAIN POLICY CONCERN

A. The Center-periphery Approach

To understand the work of ECLA, one must take into account the fact that it is an international organization and, therefore, that it is primarily interested in the relationships among the different countries of the region and between the region as a whole and the rest of the world. This does not mean that ECLA does not study the economies of individual countries. However, when it does so, it tends to emphasize more those aspects related to the interrelationships of the particular economy under study with the rest of the world, including the other countries of the region.

Perhaps for this reason or because it felt this to be the most important aspect of the development of the Latin American countries, ECLA has adopted what might be called a center-periphery world view. The most important and original work done by ECLA starts out with this dichotomy. The center (the U.S., Japan, and perhaps Europe) is economically developed, with high per capita incomes and industrialization levels, as well as fast technological development. The periphery (Latin America, Africa, Asia) is composed of poor countries which tend to produce raw materials for the center and whose technological development is scarce. In fact, in this view, the periphery's development is by and large dependent on that of the center. The analytic approach consists of the study of the interrelationships between these two groups of countries. This approach explains some of the ideas ECLA had on industrialization through import substitution, foreign and technical assistance, and others. I develop in detail below the Commission's point of view on import substitution and make a critical appraisal of this approach. The remainder of this section summarizes briefly some of the other outstanding policy proposals in ECLA's 28-year history.

B. ECLA's Main Commitments

There are two offspring of the concept of import substitution via tariff protection that should be mentioned here because of their importance in ECLA's work.[1]

The first is the idea of "industrialization towards the outside." ECLA recognized that the market size of most Latin American countries would seriously limit the possibility of "efficient" import substitution. It therefore advocated, as a first step, economic integration among the countries of the region as a basic tool to enlarging the market size for regional producers without

---

[1] See Iglesias (1974).

subjecting the new industries to competition from the center. This idea was eventually endorsed by all governments of the region. In practice, however, it has never been completely implemented. Today the Latin American Association for Free Trade (LAFTA), the Central American Common Market, the Andean Group, and the Caribbean Free Trade Association (CARIFTA) are all making some progress toward the ideal of free trade within the region.

The second is the idea of "internationalized industrialization." ECLA eventually recognized that Latin America could only realize its full potential economic growth rate if it produced industrial goods, not only for its own markets but also for export to the rest of the world. It also became clear that this last market would become more and more important in proportion to the increased efficiency and sophistication of Latin American industrial production. However, most industrialized countries were, to some extent, protecting their own industries through tariff and/or nontariff barriers. Therefore, ECLA championed the idea of preferential treatment for the less developed countries. From an institutional point of view, this lead to the creation in 1963 of the United Nations Conference on Trade and Development (UNCTAD) and to the eventual adoption of different schemes on preferential tariffs for the less developed countries.

In a different area, the Commission has always been concerned with the need to achieve better income distribution for the countries of the region. It has explicitly recognized that the effort to achieve such an improvement in income distribution should not seriously interfere with the growth possibilities of these countries' economies. It has advocated all kinds of policies to achieve these aims, including tax and income policies. However, ECLA has also consistently proposed "structural" changes to reach these objectives including land and business enterprise reforms. It is well known how difficult it is to devise a set of policies which will, in the relatively short run, produce substantial income redistribution compatible with a high growth rate. This difficulty is compounded by the fact that any such set of policies must be politically acceptable. It is, therefore, not surprising that ECLA has had less success in this field than in most others.

The Commission has always believed that most Latin American countries should adopt a planning system in order to accelerate their development rates. Although ECLA recognized the preference of most Latin American countries for a free enterprise system as legitimate, it advocated an important government role in the economy. It did not believe that in today's world a laissez-faire system could be relied on to allocate resources efficiently or that it would provide fair distribution of income. Moreover, ECLA considered that in most countries of the region the private sector would be unable to establish enterprises requiring high volumes of capital and/or high levels of technology. It, therefore, favored the existence of some government-operated enterprises.

The Commission's support of some government intervention would, in my opinion, be reasonable by the standards of most people in free market economies. Some might object to the idea of governments running business enterprises. However, ECLA's position has also provided (most certainly without intending to) the intellectual support for a large-scale public intervention in some economies, ranging from total control of foreign trade and exchange operations and price and wage fixing to the nationalization of most large- and medium-scale private operations. At the same time, surprisingly enough, planning as envisioned by ECLA has received scarce attention in most countries. During the sixties, almost all the countries of the region prepared development plans which in those years were a prerequisite for receipt of foreign aid from such Washington-based international organizations as the Agency for International Development (AID), the Inter-American Development Bank (IDB), the International Monetary Fund (IMF), and the International Bank for Reconstruction and Development (IBRD) or World Bank. Rarely, however, were these plans seriously used to guide future actions. The Planning Ministries which were created in those years act today more in the capacity of "useful research departments" than as the global planning offices advocated by ECLA.

III. ECLA TODAY

A. Latin America's Recent Economic Development[2]

During the Commission's lifetime, the economy of Latin America has changed considerably. In 1950, GNP for the region (measured in 1970 dollars) amounted to $60 billion, while in 1974 it reached $220 billion, i.e., about the size of the 1950 European GNP. At the same time, the larger economies of the region had reached a GNP level similar to that enjoyed by the larger countries of Europe in that year.

Industry's share of GNP increased from 18 percent in 1950 to 24 percent in 1974, while industry's proportion of exports increased during the same time, from 6 percent to 18 percent. Moreover, during 1974, gross investment represented 23.5 percent of GNP. ECLA estimates that if this share is maintained until 1985 all the capital in existence in the region in 1950 could

---

[2]Data taken from Iglesias (1975).

be created in one and one-half years. From 1950 to 1975, the following increases in production took place: a) steel production increased 15 times; b) energy, eight times; c) cement, four times; d) automobile production increased from near zero to 1.6 million units; e) machinery production increased nine times.

Latin America is today a very important market for foreign capital goods, consumer durable goods, and chemical products, in spite of fast increases in its own industrial production. In 1973, the U.S., Europe, and Japan exported about $11 billion of these products to the region. For the U.S. alone, the Latin American market for these products is three times as important as the Japanese market and about as large as that of the European Economic Community.

Finally, in spite of the area's substantial economic growth, the standard of living of the lowest income groups has not improved significantly. ECLA estimates that of the 300 million inhabitants of the region, about 100 million live under conditions of extreme poverty. It also estimates that the $100 increase in average per capita income during the sixties represents only a $2 per capita increase for those in the lowest 20 percent income group.

B. The Commission's Search for New Proposals

After studying the principal ECLA writings, there is no doubt in my mind that the Commission consistently advocated during its first decades a very definite "model" which, however, evolved through time. The parameters of this model and some of the policies deriving from it were adapted to the conditions of the specific countries under study and to the economy of the rest of the world. Basically an import substitution model, it stressed the need for income redistribution measures. Planning, as a way to make rational policy decisions, was recommended.

During the last 25 years, however, conditions have changed considerably in Latin America, and it is, for several reasons, no longer possible to speak of an ECLA model today. On the one hand, as described above, the economy of the region has grown substantially. Industrialization has proceeded rapidly, and today several countries are fast becoming important exporters of industrial products, some of them highly sophisticated. Now, many countries in Latin America are more interested in export promotion than in import substitution.

On the other hand, many countries have also become aware of the costs of a poorly defined import substitution policy. It is only fair to mention here that ECLA has several times pointed out in its writings the dangers of "excessive" protection to domestic activities. In any event, several Latin American countries are now reacting to their past policies and are reducing significantly their customs duty levels, while at the same time taking other measures to equalize as much as possible the incentives for both nontraditional export and import substitution production.

The economics profession in Latin America has also made substantial progress. At the time ECLA was created, there were hardly any economists in the region. It should, therefore, come as no surprise that the writings of the Commission received very little critical analysis initially and were easily accepted by policymakers eager for expert guidelines. Today, the situation has changed radically and most, if not all, governments have their own capable economic advisers. Since these have different ideological backgrounds and were trained at different schools, it should be obvious that a single, narrow model, like the one professed by ECLA during its initial years, cannot receive wide support in the region any more.

The Commission is, of course, aware of all these changes and new difficulties. In the recent past, it has stressed export promotion over import substitution. The important role ECLA played in UNCTAD and in the promotion of preferential tariff schemes for the underdeveloped countries could be cited again here. The Commission also recognized that its import substitution scheme would eventually tend to put the economies of the Latin American countries in a position very vulnerable to any reduction in exports earnings. This is a risk because initial industrial development tends to require imported raw materials or components. Balance of payments problems tend to reflect themselves in the reduction of those imports and, therefore, in the industrial output. The Commission recommended export diversification policies to offset this difficulty.

However, ECLA's work has lately been more influenced by the position of the underdeveloped countries vis-à-vis the more developed nations. Such matters as the "new international economic order," as affecting both international trade and monetary reform, have received substantial attention, as have subjects like foreign aid, foreign investment, and multinational corporations. My personal impression is, however, that this work has not produced very important new ideas which can be attributed to the Commission, except for the original--but by now old--approach of center-periphery. However, the Commission now regards this polarity differently. In line with the increased development of the region and with the considerable bargaining power represented by its substantial imports from the center, the Commission is now searching for a new, more businesslike relationship. This realistic view might eventually provide some useful policy guidelines.

As indicated, the Commission has for many years championed the idea of economic integration as the most important aspect of the economic relationships among the countries of the region, but things have progressed at a decreasing rate. ECLA is, therefore, searching now for new means of economic cooperation among the countries of Latin America.

To achieve development through internal means, the Commission has recently reemphasized social development as an objective of its studies; work in this area was initiated by ECLA in the early fifties. More than ever, the Commission considers that the countries of the region should seek both a high economic growth rate and a just social order, and that the latter might reinforce the former. As a matter of fact, it has been stated that "the objective of development in Latin America should be to constitute a new society and a new type of person. Social participation in all the forms of the development process has to be increased to achieve a more just society."[3]

ECLA is now searching for new ideas along these lines. Latin America's economic growth has been very fast in the recent past and is likely to continue so for quite some time. However, as outlined above, the record on income distribution and social participation is still very poor. Experience in other parts of the world assures that economic growth will eventually improve the standards of living of the lowest income groups substantially. The question is should we wait that long, or perhaps, can we afford to wait that long without risking the social disorder which might interrupt the growth process?

The Commission seems to feel that the region should and can take an active role in hurrying the process of social development along, without affecting growth. Besides the traditional income redistribution measures, ECLA is proposing structural reforms such as control over natural resources, land-tenure reform, and the promotion of "social ownership" of those sectors in which it is necessary to achieve an independent and self-sustaining growth rate. Moreover, it has recently emphasized the study in depth of the social and economic characteristics of those with the lowest per capita incomes in an attempt to draft proposals which might eventually eradicate extreme poverty in the region.

---

[3] Naciones Unidas/CEPAL (1973).

IV. ECLA'S COMMERCIAL POLICY PROPOSALS: A CRITICAL APPRAISAL

A. A Change in Attitude

In this section, the import substitution policy proposed by ECLA is discussed. This is, in my opinion, the idea around which the Commission's initial complete set of development policies revolved.

Somehow in the background of this concept is the notion of a change of attitude by the countries of the region. It is argued that, in the past, the Latin American countries were essentially suppliers of basic raw materials and food-stuffs for the more developed countries, especially in Europe. This implied that the export sector of the region was constituted mostly by foreign companies, that it had relatively advanced levels of technology, and that it was paying relatively high wages. With the proceeds of these exports, the Latin American countries financed imports of most industrial goods. Growth was limited to the rate of expansion of the demand for basic raw materials. Foreign investment was exclusively oriented toward this production, and technological development was also limited to that sector. The countries remained backward, except for the export sector.

According to ECLA, the economic crisis of the thirties and the two World Wars changed the attitude of the Latin American countries. The change was gradual, in some countries occurring earlier and in others more recently, but in all cases it was clearly distinguishable. The countries of the region became less and less interested in supplying basic raw materials per se to the developed countries and more and more interested in following such policies which would maximize the rate of economic development of their own countries. In pursuing this latter aim, the Commission holds, the countries of the region began to protect internal activities and to follow an import substitution policy.

This change in commercial policy was accompanied by many changes in the other economic variables. The countries became concerned with the problem of capitalization of their industrial development. Foreign investment had to be attracted into these new activities, internal credit mechanisms had to be developed, and governments had to increase taxation in order to channel more resources toward industrial development. Additional foreign exchange was required to purchase capital equipment and, therefore, the governments tended to ban, or seriously limit, the importation of "luxury" goods such as whisky, expensive cars, furs, jewelry, etc. Efforts were made to spread the knowledge of the advanced technology as widely as possible, either through technical assistance or through foreign investment. Education was expanded rapidly, and technical schooling was emphasized. Since the interest was in development, not merely growth, some actions were taken to spread the gains of the growth process as widely as possible through income redistribution measures.

Although the preceding paragraph describes very succinctly, but adequately, the main policies followed by most Latin American countries between the thirties and the late sixties, these policies were not implemented immediately as a coherent set. It is my understanding that in the most important countries of the region balance of payments problems induced the governments to raise customs duties on imports of industrial products. These measures, in fact, started the import substitution process. The remaining policies were then adopted one by one to solve the different problems which the import substitution process brought about.

It is difficult, if not impossible, to evaluate the impact of the writings of ECLA on the measures adopted by the different governments. This is discussed in the last section. Suffice it to say that the Commission provided a rationalization for the import substitution process as one of the cornerstones for the development of the region. In addition, ECLA proposed a coherent set of complementary policies to make this process as effective as possible.

B. ECLA's Proposals on Import Substitution

The Commission observed that one of the main development problems most Latin American countries faced were continuous balance of payments crises. To explain these, ECLA studied, among other things, the terms of trade between Latin America and both the U.S. and the U.K.[4] It found a tendency for these terms of trade to move against Latin America.

ECLA then proceeded to explain this tendency. The essence of the argument is that the gains from technological progress in the production of basic raw materials and foodstuffs are passed on to consumers via a reduction in the price of the product, while the same gains in the production of industrial goods are translated into higher incomes for the producers of these goods. In other words, if one takes into account that the less developed countries export mainly basic raw materials and the more developed countries relatively more industrialized goods, technological progress tends to lower the price of the exports of the less developed countries and raise the price of their imports; this explains then the tendency in the terms of trade movements. The Commission provides many arguments for this curious behavior of the gains from technological development in both cases. In one of the earlier writings,

---

[4] Naciones Unidas (1951).

62

ECLA lists the most important of these arguments,[5] which relates, as one would expect, to the relative forces of supply and demand.

According to ECLA, the relative importance of the raw materials within the aggregate value of production diminishes because:

(1) technical progress tends to induce a more refined or complex processing of basic raw materials and, therefore, diminishes the share of raw materials in the value of the final product. The examples of the wheelbarrow, the automobile, and the airplane are commonly cited;

(2) technical progress tends to allow a better utilization of the basic raw material and its subproducts and, therefore, also reduces the share of the basic raw material inputs in the value of the final product;

(3) technical progress tends to substitute synthetic products (plastics, for instance) for basic raw materials and, therefore, diminishes the demand for the latter;

(4) the income elasticity of demand for most basic raw materials is very low, while this same elasticity is much higher for most industrial goods and for services. ECLA points out that even in the case of foodstuffs, as income grows, the demand for processed food increases much faster than the demand for unprocessed food. (The Commission, by the way, attributes this phenomenon to technological progress, which is responsible both for the possibility of increases in per capita income and for providing alternative products to diversify consumer demand.)

As a consequence of these factors, the demand for imports by the more developed countries (the center) from the less developed countries (the periphery) tends to grow at a slower rate than does income in the former. This "natural" tendency is, according to ECLA, very often reinforced by the fact that the center tends to take measures to protect its own raw-material-producing units from suffering the full effects of this low-income elasticity of demand. The most common protective measure consists of raising the import duties on those raw materials which are produced by the center itself; thereby, import demand for these products grows even slower or not at all.

ECLA concludes that, due to this very low-income elasticity of demand by the center for the periphery's exports, the periphery can only grow at a very slow pace. However, the periphery has the natural and human resources to grow much faster. The Commission further pointed out that the low level of productivity at the periphery provides precisely the necessary condition for a

---

[5] Naciones Unidas (1952).

very high rate of growth which should allow these countries eventually to reach the per capita income levels of those which are more developed.

Moreover, it is agreed that the slow pace of development of the periphery's exports tends to result in an excess supply of labor. This will tend to be employed in other activities within the country, since the Commission assumes, I believe correctly, a rather low international labor mobility. Industrial activities are singled out as those which are more desirable because of their higher productivity levels. It is argued that through industrial development these higher productivity levels are spread through the economy and per capita income levels are raised.

Together with the increase in the level of per capita income, the demand for imports also increases. But, as already suggested, the demand for imports by the periphery grows at a higher rate than does income because the periphery imports mainly capital and other industrial goods. In some of its writings, the Commission contends that even in the absence of per capita income growth at the periphery, the per capita demand for imports will grow through time. This happens, they argue, because the availability of sophisticated industrial goods grows continually and changes the composition of demand in favor of more expensive imports.

The tendency of the periphery's exports to grow at the most as fast as income, and of its imports to grow faster than income, explained, according to ECLA, the continuous series of balance of payments crises by the less developed countries. Although foreign investments and loans tended to reduce the impact of the periphery's commercial trade deficit on the balance of payments, they did not, in general, amount to enough to offset the trade deficit.

Having explained the problem, ECLA turned its interest toward exploring alternative solutions. The most obvious seemed to be to expand exports. The Commission undertook several studies to determine the price elasticity of demand for the basic raw materials and foodstuffs traditionally exported by Latin America. It concluded that these price elasticities were extremely low for the vast majority of these products. This meant that if all countries at the periphery tried to expand export production, the value of their exports would increase very little and would, therefore, not contribute significantly to reduce the balance of payments disequilibrium.

The Commission recognized that there were some exceptions, the petroleum exporting countries among them. It also acknowledged that any one country at the periphery could initially expand its export value considerably by lowering the price of its export products somewhat, but it ran the risk of a price war which would eventually only benefit the center. The possibility of increasing nontraditional exports to solve the balance of payments disequilibrium appeared only later in the recommendations of the Commission.

Alternative solutions discussed by the Commission included either a reduction in wages until import substitution would become profitable or a compression of total income until imports were reduced enough to achieve balance of payments equilibrium. The first was rejected because it was considered absolutely "unrealistic," and the second because it was undesirable and ran against the very objective of the economic policy of the countries of the periphery, namely to increase the rate of economic development.

ECLA turned, therefore, toward import substitution through protection as the only feasible solution to the problem at hand. I will repeat here, as closely as possible, the argument given by the Commission, in one form or another, during its initial and most fruitful decades; I comment on it in section IV. C.

To illustrate the reasoning, I refer to an example which is used by ECLA in what I consider one of its most representative and well-written documents.[6] A given country employs one million people in its export industry, each producing an average of $100 per year. With these $100 million the country imports an equivalent amount of consumer durable goods, machinery, and other products. At a given moment in time, there are another one hundred thousand workers and capital available either to expand export production or to produce industrial goods which, under the alternative use of resources, would have been imported. At international prices, the industrial goods that can be produced with the marginally available human and capital resources amount to $70 per worker.

If exports could be expanded without affecting the price, it is obvious that the best solution would be to use the available resources to expand those exports by $10 million and import an equivalent amount, since the industrial production for internal use would amount to only $7 million. Unfortunately, according to ECLA, an expansion of export production would only lower the price of the exported goods. In fact, in this example, a reduction in the price of 9.1 percent would imply no increase in the value of exports in spite of a 10 percent increase in their physical volume. If these were the elasticities, the Commission points out, it would be better to use the available resources for internal production instead of for exports, in spite of the fact that a worker produces for export $90.9 (marginally, ECLA says) and only $70 for internal production. In the terms of this example, ECLA continued, the marginal resources available (capital and one hundred thousand men) should be applied

---

[6]Naciones Unidas (1952, pp. 28-30).

to exports if this reduces output per man in the export sector at most to $97.3, that is, if it produces a net increase in the export value of $7 million or more. Otherwise, it would be in the best interest of the country to expand industrial production for internal use even if this means that the hundred thousand men produce only $70 each per year. By comparing the $97.3 and the $70 dollars, ECLA concluded that industrial production for internal use could cost up to 28 percent more than export production and still be convenient for the country. Implicit in the argument is the fact that, if the protectionist policy is followed, the additional labor force (the hundred thousand men of the example) can be employed without a reduction in the real wage rate.

The Commission also argued that two types of protectionism should be distinguished. One, derived from the reasoning above, does not imply any reduction in international trade at all. Since the value of exports is a more or less given figure for the countries of the periphery, and the countries only protect internal activities to occupy additional resources which could not be used to expand exports any more, international trade is in no way diminished by this kind of protectionism. In other words, it is argued, this protection does not impose any burden on the rest of the world, but does benefit the countries of the periphery. The other kind of protectionism goes further and provides the incentive for a transfer of resources from export production to import substitution and, in so doing, reduces the flow of international trade.

ECLA also provided some guidelines for the allocation of resources among the different alternative uses within each of the two broad categories: production for exports and internal use. Unfortunately, the criteria suggested vary among the different documents. In some, a case is made for a marginal product of capital criterion and, in others, for a marginal product of capital per worker guideline. In addition, the Commission sometimes suggested that imports of "luxury goods" be avoided. In some of its early writings, it suggested that the countries of the periphery should protect those internal industrial activities which can be produced relatively "efficiently" and which eventually have a chance to compete in international markets. The general impression one receives of these recommendations is that ECLA favored a discriminating customs duty structure determined on the basis of factors such as those described above, plus a few others which become more important in its later work as, for example, the contribution to the spread of modern technology and the requirements of the agreements within the different free-trade zones.

C. A Critical Appraisal of ECLA's Proposal

I offer now a few comments on the Commission's proposal on import substitution. Most of what follows has been said in one form or another as the proposal has already received substantial critical analysis. I refer only to those aspects which seem to me most important.

In the first place, it is around this idea that the Commission has done its most serious professional work, and for which the approach of center-periphery is perhaps most useful. Although the idea of protecting local activities is very old, ECLA has provided a new analytic framework to justify it. There is also no doubt in my mind that this work of the Commission is of the greatest importance from the point of view of economic policy. Unfortunately, it is also true that this ECLA proposal has induced, or reinforced, wrong economic policies in many Latin American countries. Very often this has happened because the policymakers did not properly understand the Commission's recommendations and went too far in their execution. However, the Commission's analysis has several weak or sometimes even mistaken aspects which, if corrected, change its policy conclusions. Let me comment on some of them.

(1) It is in no way obvious that the terms of trade have a tendency to move against the countries of the periphery. I will not review here the extensive research that has been done on the subject. It is well known today that the tendency of the terms of trade varies as a function of the time periods being studied and according to the assumptions that are being made about improvements in the quality of industrial goods. These facts invalidate one of the basic assumptions of the ECLA framework and have as well implications for its policy recommendations.

(2) Even if one accepts that the price elasticities for basic raw materials tend to be very low and that, therefore, the countries of the periphery cannot expand their export volume of these products without producing a more or less proportional reduction in their prices, it is not at all obvious that these countries could not expand nontraditional exports to solve their balance of payments constraints. In fact, the countries developing most successfully have done precisely that and include several countries in Latin America. The export of nontraditional products requires at least an adequate foreign exchange policy as well as reasonable treatment of foreign investments, which will be responsible initially for the expansion of these activities.

In its later work, the Commission recognized the importance of the promotion of nontraditional exports and assumed, as noted above, a very active role in facilitating the access of these products to the markets of the center. However, during most of its existence, it did not consider these exports as a practical alternative to import substitution. As a matter of fact, it only changed its position significantly once it observed the success that some of the countries of the region had had with this policy.

(3)   A surprising fact is that changes in the exchange rate as one way of closing the balance of payments gap were not considered at all by ECLA initially, and later were discarded with hardly any discussion. In the initial ECLA model, a monetary devaluation would not significantly affect export earnings;[7] but would reduce imports by making them more expensive. For reasons which I fail to understand, the Commission did not consider the effect this would have on the expansion of production for internal consumption by making these activities more profitable. It seems to have considered devaluation as only one way of compressing imports to conform to the given export level and, therefore, it judged this policy to be more or less equivalent to any other policy which would reduce the level of income to a level compatible with given foreign resources. As previously observed, ECLA considered this an unsatisfactory solution because it did not allow the countries to use all their potential growth possibilities.

The evidence from Latin America, as well as from the rest of the world, indicates that movements in the real exchange rate tend to produce important readjustments in resource allocations. The importance of these readjustments in the promotion of nontraditional exports has already been noted. At the same time, these movements in the exchange rate also produced powerful, but economically efficient, import substitution effects by inducing resources to flow toward those sectors in which their marginal product was highest. It is, therefore, surprising that the Commission ignored for so long such an important policy tool.

(4)   The Commission's reasoning led it to suggest that the protection of some industrial activities for internal consumption was necessary to assure that the marginal resources would be used by the countries of the periphery in such a way as to maximize their contribution to the total product. I refer again to the numerical example described above, which suggests that the one hundred thousand men and the available capital should be employed in the import

---

[7] I am aware of the fact that a devaluation induces an increase in export production which, according to the ECLA assumptions, would be more or less compensated by a reduction in the price of the exports. Although this increase in export production might have been the reason why the Commission did not consider a devaluation as an adequate measure, I could find no argument along these lines in their writings. Moreover, this objection would suggest the convenience of a tax on traditional exports. This would then make possible the expansion of nontraditional exports, in which respect even the Commission could hardly argue that the periphery has any monopoly power whatsoever.

substitution sector if their employment in the export sector reduced the average product per man in that sector below $97.3. Since these same resources produce only $70 in the import substitution sector, a customs duty was suggested as desirable to assure the most efficient use of the available resources.

I will not discuss the Commission's obvious confusion of the concepts of marginal and average product, which at one time led it to criticize neoclassical economists. It is true that, given the assumptions made by ECLA, its conclusions would seem to be essentially correct. However, by applying traditional economic analysis, the Commission could have reached the same conclusions in a much more elegant and direct way, and some of the limitations of these assumptions might have made themselves more evident to the Commission.

Due to its commitment to the center-periphery approach, ECLA conceived of the producers of basic raw materials basically as monopolists. Their marginal revenue was below their average revenue, and the marginal cost was determined by the value, at international prices, of output in the import substitution sector. The optimum output for the export sector was at a point where the two marginal values were equal. If one now turns to the balance of trade and assumes inelastic export revenues, as the Commission does, it is possible to conclude that an adequate customs duty is an efficient solution to the balance of payments gap as well as to the allocation of resources problem.

Unfortunately, the center-periphery approach tends to obscure the fact that the countries of the periphery are not united and do not, therefore, have a common economic policy. It might well be true that the periphery as a whole is a virtual monopoly in the production of some basic raw materials and food-stuffs, but it is obviously wrong to assume that, therefore, one country has such a monopoly power. It is equally wrong to suggest for any one country a policy that is derived from an analysis in which all countries of the periphery are considered as one.

It is my understanding that for most countries of the periphery ECLA still holds that the price in the international markets of their most important export products is the best measure of the marginal revenue in that sector. The most obvious solution to the resource allocation problem analyzed by ECLA, namely an export tax of a magnitude equivalent to the difference between average and marginal revenues at the point where the latter are equal to marginal costs, seems to me absurd, except perhaps in the cases of those rare countries which might really have a monopoly position or which, for any given product, have reached a cartel agreement with other countries. Such a tax would only inhibit the exports of the country that imposes the tax without at all assuring a relative reduction of world output of the taxed product.

Further, I would question whether the countries of the periphery have in fact monopoly power in the production of most basic raw materials, even assuming that they act as one country in their pricing and production policies for these products. On the one hand, the center countries are very often also important producers of basic raw materials and foodstuffs and could, with relatively slight increases in cost, expand output substantially. On the other hand, in the past the center has developed synthetic substitutes for basic raw materials which compete effectively with natural products and is likely to do the same in the future. Moreover, technological progress itself has made it possible to substitute one basic raw material for another in the production of many final products. All these factors tend to reduce, or even eliminate in the long run, any monopoly power the countries of the periphery might have. There are some possible exceptions such as petroleum and bauxite although, taking a long view, many would argue that these are no different from any other basic raw material or foodstuff.

A question that puzzles me is why the Commission did not take a much stronger position in favor of the creation of export cartels or product agreements for basic raw materials and foodstuffs. It seems to me to be the logical corollary of its analysis. The explanation could not have been that the Commission felt that the countries of the periphery did not have the necessary monopoly power to make such agreements worthwhile, since this would contradict the most important part of the Commission's analytical framework. Could it be that the Commission considered cartels to be politically impossible unless supported by the developed countries themselves?

(5) The final critical point I would like to make refers to ECLA's apparent inability to formulate coherent guidelines for the determination of tariff structures by the countries which adopted its commercial policy proposals. In many cases, this lack of structure might have induced some countries to adopt extraordinarily high, effective protection rates for some industrial goods and none for others.

It is a fact that, in many Latin American countries, anyone wanting to market a product that formerly was imported could set his own protection rate. Government officials, having the ECLA model in mind but not understanding it at all properly, were more than happy to grant any protection that fostered additional activity in the industrial sector and that "saved" the country some foreign exchange. This led to an extremely inefficient allocation of resources as well as to the eventual reduction in the flow of trade. The rationalization of duty structures today is, of course, very difficult because of the interests involved.

D. An Alternative to ECLA's Commercial Policy Proposal

The preceding discussion of the Commission's suggestions on commercial policy leads me to propose a set of alternative policies. These measures, based on the realistic assumption of the existence of market economies in the region, would reduce customs protection to relatively low levels and to a narrow spread. The remaining protection is justified on grounds of product diversification and adoption of new technologies. Nontraditional exports are promoted but only to the point where the incentive to produce them is equal to the incentive to produce them for internal consumption. Several additional measures are suggested to reduce the vulnerability of the economies to fluctuations in basic raw material and foodstuff prices. "Efficient" economic integration is stressed, and the benefits of cartel formation are discussed. The set of measures that will be suggested will not be justified to any extent. These are all well known and have received considerable critical analysis in the economic literature.

The specific measures proposed here are the following.

(1)   The exchange rate is preferable to the imposition of customs duties on imports as the main policy variable to be used to correct balance of payments disequilibria resulting from different tendencies in import and export prices. This method has the advantage of not distorting resource allocation, assuming that this allocation is more or less reasonable to begin with.

(2)   Customs duties should be restructured, if necessary, along the following lines.

(a) In general, no duty should exceed a relatively low level, say, 20 to 30 percent.

(b) All goods should be subject to some import duty, and the structure should be such that effective protection rates are not too different for processes of similar labor intensity, technological complexity, and external economies.

(c) The resulting protection for all internal production (which will be positive but in general low) is justified on the basis of the need to diversify this production to avoid the disastrous effects of possible trade crises such as those that have occurred in the past. Low maximum protection rates imply that the cost of this diversification will also be low. In fact, the (average) protection rate for each country should be a function of its own production conditions, of the level of diversification it wants to achieve, and of the other measures it will or is able to take to insure export earnings stability. Economies of scale in the production of most basic

71

industrial goods are such that only a few countries in Latin America, because of their size, could achieve a highly diversified and relatively autonomous economy without incurring prohibitive costs. Practically all countries of the region will have to reach some compromise between efficiency in production and diversification of the economy.

(d) High customs duties for "luxuries" should be avoided. If countries want to restrict the consumption of such goods, an excise tax is preferable. In Latin America, as elsewhere, high duties imposed to "save" foreign exchange only lead to inefficient import substitution of the final product without an important saving of foreign exchange because a high proportion of the value added is constituted by imported raw materials and spare parts.

(e) In spite of the known arguments against infant industry protection, and mainly because capital markets are quite imperfect in the region, making it very difficult for the private sector to finance present losses, I would favor somewhat higher effective protection rates for new activities of high technological complexity. However, these higher rates should be reduced to normal levels within relatively brief periods, and this should be well known to everybody concerned.

(3) To further reduce the vulnerability of the economies to a decrease in traditional exports earnings, and to equalize, as much as reasonable, incentives for export and internal production, I would propose some steps for the promotion of nontraditional exports, such as the granting of special credits, government support for the organization of and participation in international trade fairs, promotion of products through the consulates, and other similar measures.

(4) Another way of reducing the cost of an increase in diversification is to continue and, if possible, accelerate the movement toward economic integration in the region. In this way, most Latin American nations, which have very small markets, can take advantage of the economies of scale made possible by the increased number of subregional markets.

The purpose of increased diversification is achieved only if the free intraregional trade is solidly based, since what is being diversified is the economy of the integrated group of countries and not the economies of each country. Moreover, a reduction in the cost of this diversification is likely to be achieved only if integration is accompanied by a reduction in the customs duties that apply to imports from third countries. This should be easily arranged because the existing production units will benefit from the economies of scale and should, therefore, not oppose such a move. I feel very strongly that regional or subregional economic integrations carried out in a relatively rational way are, by far, the most efficient ways of increasing economic diversification and of reaching a rate of technological development such that the vast majority of the economies of Latin America might achieve relatively high and self-sustained rates of growth. However, I am also aware of the tremendous practical and political difficulties these movements face today, so much so that the Commission, which championed the idea of economic integration for so long, is now searching for alternative ideas on intraregional trade without abandoning, of course, its support of the integration movement.

I should add here that such an integration would also enormously facilitate negotations to take advantage of such bargaining power as might exist in the region (or subregions) for the purchase of many import goods or for the sale of some of its raw materials, foodstuffs, and even industrial products. The fact is, and I repeat here, that very few countries in Latin America have the actual or potential market size to take advantage of economies of scale in the production of most industrial products, to achieve a self-sustained and relatively high rate of growth, and to negotiate favorable terms, whenever possible, for their exports or imports.

(5)   In my opinion the problem of instability in the export earnings of the countries of the periphery is much more serious than the sometimes unfavorable tendency of the terms of trade. As long as exports depend heavily on one or two basic raw materials whose prices tend to fluctuate significantly, the countries of the periphery should take measures to reduce the impact of such fluctuations. One way of doing this is to build up foreign exchange reserves to the point where they constitute an adequate reserve in case of a reduction in export earnings. Another way would be to increase substantially such international funds as already exist for the same purpose. Finally, wherever possible and practical, the countries of the periphery might participate in international product agreements to regulate prices and output of basic raw materials and foodstuffs. Although these latter have not worked too well in the past, the increased maturity of the countries involved, as well as the growing internationalization of trade, might make these agreements increasingly efficient.

(6)   Although I believe, as pointed out above, that the countries of the periphery, even taken as a group, have relatively little if any monopoly power in the markets of most basic raw materials and foodstuffs, there are probably some exceptions. In these cases, the countries concerned should form export cartels or other similar arrangements in order to maximize incomes. I am invoking here the Commission's argument but suggesting an alternative policy which seems to me more effective, although I am also aware of the many difficulties cartels have had in the past.

The measures proposed here are obviously different from those suggested by ECLA in its earlier period, and differ to a considerable degree from those which most countries in Latin America have adopted. However, during the last decade, several countries in the region have moved toward a scheme that resembles more the one suggested in this paper than the old import substitution model.

It is evident that the allocation of resources will differ substantially from one scheme to the other. Specifically, diversification will result relatively more from the promotion of industrial exports than from the production of import substitutes. Moreover, because of a more evenly distributed protection rate, internal production might, in absolute terms, actually be more diversified under a scheme of the sort proposed here than under an import substitution scheme like the one in fact adopted by many Latin American countries, with features like high tariffs on the importation of some products and no tariff on others. Moreover, the marginal social contribution of resources to the total product should be fairly equal in all sectors of the economy,[8] something which does not happen with a highly discriminating tariff structure. Finally, the exploitation of a possible monopoly power in the production of some basic raw materials or foodstuffs by the periphery as a whole is adequately taken care of with the cartel formation suggestion.

ECLA was concerned with the labor surplus that would result as a consequence of the slow rate of growth in the export sector. It, therefore, proposed to employ that surplus "productively" in the import substitution sector. Does the proposal offered here take care of this problem?

The measures suggested above apply to commercial policy and, therefore, regulate the relative incentives allowed to the production of different products, both internally and externally. Because these measures seek to keep discrimination to a minimum, resource allocation will not be biased significantly either against or in favor of the use of labor. Employment will tend, therefore, to be determined by other factors, including especially wage rate policies, interest rate policies, social security legislation, other tax policies, etc. Commercial policy is designed so as to maximize the efficiency with which labor input is absorbed by the economy, assuming that the policies adopted in other areas of the economy are also "rational" and consistent. I should point out finally that the highly discriminating tariff structure proposed by ECLA very often induced the countries to protect relatively more the capital-intensive industries and, therefore, actually produced a relative reduction in the demand for labor.

---

[8]The exception is in the traditional export sector, since the purpose of the commercial policy here proposed is to reduce the dependence of the economy on one or two export products.

V. THE COMMISSION'S IMPACT ON PUBLIC POLICY IN LATIN AMERICA

There are two questions to be answered under this heading. In the absence of ECLA, which alternative economic policies would the countries of the region have followed? And, given this alternative set of policies, would income have grown faster or slower, or would it have been better or worse distributed? There is no way to reply seriously to the first question. However, if one were to assume a set of alternative policies, perhaps one could, through econometric history, make some inference as to the "cost" of the policies that were actually followed. This would require, unfortunately, a research effort exceeding by far the scope of this paper. I will, therefore, limit myself to presenting a summary of current opinion on the subject.

The prevailing judgment is that ECLA's impact on public policy in Latin America has been, in very general terms, substantial. Some have even said that Latin America was being created by the Commission. It is also thought that ECLA's impact which was felt mainly during the first two decades of its existence has diminished in the more recent past. The reasons for this are twofold. During the initial phase of its existence, the Commission developed and could, therefore, "sell" a new set of economic policies which, as will be explained below, were an answer to the problems and doubts of several of the most important countries of the region. The same conditions do not exist today. The Commission is now in search of a new set of policy recommendations which might regain for ECLA some of its past preeminence.

In judging the impact of the Commission's recommendations on public policy, one must distinguish two aspects. First, there are those cases in which ECLA rationalized a given set of policies the countries were already following and in doing so reinforced those policies. The second aspect is constituted by those ideas which were developed by ECLA and then "sold" to the countries.

Opinion is almost unanimous that the Commission has been more successful in the first aspect. It is evident that several of the larger Latin American countries initiated an import substitution policy years before ECLA was created. Many of them did so after the economic crisis of the thirties, and others during World War II. These policies were initiated under the pressure of severe trade crises. It is also evident that after such experiences, which produced in some countries tremendous shortages, the governments were reluctant to return to free-trade policies under which they would run the risk of suffering similar difficulties again. ECLA's intellectual justification for the import substitution process was, therefore, highly welcomed and easily accepted. One should recall again that during those years Latin America did not have any economics profession to speak of, so that the Commission's writings received little internal critical analysis. Comments by such institutions as the International Monetary Fund were very often discarded as revealing more interest in the well-being of the developed countries than in that of the periphery.

In addition, the Commission offered a coherent set of complementary policies on government financing, income redistribution, land reform and agricultural development, infrastructure, and so on. Given the lack of expertise in most of the countries, and the distrust of advice from the more developed countries or from international institutions in Washington, Paris, or Geneva, it is hardly surprising that the Commission filled a real need and was, therefore, very influential.

It is also evident that the apparent impact of the Commission's trade policy recommendations was not at all uniform. Countries in the southern extreme of the region adopted strong protective measures relatively early, whereas the Central American and Caribbean countries proceeded more cautiously; eventually, however, most of these countries also followed the same scheme. Ecuador and Venezuela, which until very recently had relatively low levels of customs duty protection, are only now raising tariffs to "industrialize" their countries. My impression is that the impact of ECLA's position depended to a large extent on the objective conditions of the country (balance of payments position, size of the country, training levels of the labor force, etc.) and these were such that the Commission exerted maximum impact in the southern part of Latin America, including Brazil. However, I share the common opinion that the Commission's ideas on trade policy either reinforced the position of some countries or induced many others to adopt some protective measures for their import substitution activities.

During the last ten or fifteen years, the region's general interest turned away from import substitution toward export promotion. The Commission had very little influence on this change of policy. Brazil was perhaps the first major country in the region to adopt this policy, and its success was soon emulated by others. The Commission strongly supported the move and was instrumental in the organization of UNCTAD, as previously noted, and of winning approval for different preferential treatment schemes. In this respect, the impact of ECLA was not so much on the policies of the region's governments but on those of more developed countries which opened up their markets substantially for most industrial products manufactured by the periphery.

I would put ECLA's ideas on planning and economic integration in the category of those which were developed by the Commission and then "sold" to the countries of the region. Although it is true that perhaps no country has permanently adopted a planning scheme of the type envisioned by ECLA, most countries now devote considerable resources to obtaining enough information about the economy to be able to make more rational decisions. In addition, policy alternatives are being analyzed, and the coherence of different schemes is evaluated. In a way, all these actions have been directly or indirectly influenced by the Commission's suggestions on planning.

ECLA can also be credited with the fact that all the countries of the region, in their public statements at least, favor a vigorous movement toward economic integration. In addition, as is well known, there exists the institutional framework to carry such a movement forward, and some progress is constantly being made. The Commission feels, and I share this view, that it has been particularly influential in the case of the Central American Common Market. The region is, however, far from reaching a truly operating free-trade zone, let alone a customs union, not even in any one of the subregional working arrangements. At the same time, the idea of a regional development bank, which I believe originated with ECLA, was implemented successfully in the form of the Inter-American Development Bank.

There is, finally, the idea of a more just income distribution as well as the more general concept of social development. In this respect, I believe, the concern of ECLA is shared completely by the governments of the region. Progress, however, has been slower than desired by all parties. The structural reforms proposed by the Commission are not always considered the most appropriate or, even if they are, they cannot, for political reasons, be implemented. A reasonable fear that social development measures might reduce the rate of growth of the economy to the point where those to be benefited will actually be worse off is also present. I believe that unless a way is found to make the aim of economic growth compatible with that of social development in the short run, progress in the latter area is bound to be relatively slow and will tend to follow more or less naturally the former.

The Commission's impact should not, however, be judged only by its ideas and by the rate at which they were adopted by the governments. ECLA's ideas, which were relatively novel and were based on assumptions not shared by everybody, produced a reaction in the region as well as abroad. In the region, they generated considerable interest in the study of economics, and a large number of Latin Americans began pursuing graduate studies abroad. This interest found its counterpart in the work of several foreign economics departments which undertook studies of the problems of the region. The several foreign exchange programs that were created as a result have meant a tremendous improvement in the quality of the work of the economics profession in Latin America and have resulted in the establishment of several very good local economics departments. In turn, Latin American economists have become influential in the shaping of economic policy in their countries.

One could perhaps say that the most important and permanent impact of ECLA was a by-product, namely, the awakening in the region of a serious desire to study economic phenomena. In the absence of ECLA, this might have taken much longer.

REFERENCES

1. Iglesias, E., "Exposicion ante la Asociacion de Industriales Latinamericanos," mimeo, Rio de Janeiro, 1974.

2. _____, "Exposición de la Sesión Plenaria del 7 de Marzo de 1975 del Decimosexto Período de Sesiones de CEPAL," mimeo, Port of Spain, Trinidad, Tobago, 1975.

3. Naciones Unidas, Estudio Económico de América Latina 1949, document E/CN. 12/164 Rev. 1, 1951.

4. _____, Problemas Teóricos y Prácticos del Crecimiento Económico, document E/CN. 12/221, 1952.

5. Naciones Unidas/CEPAL, "Evaluación de Quito," Santiago de Chile, 1973.

DEVELOPMENT POLICIES AND PROBLEMS:
THE BRAZILIAN EXPERIENCE

Carlos Geraldo Langoni*
and
Edy Luiz Kogut*

Fundacão Getúlio Vargas,
Rio de Janeiro, Brazil

The main objective of this paper is to give an overview of the Brazilian economy in the 1964-1975 period. Most of the discussion centers on the policies adopted since 1964 to control inflation and to open the economy.

We divide the presentation into three parts. The first is a brief review of Brazilian economic growth, inflation, and foreign trade since the 1950s. The second part is a discussion of anti-inflationary measures and export incentives put into practice since 1964. Finally, we summarize what we believe to be the major problems facing the Brazilian economy at the present time.

I. A BRIEF REVIEW OF THE BEHAVIOR OF THE BRAZILIAN ECONOMY

A. Economic Growth

Table 1 shows the behavior of the Brazilian economy in terms of economic growth from 1948 to 1975. The average growth in this period was about 7.0 percent, which can be considered high according to international standards.

From 1960 to 1970, the rate of growth of GDP averaged 6.4 percent, higher than the 3.9 percent of the U.S., the 4.9 percent of West Germany, or the 5.5 percent of Italy, although lower than the Japanese average of 11.1 percent. Per capita figures are less impressive, reflecting the high rate of growth of the Brazilian population. One interesting fact in Table 1 is the great variability of the rates, suggesting how difficult it is to achieve a sustained path of growth over long periods of time.

Thus, by any international standard, high rates of growth are observed, for example, 10.1 percent in 1954, 10.3 percent in 1961, 11.3 percent in 1971, and 11.4 percent in 1973; side by side with disappointing rates such as

*We would like to thank the participants at the Conference, particularly Arnold Harberger, Larry Sjaastad, and Allan Meltzer, for their valuable comments and suggestions. They are not, of course, responsible for our own errors.

Table 1

Rates of Growth of the Real Product,
Agriculture, Industry, and Services
(percent)

Year	Agriculture	Industry	Services	Total
1948	6.9	11.3	5.8	7.4
1949	4.5	10.3	6.0	6.6
1950	1.5	11.3	7.1	6.5
1951	0.7	6.4	9.9	6.0
1952	9.1	5.0	10.8	8.7
1953	0.2	8.7	-0.1	2.5
1954	7.9	9.5	13.0	10.1
1955	7.7	10.6	3.5	6.9
1956	-2.4	6.9	4.7	3.2
1957	9.3	5.7	8.9	8.1
1958	2.0	16.2	5.4	7.7
1959	5.3	11.9	1.2	5.6
1960	4.9	9.6	13.0	9.7
1961	7.6	10.6	11.9	10.3
1962	5.5	7.8	3.3	5.3
1963	1.0	0.2	2.9	1.5
1964	1.3	5.2	2.1	2.9
1965	13.8	-4.8	1.3	2.7
1966	-3.2	11.7	5.8	5.1
1967	5.7	3.0	5.8	4.8
1968	1.4	15.5	8.9	9.3
1969[a]	6.0	10.7	-	9.0
1970[a]	5.6	11.8	-	9.5
1971[a]	11.4	11.1	-	11.3
1972[a]	4.5	13.8	-	10.4
1973[a]	3.5	15.0	-	11.4
1974[a]	8.5	8.2	-	9.6
1975[a]	3.4	4.2		4.0
Average	4.8	8.8		7.0

Notes: (a) Preliminary estimate.

Source: Centro de Contas Nacionais, Instituto Brasileiro de Economia, Fundacão Getúlio Vargas, Rio de Janeiro.

2.5 percent in 1953, 3.2 percent in 1956, 1.5 percent in 1963 (the lowest), and 2.7 percent in 1965. In at least four years (1953, 1963, 1964, and 1965), the GDP rate of growth was close to or smaller than the demographic rate, resulting in negative or zero rates of growth of per capita income.

The disaggregation by sectors also stresses important patterns of behavior. The industrial sector is the one which presented the highest rates of growth and also the smallest variance. The average industrial rate of growth was 8.8 percent in the 1948-1975 period, which contrasts with 4.8 percent shown by the agricultural sector. As expected, the behavior of the agricultural sector is rather erratic, reflecting the great sensitivity of production to climatic conditions, which by itself is clear evidence of the traditional nature of Brazilian agriculture.

Table 2 shows the behavior of the most important industrial sectors for the 1958-1969 and 1971-73 periods. As might be expected, the sectors with the highest rates of growth are those either with high income elasticity (particularly durable goods), or the intermediate industries with great technological content (chemical products and machinery). The growth of traditional industries like food products and textiles tended to be smaller when compared to modern industries like machinery, electrical and communication equipment, and transportation equipment.

Since these differences in growth performance have maintained for a long period, the result is a significant change in the structure of Brazilian industry. The share of the "modern" sector increased from 29.1 percent in 1949 to 55.4 percent in 1969 (Table 3).

B. Inflation

Table 4 summarizes the Brazilian experience with inflation from 1950 to 1975. Rates of inflation vary from a minimum 7 percent in 1957 to a maximum 92 percent in 1964. Many combinations of inflationary trends and growth performance figures may be found in the Brazilian case. From the mid-1950s, we may distinguish three basic periods:
1) acceleration of growth and of inflation between 1957 and 1961;
2) deceleration of growth and acceleration of inflation in the 1962-65 period;
3) acceleration of growth and reduction of inflation from 1966 to 1973.

Since 1973, one observes again an acceleration of inflation (35.4 percent in 1974, 30 percent in 1975, and about 46 percent in 1976) with growth of real output tending to decline (9.4 percent in 1974 but only 4 percent in 1975).

81

Table 2

Real Growth of Industrial Output by Sectors
(percent)

Sectors	1958-1969[a]	1971[b]	1972[b]	1973[b]
Nonmetallic mineral products	96.0	4.35	13.67	16.36
Metallurgy	109.0	12.09	12.06	7.19
Machinery	311.0	23.03	15.12	26.84
Electrical and communication equipment	177.0	16.39	22.11	28.63
Transportation equipment	200.0	24.30	23.47	24.32
Printing and publishing	91.0	6.99	6.96	10.09
Rubber	117.0	12.92	13.02	12.39
Chemical	133.0	8.99	16.97	25.36
Textiles	54.0	16.60	3.82	6.89
Clothing	61.0	-5.74	5.02	14.10
Food products	81.0	0.42	18.73	3.34
Beverages	73.0	4.85	4.77	17.81
Tobacco	85.0	11.44	5.96	6.40

Notes: (a) Accumulated rates.
           (b) Annual growth.
Source: Santos (1974, Table 3).

Table 3

Distribution of Industrial Output by Sectors
(percent)

Sectors	1949	1959	1969
Textiles	20.10	12.00	10.25
Food products	19.70	16.60	11.64
Nonmetallic mineral products	7.40	6.70	6.03
Clothing, footwear	4.30	3.60	2.75
Beverages	4.30	2.90	2.56
Printing and publishing	4.20	2.00	0.15
Wood	3.90	3.30	2.64
Furniture	2.20	2.20	1.56
Leather products	1.30	1.10	0.56
Tobacco	1.60	1.30	1.64
Others	1.90	1.60	1.79
Subtotal	70.90	54.30	44.57
Chemical	9.40	13.40	17.90
Metallurgy	9.40	11.90	11.25
Transportation equipment	2.30	7.60	8.82
Electrical and communication equipment	1.70	3.90	6.45
Machinery	2.20	3.50	6.12
Paper	2.10	3.10	2.66
Rubber	2.00	2.30	2.23
Subtotal	29.10	45.70	55.43

Source: Santos (1973, p. 170).

These observed behaviors of rates of growth and rates of inflation are consistent with the predictions of the recently developed models of the determinants of both inflation and the level of economic activity.[1] According to a monetary version of these models, the first impact of an increase in the rate of growth of the money supply is to stimulate economic activity and, only after a certain lag, will prices come under pressure.[2] In the long run, increases in the rate of monetary growth will eventually be completely reflected in prices.[3] As may be observed in Table 4, the rates of variations of prices tend to follow the movements of the money supply in the long run. Thus, the rate of growth of the money supply increased from an average 20.4 percent in the 1950-55 period to 72.3 percent between 1962 and 1965, and then decreased to 33.9 percent in the period 1966-1973. Following these movements, prices increased from 16.0 percent in 1950-55 to 63.1 percent in 1962-65, and then decreased to 22.1 percent in 1966-1973. In the long run, there seems to be a clear positive relationship between the behavior of the money supply and inflation.[4]

The use of continuously overexpansive monetary policy to raise the level of employment or to raise revenue through a tax on real cash balances eventually leads to an acceleration of inflation. This practice gradually reduces the level of private investment through its disruptive effect on voluntary savings and the increased difficulty of evaluating expected rates of return. The Brazilian evidence of 1963-65 and 1975-76 suggests that the output losses associated with the allocative costs of imperfectly anticipated inflation are much higher than the eventual gains related to the transitory increases of government-forced savings. We should also consider that inflation is one of the objective factors behind the increasing participation of the state in the Brazilian economy. On many different occasions, unexpected changes in the rate of inflation have generated significant redistributive effects, especially against those who depend mainly on contractual income. The data also show, as in the 1964-67 period for example, the negative short-run effect of policies directed toward the reversion of the inflationary trend on real output.

High-powered money has been the dominant element in the expansion of the money supply in Brazil. The money multiplier declined from 2.0 in 1960 to 1.6 in 1963. From 1963 to 1967 it stayed around 1.6-1.7. It has been

---

[1]See Laidler and Parkin (1975).

[2]Laidler (1975). In Brazil, industrial output seems to be the best proxy for economic activity because of the erratic nature of the agricultural sector.

[3]For empirical evidence in the Brazilian case, see Lemgruber (1975).

[4]For a stronger evidence of this relationship, see Pastore (1973).

Table 4

Inflation and Growth

Years	Rates of Variation of the Money Supply[a]	Rates of Variation of Prices[b]	Rates of Variation of Real Product[c]	Rates of Variation of Industrial Product
1950-55	20.4	16.0	6.8	8.6
1956	21.8	24.4	3.2	6.9
1957	32.1	7.0	8.1	5.7
1958	23.0	24.3	7.7	16.2
1959	42.9	39.5	5.6	11.6
1960	38.8	30.5	9.7	9.6
1961	52.5	47.7	10.3	10.6
1956-1961	34.7	28.2	7.4	10.2
1962	64.1	51.3	5.3	7.8
1963	64.6	81.3	1.5	0.2
1964	81.6	91.9	2.9	5.2
1965	79.5	34.5	2.7	-4.8
1962-65	72.3	63.1	3.1	2.1
1966	13.8	38.3	5.1	11.7
1967	45.7	25.0	4.8	3.0
1968	39.0	25.4	9.3	15.5
1969	32.5	20.2	9.0	10.7
1970	25.8	19.3	9.5	11.2
1971	32.3	19.5	11.3	11.2
1972	38.3	15.5	10.4	13.8
1973	47.0	15.1	11.4	15.0
1966-1973	33.9	22.1	8.8	11.5
1974	34.0	35.4	9.4	9.0
1975	42.0	30.0	4.0	4.2
1976[d]	30.0	46.0	-	-

Notes:

(a) The money supply is defined as demand deposits plus currency held by the public.

(b) General price index ("Disponibilidade Interna").

(d) Estimated values.

Sources:

(a) Central Bank of Brazil.

(b) and (c) Instituto Brasileiro de Economia, Fundacão Getúlio Vargas, Rio de Janeiro.

growing steadily since 1967 to 1.9 in 1972, and is presently about 2.4 (June 1976). The growth between 1972 and 1975 is apparently due to decreases in the reserve requirements and to the possibility of using indexed Treasury bonds as legal reserves.[5]

C. Trade

The import coefficients declined from an average 13 percent in the immediate postwar period to about 8 percent during 1958-1961, when a large part of the import substitution took place. It fell further (to 5.9 percent) between 1962 and 1967. However, it is difficult to separate in this period the net effect of policy measures from the declining trend in the economy.[6] The import coefficient started to increase again in 1967 due to a clear change in the development strategy directed toward a substantial opening of the economy, reaching 12 percent in 1974.

Table 5 summarizes the main features of the trade balance. It is evident that until 1966 the volume of exports was almost stagnant. In the import substitution period of 1957-1961, there is a decrease of 11 percent in the value of exports with respect to the 1952-56 period. We discuss below why this has happened. Beginning in 1967, exports started to grow rapidly from US$1,654 million to US$8,655 million in 1975, an increase of about 423 percent. Until 1973, the policies succeeded in keeping the trade deficit under control and, in fact, through the liberalization of capital inflows, allowed for the accumulation of reserves up to US$6,400 million (Table 6). As a consequence of both the increase in the price of oil and the acceleration of inflation itself, trade deficits have tended to increase in recent years, reaching US$4,563 million in 1974 and US$3,515 million in 1975, and the external sector has again become an important constraint to Brazilian growth.[7] The external debt also showed considerable increases in 1974 and 1976, totaling close to US$28 billion at the end of 1976 (Table 6).

---

[5] In 1975 the reserve requirement was 25 percent, of which only 3.7 percent was required to be in cash. A large portion (14.3 percent) was allowed to be in the form of Treasury bonds (receiving interest) or in stocks (1 percent). Loans to small enterprises and to export firms were deductible from required reserves (4 percent and 2 percent, respectively). In 1976 there was a greater emphasis on the reduction of the multiplier as a means of offsetting the impact of the expansion of the monetary base on the money supply. Thus, there was an increase in the overall reserve requirements and in the fraction kept in a cash form. The rediscount rate was also raised.

[6] The Brazilian income-demand elasticity for imports tends to be greater than one.

[7] Another important component of the increase in the demand for imports seems to be the uncertainty regarding future import constraints.

Table 5

Brazilian Trade Balance
(U.S. $ millions)

Periods	Exports FOB Value	Average Annual Rate of Growth (percent)	Imports FOB Value	Average Annual Rate of Growth (percent)	Balance (Exports-Imports)
1947-1951	1,314[a]		1,103[a]		211
1952-56	1,483[a]	12.7[b]	1,275[a]	15.6[b]	208
1957-1961	1,319[a]	-11.1[b]	1,252[a]	-0.2[b]	67
1962-66	1,478[a]	12.1[b]	1,186[a]	-5.1[b]	292
1967-1971	2,298[a]	55.5[b]	2,209[a]	86.2[b]	89
1971	2,904	26.4	3,245	46.9	-341
1972	3,991	37.4	4,235	30.5	-244
1973	6,199	55.3	6,192	42.2	+7
1974	7,968	28.5	12,530	108.3	-4.563
1975	8,655	8.6	12,170	-3.9	-3.515

Notes: (a) Average value in the period;
      (b) With respect to the preceding period.

Source: Central Bank of Brazil.

Table 6

Reserves and External Debt, 1960-1974
(U.S. $ millions)

Years	Reserves	External Debt	Ratio of the Net Debt to Exports
1960	345	1,661	1.04
1961	470	2,127	1.18
1962	285	2,379	1.72
1963	219	2,497	1.62
1964	245	2,623	1.66
1965	484	2,808	1.46
1966	425	2,948	1.45
1967	199	2,866	1.61
1968	257	3,378	1.66
1969	656	4,403	1.62
1970	1,187	5,295	1.50
1971	1,723	6,622	1.69
1972	4,183	9,521	1.34
1973	6,417	12,572	1.04
1974	5,251	17,160	1.49
1975	4,000	22,000	2.00
1976[a]	5,000	28,000	2.30

Notes: (a) Estimated.
Source: Central Bank of Brazil.

II. THE CONTROL OF INFLATION AND EXPORT INCENTIVES

A. The Control of Inflation

There is empirical evidence that Brazilian inflation rates may be explained by present and past rates of growth of the money supply, variations of real income, and autonomous changes in some prices, among them wage rates and exchange rates. With quarterly data, these variables explain about 65 percent of the observed variance in prices. In the long run, or when great variations of prices take place, the expansion of the money supply tends to be the dominant factor. Only in the short run do exchange rates and wage rates seem to be important.[8]

Until 1964, the government deficit was the largest source of monetary expansion. In fact, early in the 1960s, when inflation rates accelerated, the government deficit increased from 2.8 percent of GDP in 1960 to 4.2 percent of GDP in 1963 (Table 7).

Table 8 shows the values of the main items of the consolidated balance sheet of the Brazilian monetary system: foreign assets, claims on government, claims on official entities, claims on private sector, and money. One may observe that since 1964 there has been a clear trend for the contribution of the government deficit to decrease as an inflationary source. On the one hand, there was a decrease in the deficit itself which dropped initially from 3.2 percent of GDP in 1964 to 1.6 percent of GDP in 1965, and then continually went down until 1973 when the Federal budget showed a surplus. On the other hand, since 1966 the government has not borrowed from the banking system (Table 8, column 2).

Nevertheless, there is no doubt that the government deficits were extremely important in the 1962-64 period when inflation reached its peak. This justifies the emphasis that was given to the reduction of the deficit and to its financing without creation of money, which was achieved basically through the following measures:

1) increase in government receipts through a combination of:
   a. fiscal reform, with the institution of value-added taxes, the mechanics of which clearly reduced evasion;
   b. the indexation of fiscal debts. Until 1964, there was an incentive to postpone payment of taxes since inflation rates were higher than the scale of penalties for delayed payment;
   c. elimination of subsidies of public services' tariffs;

---

[8] See Pastore (1973) and Pastore and Almonacid (1975).

89

Table 7

Government Finance, 1951-1975

Years	Government Receipts (percent annual changes)	Government Expenditures (percent annual changes)	Government Receipts/ GDP	Government Expenditures/ GDP	Surplus (+) or Deficit (-) (percent of GDP)	Money Supply (M) (percent annual change)
1951	40.38	11.67	9.0	8.3	+0.7	16.4
1952	12.67	13.43	8.3	7.7	+0.6	15.4
1953	24.32	69.74	8.7	11.0	-2.3	19.3
1954	22.98	5.23	8.0	8.7	-0.7	23.7
1955	17.69	19.52	7.6	8.3	-0.7	16.4
1956	25.84	51.62	7.5	9.9	-2.4	21.9
1957	30.07	40.35	8.0	11.4	-3.4	32.1
1958	35.81	17.52	9.0	11.1	-2.1	23.0
1959	37.46	36.41	9.1	11.1	-2.0	42.9
1960	36.76	46.34	9.0	11.8	-2.8	38.8
1961	50.04	57.01	9.2	12.6	-3.4	52.5
1962	52.37	66.40	8.6	12.9	-4.3	64.1
1963	85.86	83.80	8.8	13.0	-4.2	64.6
1964	102.53	83.64	9.2	12.4	-3.2	81.6
1965	83.50	57.48	13.3	14.9	-1.6	79.5
1966	51.27	44.38	11.0	12.1	-1.1	13.8
1967	15.30	23.74	9.5	11.2	-1.7	45.7
1968	50.80	43.08	10.3	11.5	-1.2	39.0
1969	35.79	27.88	10.5	11.1	-0.6	32.5
1970	37.56	28.71	11.0	11.4	-0.4	25.8
1971	40.57	46.06	11.5	11.8	-0.3	32.3
1972	39.87	38.34	12.5	12.7	-0.2	38.3
1973	40.08	37.42	13.6	13.5	+0.1	47.0
1974	45.30	38.73	13.5	12.8	+0.7	34.0
1975	24.26	30.77	12.1	12.4	+0.3	42.0
Average Percentage Changes						
1952-1973	42.2	42.6	9.7	11.5		38.6
1952-58	24.2	31.0	8.2	9.9		21.7
1959-1964	60.9	62.3	9.0	12.3		57.4
1965-1973	43.9	38.6	11.5	12.3		39.3
1968-1973	40.8	36.9	11.6	12.1		35.8
1974-75	34.8	34.8	14.8	14.5		38.0

Source: Central Bank of Brazil.

Table 8

Main Items of the Consolidated Balance Sheet of the Brazilian Monetary System
(CR$ millions: end of period)

Years	Net Foreign Assets	Domestic Credit						Money Increase (percent)
		Claims on Government	Increase (percent)	Claims on Official Entities	Claims on Private Sector	Total	Increase (percent)	
1960	12	295	-	35	593	923	-	-
1961	27	538	82	43	816	1,397	51.4	52.5
1962	47	810	50.6	49	1,303	2,162	54.8	64.1
1963	75	1,352	66.9	88	2,020	3,460	60.0	64.6
1964	173	2,726	101.6	166	3,631	6,523	88.5	81.6
1965	1,573	4,478	64.2	483	5,688	10,650	63.2	79.5
1966	1,547	6,274	40.1	635	8,605	15,514	45.7	13.8
1967	1,306	4,178	-33.4	956	11,717	16,851	8.6	45.7
1968	875	5,581	33.6	1,250	19,562	26,393	56.6	39.0
1969	2,928	6,010	7.7	1,710	27,830	35,550	34.7	32.5
1970	4,979	5,730	-4.7	2,755	37,475	45,960	29.3	25.8
1971	7,990	6,340	10.6	3,173	55,460	64,980	41.4	32.3
1972	22,160	1,130	-82.2	4,358	80,240	35,730	31.9	38.3
1973	35,080	860	-24.0	5,850	118,960	125,670	46.6	47.0
1974	32,750	470	-45.3	8,180	190,560	199,210	58.5	34.0
1975	(a)	-9,530	-	12,040	299,290	301,800	51.5	42.0

Notes: (a) Not available.

Source: International Financial Statistics, various issues, and Central Bank of Brazil.

2) The institution of indexed Treasury bonds. One of the effects of inflation on Brazilian capital markets was to lead to a decrease in the demand for savings deposits, bonds, and other financial assets because Brazilian law limited interest rates to 12 percent while prices rose faster than this limit. This policy made it impossible to finance the government deficit through Treasury bonds. In 1964, for the first time, the government issued indexed Treasury bonds which also offer an average real fixed rate of return of 6 percent per annum.[9]

As previously noted, the inflation rate reached its peak in 1964. During this year there occurred a substantial process of "corrective inflation"; that is, the government permitted readjustment of prices which had previously been under control. Monetary expansion was still high (81.6 percent). In 1965 there was a minor decrease in the rate of expansion of the money supply (79.5 percent) and prices grew less rapidly (91.9 percent in 1964 versus 34.5 percent in 1965). Expectations with respect to inflation came down with a gradual decrease in the income velocity of money from 7.04 (third quarter of 1964) to 6.21 (third quarter of 1965). An important element in the formation of these expectations was the success in reducing the government deficit by half in approximately one year. Nevertheless, industrial output decreased by 4.8 percent in 1965.

In 1966 the rate of growth of the money supply decreased sharply to 13.8 percent. The effect on inflation was felt until the next year, 1967, when the annual rate of inflation declined from 38.3 percent to 25.0 percent. This sharp decline in the rate of growth of the money supply in 1966 did not, however, immediately affect the average yearly rate of growth of industrial output which in fact reached 11.7 percent.[10]

---

[9]The Treasury bond has a nominal value that is indexed monthly. Until 1976, the value of the bond in one certain month was indexed according to the average wholesale price indexes of the preceding fourth, fifth, and sixth months. One might know well in advance, therefore, the value of the bond. Indexation of a large number of assets is based on that made for the Treasury bonds. This way of calculating the monetary correction introduced an exogenous element in the formation of expectations with respect to the future behavior of prices. In 1976, the lag in indexation was decreased to only one month. The public debt increased from CR$11.5 million in 1963 to CR$72.8 in 1964, and to CR$97,548 million in 1975.

[10]This great increase of industrial output clearly constitutes a puzzle. Probable explanations are: a) use of idle capacity generated by the 1964 recession; b) a large increase in equity financing, from CR$454 million in 1964 to CR$1,779 million in 1966. This large increase in equity financing reflects the expectation of the public regarding the decline of inflation. This might have been a reflection of confidence in the new government, which was able to decrease substantially the Treasury deficit, and of the impact of the new laws concerning the capital market (Law 4357 of July 16, 1964, Law 4595 of December 31, 1964, and Law 4728 of July 14, 1965).

The liquidity crisis affected the industrial sector drastically in 1967 when the rate of growth fell to 3.0 percent. When a new government came to power in 1967, it tried first to end the liquidity crisis by increasing the level of real credit, and then started to adopt a gradual approach to the decline in monetary expansion. In fact, short-run real credit to the private sector moved from a negative annual rate in 1966 (-4.0 percent) to a positive and increasing rate from 1967 on (Table 9). Although more difficult to evaluate, the government also tried to affect people's expectations with respect to inflation, especially through the implementation of a broader system of price controls. With this combination of measures, it was possible to reduce inflation from 25 percent in 1967 to 15 percent in 1973. At the same time, the economy expanded from a growth rate of 4.8 percent in 1967 to 11.4 percent in 1973. As noted above, the key to the conciliation of these two objectives was the expansion of credit to the private sector; in real terms, credit grew at a yearly average rate of 24 percent from 1967 to 1974 (Table 9, columns 1 and 4). Brazilian gradualism may, therefore, be described as an exchange between decreases of public deficits and expansion of credit to the private sector, with considerable gains in terms of reduction of inflation and expansion of the product. The margins of gains are higher as long as expectations are adjusted for declining rates of inflation, allowing a smaller lag between changes in the money supply and behavior of prices. Tables 7 and 8 illustrate that, since 1966, the contribution of the public sector's deficit to the expansion of the money supply has not been significant, and the main source of Brazilian inflation became the expansion of credit from both domestic and foreign sources. This tends to make it more difficult to conciliate acceleration of growth with reduction of inflation even within the gradualism framework, especially when inflation expectations are high. Under these circumstances, one cannot count on smaller lags (and even undershootings) between reductions in the rate of expansion of money supply and a fall in the rate of change of prices, which would avoid sharp reductions in the level of credit to the private sector in real terms, a key element in the conciliation of growth and reduction of inflation.

We will return to the analysis of recent trends in Brazilian inflation in the last section.

Price and wage controls are another tool that the government has been trying to use against inflation.[11] In principle, one could argue that this might

---

[11] Industrial and agricultural prices have been controlled by two government agencies: Comissão Interministerial de Precos (CIP), and Superintendência Nacional de Abastecimento (SUNAB).

Table 9

Distribution of Credit in Brazil,[a] CR$ billions at 1974 Prices
(Deflated by wholesale prices)

Years	Short-Run Credit to the			Long-Run Credit to the			Total	Increase (percent)
	Private Sector	Public Sector	Total	Private Sector	Public Sector	Total		
1952	43.21	1.32	44.53	5.69	6.11	11.80	56.33	-
1953	40.84	1.66	42.50	5.49	5.80	11.29	53.79	-4.5
1954	41.74	1.50	43.24	5.38	6.53	11.91	55.15	+2.5
1955	40.90	1.08	41.98	5.79	6.44	12.23	54.21	-1.7
1956	38.68	0.90	39.48	5.71	5.47	11.18	50.66	-6.5
1957	45.40	0.90	46.30	7.51	5.65	13.16	59.46	+17.4
1958	42.51	0.63	43.14	7.07	5.59	12.66	55.80	-6.2
1959	38.58	0.73	39.31	6.65	5.10	11.73	51.06	-8.5
1960	40.84	0.94	41.78	6.45	4.48	10.93	52.71	+3.2
1961	36.56	0.79	37.35	5.36	3.20	8.86	46.21	-12.3
1962	40.14	0.57	40.71	6.45	3.73	10.18	50.89	+10.1
1963	33.78	0.62	34.40	5.65	2.65	8.30	42.70	-16.1
1964	33.26	0.83	34.09	5.16	1.64	6.80	40.89	-4.2
1965	39.59	2.15	41.81	7.27	3.13	10.40	52.22	+27.7
1966	37.86	1.39	39.25	9.32	2.82	12.14	51.39	-1.6
1967	50.49	1.57	52.06	14.04	5.22	19.26	71.32	+38.8
1968	68.26	1.61	69.87	20.07	5.07	25.14	95.01	+33.2
1969	84.39	1.17	85.56	27.67	7.20	34.87	120.43	+26.8
1970	99.23	2.21	101.44	38.64	7.35	45.99	147.43	+22.4
1971	122.49	1.53	124.02	48.89	7.87	56.76	180.78	+22.6
1972	154.36	1.31	155.67	76.10	9.87	85.97	241.64	+33.7
1973	196.53	1.71	198.24	102.18	12.53	114.71	312.95	+29.5
1974	226.21	2.90	229.11	88.85	13.57	102.42	331.53	+5.9

Notes: (a) Taken from the aggregate balance sheet of the Bank of Brazil, commercial banks, savings and loan companies, Federal and state savings banks, state and Federal development banks, investment banks, housing companies, and insurance companies.

Source: Carvalho, et al. (1976).

be a way of acting on the formation of price expectations.[12] It is also a widespread idea that price controls are useful for dealing with oligopolies and monopolies, which dominate many sectors of the Brazilian economy as a result of import substitution policies. In theory, there is no better way to deal with monopoly than competition, including competition from foreign sources through international trade. Even though in Brazil price controls have not led to artificial reductions in supply such as those reflected by "queues," there is no question that it is affecting long-run choices of investors, besides making short-run adjustments more difficult; an example would be those investments related to a more intensive change in the mini-devaluation scheme.[13] There is no clear evidence of the net contribution of price controls to curbing inflation. Moreover, in the period under analysis (1964-67), when there was a sharp decrease in price expectations, the government was actually eliminating price controls, particularly on public utilities and rents.

Wage controls are applied to the minimum salary, government employees' salaries, and whenever there are collective disputes between employers and employees ("dissídios coletivos"). The initial philosophy of the wage readjustment formula was to restore wage's purchasing power to its average value in the last two years, plus allowing an increase due to productivity. Since readjustments are made at the beginning of each year, and the new levels are intended to prevail for one year, a rate of inflation for the next 12 months had to be estimated.[14] Divergences between planned and realized rates of inflation brought about readjustments that underestimated the effective loss in purchasing power. In 1968 the formula was changed in order to permit the correction of any underestimation of future inflation through the introduction of a factor that would account for the difference between expected and observed

---

[12] Even if this hypothesis were true, it seems clear that this instrument can only succeed when the government is curbing the expansion of aggregate demand.

[13] This point will be discussed below.

[14] The actual formula was

$$W_{n+1} = 0.5 \ (W_n + W_{n-1}) \ (1 + r_{n+1}) \ (1 + 0.5 \ i^e_{n+1}) \ P_n \ ,$$

where W_{n+1} = the nominal wage to apply in the 12 months;

W_n = the real wage prevailing in the past year;

r_{n+1} = the rate of anticipated productivity increase;

i^e_{n+1} = the rate of expected inflation;

P_n = the price index at the end of period.

For more details, see Fishlow (1974).

inflation.[15] Then, in November 1974, due to the acceleration of inflation, a further change was made. The average to be considered is the one prevailing in the previous 12 months (and not 24 months as before), which works better in a situation of an increasing rate of inflation.

As Table 10 demonstrates, since 1962, long before wage controls, the minimum wage already showed a declining trend. During the 60s, the minimum wage decreased 33 percent in real terms. The impact of this decline in terms of income distribution is smaller than one might first imagine because, as economic growth takes place, social mobility permits individuals to leave the minimum wage bracket (Langoni, 1976).[16]

Morley and Williamson (1975) present additional empirical evidence for this hypothesis, suggesting that the increase in income inequality during the 60s was mostly due to conventional market forces and not to wage controls.[17]

Now, gradualism accepts the idea of living with inflation for long periods. This requires special devices which permit the neutralization of the classical effects of inflation, among which the most important is the disarticulation of the capital markets. If interest rates remain fixed while the rate of inflation grows, voluntary savings tend to dwindle. Moreover, because inflation increases uncertainty, long-run savings and investments are particularly affected.

One way of minimizing these distortions would be to eliminate any restrictions on the movements of interest rates. The Brazilian option was to establish an overall remuneration equal to a real rate (fixed), which varies with the liquidity and period of time of the application, plus the expected rate of inflation. This policy reestablished, to a certain extent, the flow of voluntary savings, although it introduced some new distortions into the economy. The main result was a tremendous growth of financial assets and of financial intermediation in the Brazilian economy. From 1964 on, these assets grew rapidly, from 25 percent of the money supply (M1) in 1966 to 124 percent of M1 in 1974. To what extent this important change in the structure of the Brazilian economy is affecting the ability of the monetary authorities to control the money supply is a question still open to empirical investigation.[18]

---

[15] The formula became

$$W_{n+1} = 0.5 \left(\overline{W} \left(\frac{1+0.5i_n}{1+0.5i_n^e} \right) + \overline{W}_{n-1} \right) (1+r_{n+1}) (1+0.5i_{n+1}^e) P_n .$$

[16] One indirect evidence of this upward mobility is the more favorable behavior of the average real wage in the industrial sector (Table 10).

[17] Actually this confirmed the evidence presented by Langoni (1973 and 1976).

[18] Contador (1974) has suggested that there is a high degree of substitution between these financial assets and money in the Brazilian case.

Table 10

Rates of Change of the Minimum Wage and of the Average Wage in the Industrial Sector in Real Terms

Years	Annual Rates of Change (percent)	
	Minimum Wage	Average Wage
1961	+16.04	-
1962	-16.25	-
1963	-6.80	-12.4
1964	-2.08	-3.2
1965	-7.45	-6.4
1966	-6.90	+3.8
1967	-3.70	+0.4
1968	+1.28	+6.6
1969	-5.06	+7.2
1970	-5.33	+3.4
1971	+2.82	+4.6
1972	+4.11	+7.1
1973	+9.21	+6.3
1974	+3.61	+4.6
1975	+4.00	+8.9

Source: Langoni (1975), and Central Bank of Brazil.

There are two types of financial assets when indexation is involved as indexation can be fixed ex ante or ex post. When there is an acceleration of inflation, investors tend to prefer assets with ex post indexation, and vice versa when inflation is expected to decline. With inflation picking up since 1973, ex post indexed financial assets (Treasury bonds, savings deposits) became more important as opposed to ex ante indexed assets (bills of exchange, time deposits) whose importance declined. Since most of these funds have specific applications, the acceleration of inflation is still generating a reallocation of funds, which has nothing to do with real rentability which reflects relative scarcity of resources.[19]

The existence of price controls and indexation may generate distortions. Under price controls, indexation will hardly reflect the real rates of inflation. Price controls also make it difficult for entrepreneurs to pass part of the increasing financing cost to the market. Thus, firms were recently granted, through the two largest government banks (National Development Bank and Bank of Brazil), loans with a maximum monetary correction of 20 percent a year.

With expected rates of inflation for 1976 higher than 40 percent, these loans are clearly subsidized. Further, an increasing variance in the rate of inflation has made it more difficult to channel voluntary resources toward investments with longer time periods. Thus, in Brazil, the sources of long-run financing are either forced funds managed by the state or the international capital market.

Since 1964, indexation has also been applied to the real assets of enterprises. Their previous evaluation at historical prices led to a great distortion between real and nominal returns. More recently, enterprises have been allowed also to index their working capital and to deduct the monetary correction from taxable profits.[20]

Indexation was introduced in Brazil to neutralize some of the classical distortions caused by inflation and, although it did succeed in this direction, it brought about some new distortions. Even if monetary correction were perfectly calculated and applied, the fact persists that expectations with respect to rates of inflation differ among individuals and that these differences tend to be bigger the greater is the variance of the rate of inflation. From the Brazilian experience, one cannot say that the monetary correction perpetuates inflation. In fact, from 1964 to 1973, the annual inflation rate declined substantially

---

[19] For example, until recently, saving deposits ("cadernetas de poupanca") were supposed to be applied exclusively in the construction industry.

[20] In Brazil, last in-first out (LIFO) inventory accounting is not legal.

even though the monetary correction scheme was being implemented. One can even argue, following Friedman (1974), that the existence of monetary correction allows a quicker adjustment of expectations through a faster perception of the behavior of prices. Only recently, however, is Brazil testing the effects of monetary correction during a phase of acceleration of inflation and of increasing monthly variance in the rate of change of prices.

The main problem here is not caused by the indexing idea itself but by the way in which, until recently, it was implemented, and particularly by the existence of price controls which aggravate the short-run impact of changes in monetary correction on the cash flow of firms. Because of these difficulties, some important changes were introduced into the Brazilian indexing scheme. First, a "correction" of the monetary correction was recently introduced for loans and for calculating the return on financial assets. The idea is to "purge" the wholesale price indexes from changes which are clearly related to exogenous shifts in the price level of specific products (particularly agricultural products), which may have a large short-run influence in the magnitude of the index.[21] Although the idea of normalizing the index has some theoretical appeal because it brings up the basic distinction between inflation and a once-and-for-all change in prices, it also introduces a new element of discretion in the estimation of price indexes, which by itself feeds the uncertainty component already present in any inflationary environment. Second, there was a reduction in the lag between monetary correction and current inflation since indexation is now based on the average increase of wholesale prices of the preceding second, third, and fourth months (and not on the preceding fourth, fifth, and sixth months, as previously). The justification here is to avoid having the monetary correction become involuntarily an obstacle for a rapid revision of inflationary expectations. Third, there is now an adjustment toward a hypothetical "normal" rate of inflation for the Brazilian economy of 15 percent, which value participates with a weight of 20 percent in the calculation of the monetary correction index (the other 80 percent being the average of past prices). The justification usually presented is to reduce the feedback from monetary correction to inflation. The practical result is the introduction of a substantial difference between monetary correction and inflation (particularly when the rate of inflation is well above 15 percent) with all well-known allocative distortions. Whether these allocative costs are offset by the benefits of a quicker revision of expectations is an open question. It is also difficult to know the relative importance of indexing by itself in the formation of inflationary expectations in Brazil. Given all these uncertainties, we would prefer a scheme

---

[21]The adjustment may, in fact, increase or decrease the index.

of full monetary correction combined with more liberty to set prices (which includes flexibility with respect to real rates of return), giving more emphasis to the monetary policy itself as the basic instrument for the control of inflation.[22]

B. The Incentives to Export

From the end of World War II to 1964, Brazil followed a typically inward-looking model of economic growth based on the substitution of manufactured imports. Since 1964, there has been a strong belief that Brazil needs to open its economy, giving more emphasis to exports. This would be the only way to assure, in the long run, the financing of imports necessary to the maintenance of rapid economic growth. The objective should be not only a higher overall rate of growth for exports but also a significant change in their composition in order to reduce the dependence on one or two traditional products.[23]

Many mechanisms were utilized to promote import substitution and industrialization. Until 1953, a system of import licenses was used and, from 1953 to 1957, a multiple exchange rate system.[24] The latter scheme permitted discrimination among imports. By the end of the 1950s, less than 2 percent of demand for manufactured consumer goods was satisfied by imports; for industrial intermediate inputs, the participation was greater at 12 percent; and, for capital goods, greater still, approximately one-third of the total.[25] There is no doubt that this protectionist policy succeeded in developing and diversifying Brazil's industrial structure. Nevertheless, it exacted its costs, generating, among other things, a large number of industrial sectors with oligopoly characteristics and a relatively capital-intensive industrial sector. It also resulted in a clear discrimination against certain nonprotected sectors, particularly agriculture. Moreover, it had a strong negative impact on exports. The counterpart of barriers to imports in the exchange market is the existence

---

[22] There is another conceptual error in the Brazilian capital market, which is the confusion between a real rate of return and a fixed one. As already stated, Treasury bonds and also savings and time deposits pay a real rate of 6 percent, independent of the conditions of supply of and demand for these financial assets. Since these assets are practically risk free, the value of 6 percent actually becomes an institutional limit, which avoids the problem that market rates of interest decline even further during periods in which the rate of inflation is declining.

[23] From 1950 to 1964, coffee represented more than 50 percent of Brazil's exports.

[24] In August 1957, a comprehensive set of ad valorem tariffs was introduced and the number of exchange rate categories was reduced. See Bergsman (1970, p. 32).

[25] Bergsman and Candal (1969).

of an overvalued exchange rate, and, many times, the use of domestic protected inputs reduced the degree of external competition of Brazil's exports.[26]

One of the fallacies of the strategy of economic development based on import substitution was the belief that domestic production of imports would eliminate restrictions concerning the balance of payments. As became clear later, the establishment of new industries generated additional demand for products that Brazil could not produce, for example, sophisticated capital goods, metals (aluminum, copper, zinc), some steel products, and petroleum.

Another component of this strategy, also contradicted later by the empirical evidence, was that Brazil's exports had few possibilities for growth because of "structural" reasons. On the one hand, it was argued that the supply of traditional exports was too rigid to respond to economic incentives mainly because of the distribution of land tenure. On the other hand, a systematic deterioration of the terms of trade of Brazil's primary products and the barriers imposed by the developed world to the exports of Brazil's manufactures would make impossible an opening of the economy, at least at that stage (the 1950s) of the development of the economy.[27]

The historical evidence seems to show that, over a long period of time, there has been no systematic declining trend in the relative prices of Brazil's primary products, although the figures show a relatively high variance.[28] In addition, there is strong evidence that Brazilian agricultural production does respond to economic incentives.[29]

Another misjudgment concerned the possibilities for the export of manufactures. Brazil has the advantage of being a small producer of these goods and, therefore, its exports do not influence international prices. This implies that, in a certain period, if Brazilian manufactures can sell at competitive prices, they do not face market limitations. The experience has demonstrated that, for a large number of products, competitive conditions can be attained basically through the following policies:

---

[26] For a long time, the exchange rate was also overvalued by explicit government policy.

[27] These are the basic arguments used by ECLA. For a comprehensive analysis of ECLA's points of view, see Luders (this issue).

[28] See, for example, Simonsen (1972).

[29] See Pastore (1968). More recent evidence of the rapidity of response of Brazilian agriculture to price incentives is the expansion of soybean production, which was very small in 1971 and is now one of Brazil's main exports (15 percent of total exports, including soybeans, soy cake, and soybean oil).

1) an exchange rate policy that takes into account internal and external inflation (crawling peg or the mini-devaluation scheme);
2) credit for the production and commercialization of exportable manufactures;
3) fiscal incentives.

The mini-devaluations, which started in August 1968, consist of frequent, but not regular, devaluations of the cruzeiro. The annual devaluation corresponds roughly to the difference between Brazilian inflation and the average inflation of the main countries with which Brazil maintains trade. The objective is to keep the exchange rate approximately constant, in real terms, in order to avoid the reduction of exporters' profits in real terms (when there is no decline in international prices), and to discourage the demand for imported goods.

An additional advantage of this system is that it minimizes the speculation in foreign currency which generally occurs before devaluation in a fixed parity system. The gradual drop in the price of imports denominated in cruzeiros and the increase of the domestic costs of exportables, resulting from fixed parity in an inflationary environment, eventually induces the certainty that the existing rate cannot prevail for long. This tends to lead to large purchases of foreign currency, which hasten the devaluation. Since these purchases are made with resources previously applied to other types of investments with higher social rates of return, it is easy to understand how they jeopardize the efficient allocation of resources.

Under the mini-devaluation system, these speculative movements of foreign exchange are greatly reduced, since the timing of the mini-devaluation is irregular and its value rather small. Moreover, the devaluation tends to be smaller than the monetary correction, so it is usually more efficient to buy financial assets (with monetary correction) than foreign exchange.

In principle, the formula should be flexible in order to permit adjustments for changes in the terms of trade. In practice, price and interest rate controls, the size of the external debt, and the short-run inflationary feedback have prevented larger devaluations, which would be necessary to correct for exogenous changes in relative prices like those prevailing in 1975 and 1976.

The exchange rate policy was, nevertheless, a key factor in explaining the growth of exports of basic products at a cumulative rate of 232 percent between 1964 and 1973. Other important factors were:
1) favorable international prices, particularly for some agricultural products (sugar, soybeans, cocoa);

102

2) a stronger commitment by the government with respect to production in the agricultural sector;[30]

3) the improvement of commercial schemes, especially for iron ore, manganese ore, and coffee.

To explain the 1,000 percent increase in manufactured goods exports from 1964 to 1973 (from US$165 million to US$1,841 million), it is necessary to take into consideration the impact of fiscal incentives.

A justification for giving incentives to manufactured goods is that, to a certain extent, they offset distortions already existing in the economy.[31] An obvious one is taxes. As, in general, the indirect taxation burden tends to be relatively higher in developing countries, so (at least for this reason) the relative prices of their manufactured goods tend also to be higher. This idea led the government to exempt exports of manufactured goods from indirect value-added taxes.[32] It is important to realize that the implementation of a scheme of fiscal incentives was facilitated by the fiscal reform program that created value-added taxes in Brazil.

There are, however, some additional fiscal incentives that must be interpreted in broader terms, such as government advances to exporting firms, the magnitude of which corresponds to the same indirect taxes which were exempted. Justification for these subsidies relies on the assumption that the social return from the export of manufactured goods is higher than the private one. There is no doubt that the diversification of exports reduces the risk of a balance of payments crisis caused by unexpected changes in the prices of primary products, which may eventually jeopardize the performance of the whole economy. In a way, the levels of tariff protection imply an overvalued cruzeiro.

Also, to the extent that access to broader markets may allow domestic firms to explore economies of scale, there is an additional justification, since it may be expected that a fraction of these gains will be transferred to other domestic sectors or to final consumers through lower relative prices. Moreover, industrial exports expose Brazilian manufactures to a discipline of international

---

[30] There have been, however, some biases against the exports of basic products, for example, the transitory imposition of taxes and quotas. For a comprehensive analysis of these biases, see Senna (1976).

[31] Sjaastad (1975) and Fishlow (1976) seem to agree with this point.

[32] The exemption of taxes does not run against GATT rules.

competition lacking in the domestic market, which usually stimulates quality improvements and facilitates the absorption of new technology.[33]

As should be expected, the success of Brazil's export incentives has aroused the protests of potential competitors, mainly with respect to products whose export growth rates have been extremely rapid, clothing and footwear, for example.[34] It is reasonable to assume that external resistance will tend to be greater in the near future. Besides political bargaining, there are other ways of minimizing these resistances. The major one is geographical diversification with emphasis on the new markets (Africa, Asia, and the Middle East). Fortunately, geographical diversification is already happening with most of Brazil's exports. Thus, in 1947-1951, for example, 48.1 percent of Brazilian exports and 46.4 percent of imports were traded with the U.S. In 1974 these same figures were, respectively, 21.1 percent and 27.7 percent, with a substantial increase in European Common Market participation.

The preceding paragraphs make clear how complex problems relating to foreign trade are in a developing economy. In principle, one cannot simply dichotomize the alternatives: import substitution versus export promotion. Given a certain target of growth, one has to accept a minimum level of imports, which will have to be paid for through exports or be financed by foreign loans. By the same token, a certain wanted volume of investment usually implies a certain inflow of foreign capital to complement domestic savings. Since, in practice, a country cannot increase indefinitely its foreign debt, export promotion again enters the picture as a fundamental tool of development.

Import substitution should be considered more as a strategy of industrialization than as a mechanism to eliminate trade deficits. One has to take into consideration that, besides eventual inefficiencies brought about by this policy, additional demand for new imports seriously limits reductions of the import coefficients over time. Even as a tool for industrialization, the Brazilian experience showed the necessity to prevent having final consumers and other sectors bear the full burden of this strategy. Eventually, import substitution may even jeopardize the export sector by increasing the costs of some of its inputs.

---

[33] According to the Department of Foreign Commerce of the Bank of Brazil (CACEX), the number of firms exporting manufactures increased 464 percent from 1967 to 1974.

[34] Exports of shoes increased from an average US$18.9 million in the 1968-1972 period to US$165 million in 1975 (more than 760 percent). Exports of cotton fabrics increased from US$10.3 million to US$50 million in the same period (a near 400 percent increase).

It is possible to imagine a development strategy which tries to explore the possibilities of complementarity between export promotion and import substitution. Saving and generating foreign exchange are not necessarily mutually exclusive factors. Newly protected industries may eventually participate in the export promotion effort, with substantial gains in terms of production efficiency. This may even facilitate the implementation of a policy, which has been suggested frequently, of gradually declining effective protection in order to avoid the common situation of a permanent infant industry.

The Brazilian experience also illustrates how important the role of the exchange rate can be in minimizing trade disequilibria. It also seems reasonable to extend the infant industry argument to a newcomer exporter. This argument, coupled with the ideas of offsetting distortions, generating externalities, appropriating economies of scale, and stimulating technological improvements, helps to justify transitory fiscal incentives to exports.

III. MAJOR CURRENT PROBLEMS

As a result of seven years of rapid economic growth from 1968 to 1974 Brazil has to a large extent modernized its economic structure and substantially raised its per capita income. There are, however, some important problems facing the country on its way to a higher stage of economic development. Long-run problems include the increasing participation of the state in the economy and the controversial question of the inequality in the distribution of income. Short-run problems are the balance of payments disequilibrium and the acceleration of inflation.

A. Participation of the State in the Economy

The presence of the state in the Brazilian economy is gradually becoming more important and complex. Government expenditures as a proportion of GDP increased from 19.4 percent in 1949 to 27.7 percent in 1973. Baer, Kerstenetsky, and Villela (1974) estimated this figure to be only 50 percent of the global figure obtained if government enterprises are included. The Brazilian government is responsible for 60 percent of all investments in fixed capital (machinery and equipment).

What is most interesting is that the advances in the participation of the state in the economy have occurred irrespective of the political regimes, so that it is not possible to adopt any naive "ideological" explanation for this development.

105

One of the basic aspects of state intervention in the Brazilian economy is the existence of large government enterprises in sectors such as electrical energy, communications, transportation, exploration of mineral resources, and steel production.[35] In some industries, such as oil, exploration for iron ore, and communications, there prevails a monopoly situation. In others, such as steel, there is some competition with private firms. These enterprises are organized in two alternative forms: "public" enterprises, in which the government retains all control; and "mixed" enterprises, in which the government is the major stockholder but in which private investment is also present.

Some of the objective factors that have led to the development of state enterprises are economies of scale, externalities, and capital market imperfections (especially with respect to access to long-run funds, caused by inflation). Furthermore, it is necessary to add a political preference for domestic control vis-à-vis foreign control. In fact, in some of the aforementioned sectors (communications and transportation, for example), the state became a substitute for foreign monopolies, whose profitability was drastically affected by price controls. One evidence of the importance of the objective factors noted above in the determination of the sectoral allocation of state enterprises (suggesting another dimension of their importance) is the fact that, among the 20 largest Brazilian firms in terms of stockholder's equity, 15 are government enterprises.

The presence of the government in the financial sector is also high. Besides the Bank of Brazil, which holds close to 25 percent of all bank deposits, the government controls 15 commercial banks and 11 development banks.[36]

The government is also becoming the most important source of long-run funds for investment, which are guaranteed by "forced" savings. Actually most of these funds are being centralized in the National Development Bank and in the National Housing Bank, which also have the responsibility to allocate these funds among different investment opportunities. These forced savings are the result of income and sales taxes (PIS/PASEP) and of a payroll tax (FGTS).[37]

---

[35] Major government enterprises are: Loide Brasileiro (1937, navigation); Companhia Siderúrgica Nacional (1941, steel production); Companhia Vale do Rio Doce (1957, iron ore); Petrobrás (1953, oil); Rede Ferroviária Federal (1957, railroads); Eletrobrás (1962, electricity generation); Embratel (1965, telecommunications); Embraer (1969, airplanes).

[36] It seems easier to understand the presence of the government in the development type of bank than in the commercial type.

[37] In 1975 the contribution to PIS/PASEP was divided into two parts:
a) a 5 percent income tax, deductible from the total income tax to be paid;
b) a 0.5 percent tax on total sales.
The FGTS contribution is an 8 percent payroll tax. These funds have also social functions, which are to guarantee an additional monthly wage equivalent to the minimum wage in the case of PIS/PASEP, and to work as a pension fund in the case of the FGTS.

Another form of indirect intervention by the state in the economy has been an extensive use of fiscal incentives. Originally these were designed to correct regional imbalances. Thus, these incentives benefit the Brazilian Northeast and North, which are the poorest regions in the country, aiming to stimulate investments in these areas through the use of funds derived from personal and corporate income-tax exemptions. Nowadays, they cover sectors like forestry, tourism, and fishing, independent of regional location. Until recently, fiscal incentives in Brazil benefited disproportionately the use of physical capital relative to labor, which helps to explain the relatively small impact of these investments on the poorest areas in terms of labor absorption. Only in 1976 did the government introduce incentives for programs of training and nutrition within firms.

Until now, the Brazilian economy has achieved a reasonable balance between private enterprise and public sector, at least in the sense that the presence of the state has not yet reduced the stimulus for private investment. As a matter of fact, through institutions like the National Development Bank (providing long-run financial and risk capital), the National Housing Bank (acting as a second-line bank for the housing sector), and the Bank of Brazil (especially through its action in the agricultural sector), the government has been acting explicity toward the development of the private sector. The question is to what extent this situation will be maintained given the difficulty of tracing the borderline in the relationship of substitutability and complementarity between the state and the private sector. We should also consider the workings of what could be called the "efficiency paradox." As long as government enterprises have been successful in increasing their efficiency over time, it has been difficult to avoid their expansion on the exclusive bases of market criteria. One of the main issues in Brazil nowadays is exactly how to avoid the diversification of the activities of large state enterprises like "Vale do Rio Doce," whose profit rate is extremely high.

Finally, it is also important to take into account the costs imposed on the private sector by the increasing complexity of economic legislation and of different forms of government control, some of which we have already mentioned.

Of course, the optimum balance between the state, domestic private enterprise, and foreign capital is a complex question which goes beyond the limits of economic theory. However, the historical experience of many countries, especially in Latin America, suggests that political stability seems related to success in achieving this dynamic balance, which by itself becomes a key factor for sustained development.

B. Income Distribution

Interpretation of the nature of the changes in income distribution in Brazil has been a controversial issue. There is no quarrel about the <u>direction</u> of the changes. Different studies have shown a clear trend toward increasing inequality, although the analyses are limited to a comparison of the 1960 and 1970 years.[38]

The distinguishing feature of the Brazilian case is that all groups have presented a real gain in absolute income over time, but those at the top of the distribution benefited proportionately more. Furthermore, the increase in inequality occurred only in the urban sector (secondary and tertiary), which is exactly the one with the highest rate of growth.

Divergences of opinion derive from the analysis of the factors that have led to increasing inequality as well as to its social consequences. Some argue that the increased inequality should be attributed mainly to the wage policy followed after 1964.[39] Others suggest that the increased inequality may well be a transitory phenomenon of disequilibrium resulting particularly from lagged adjustments of labor supply of different skill content to demand, in relation to varying speeds of adoption of improved technology and to sectoral growth.[40] In other words, according to this hypothesis, the main cause of the increase in inequality observed in Brazil lies in the imbalance of the labor market during the stage of accelerated growth, reflecting the dichotomy between unskilled and skilled labor as well as that between modern and traditional sectors.

According to this second hypothesis, it should be possible to show that this phase of increasing inequality coincides with a stage of intense social mobility, with a substantial enlargement of opportunities for people to move from one social status to another. In Brazil, we have found that income was more unequally distributed exactly in those sectors that presented a higher average income level, a higher rate of growth, and a higher average skill. Thus, we are not facing a frozen social structure. In the Brazilian case, inequality was also creating, through market "quasi rents," the signs and stimuli that will lead to a correction of the actual disequilibrium.[41]

---

[38] This increase in inequality, which has been widely noted in both the technical and the popular literature, actually applied to the economically active population receiving monetary income. Morley and Williamson (1975) argue that when the groups classified in the census as receiving zero income are included in the analysis, it is no longer clear that inequality increased over the period, for the Lorenz curves for 1960 and 1970, constructed on this basis, cross each other. For the basic empirical results, see Langoni (1976).

[39] Fishlow (1973).

[40] Langoni (1976).

[41] University enrollment, for example, increased 61.8 percent from 1970 to 1972.

This interpretation is consistent with the "tunnel" hypothesis which suggests that the key to defining the tolerance of any society with respect to relative inequality is the expected degree of mobility.[42]

In Brazil, the speed of the adjustment process will be influenced by many institutional variables and economic events, but the crucial elements seem to be the pace of expansion of the educational system and the reduction of population growth.[43] In the meantime, short-run policy must be geared to the alleviation of the consequences of poverty, especially by enlarging social security and by expanding health and nutrition programs, particularly for children.

In short, the existence of large inequalities creates an additional pressure for the maintenance of rapid growth and, of course, the hope for a more balanced path, in order to avoid a change in the expectations of future affluence of the majority of Brazilians, which could affect social and political stability.

C. Acceleration of Inflation and Balance of Payments Deficits

As noted in Part I, the Brazilian rate of inflation started to increase again in 1974 and reached a level of 46 percent in 1976.

The main causes of the acceleration of Brazilian inflation after 1973 were the great expansion of foreign and domestic credit and the lack of an appropriate instrument to deal with the monetary problems of a relatively open economy. This "credit" inflation contrasts clearly with the "fiscal" inflation of 1964. As Table 8 shows, from 1968 (and until 1973) when the outward-looking policy started, the relative importance of net foreign assets to the expansion of the monetary base increased sharply. This accumulation of reserves was not caused by significant trade surpluses but by a massive inflow of financial capital in response to favorable interest rate differentials between the domestic and the international capital markets, once legal barriers between them were removed.[44] Behind these favorable interest rate differentials were exceptional conditions of the Eurodollar and the American markets for financial capital, until the time of the oil crisis at the end of 1973. These conditions, combined with the Brazilian mini-devaluation policy, whose mechanics assured that the exchange risk component of the cost of borrowing abroad was generally smaller than domestic inflation, gave rise to substantial inflows of capital. Thus, the net

---

[42]Hirschman and Rothschild (1973).

[43]For a more detailed discussion, see Kogut and Langoni (1975).

[44]Through Resolution 63 of August 1967, the Central Bank allowed Brazilian banks to borrow money abroad and to lend it to Brazilian firms. Previously, this was only permitted to firms (Law 4131/62, with the modifications of Law 4390/64).

inflow of foreign financial capital grew from US$583 million in 1968 to US$4,298 million in 1973. This increase was enough not only to cover the current account deficits but also to contribute to the rise in the stock of foreign reserves to a level of US$6.4 billion at the end of 1973.

Theoretically, open market operations are the appropriate instrument to deal with unanticipated variations in the money supply, such as those caused by deficits or surpluses in the balance of payments. In Brazil, open market operations started simultaneously with the opening of the economy in 1968. However, the emphasis on interest rate controls seriously limited the effectiveness of these operations, since the controls indirectly determined the maximum amount of Treasury bills ("Letras do Tesouro Nacional") that could be sold to the public during a given period of time. By the same token, changes in the discount rate were also administered, with the intent of reducing interest rates and, therefore, could not be used as a tool to offset excessive expansions of the money supply.[45]

The difficulties of controlling excesses of liquidity brought about by balance of payments surpluses are well illustrated by the gradual increase in the minimum repayment period required for external loans, which reached 12 years in 1973.[46]

Furthermore, as an additional consequence of interest controls, the accumulated stock of Treasury bills held by the public was considerably smaller in 1974 than the one that would be required to offset an unexpected decline in real liquidity.[47]

The lack of instruments to deal with changes in the endogenous component of the monetary base resulted in a reversal of the declining trend in the rate of expansion of the money supply, which was observed beginning in 1964 (with the exception of 1967, already commented on). From 1971 on, the rate of change of the money supply started to accelerate again, from an annual rate of 25.8 percent to an annual rate of 47 percent in 1973.

---

[45] Accordingly, the basic rediscount rate was reduced from 22 percent per year in 1968 to 18 percent per year in 1973. It was only in 1976 that the government decided to free interest rates, apparently becoming less concerned by the rates reached by Treasury bills. As a result, the volume of Treasury bills held by the public increased from an average 13 percent of the money supply in the 1973-75 period to 20.9 percent in August 1976.

[46] These measures are also consistent with the objective of improving the debt profile.

[47] Such a decline was observed in the second semester of 1974, when there was a substantial loss of foreign reserves caused by sharp changes in the Eurodollar market, associated with initial difficulties in the recycling of petrodollars. During 1975 the government used so-called "compensatory financing," which consisted of loans by the Central Bank to banks at subsidized interest rates for a limited period of time.

Thus, there was a considerable inflationary potential in the Brazilian economy even before the impact of the oil price hikes. In fact, one can say that the preexisting excess of liquidity facilitated the transformation of the sharp increase in the oil price into an inflationary component, which added to its direct impact in the exacerbation of inflationary expectations.

Since 1974, the foreign reserve component of the base ceased to be expansionary, and domestic credit expansion became the major source of inflation. In 1975, for example, the loans of the Bank of Brazil to the private sector rose by 72 percent, mostly due to a policy of subsidized credit, especially to the agricultural sector.

The difficulties of adopting a consistent restrictive monetary policy in the 1974-76 period reflect the smaller possibility of conciliating reduction of inflation without affecting the behavior of real output in the short run when credit inflation combines with unfavorable inflationary expectations, as noted above. It may well be that to succeed once again in conciliating rapid growth with a reasonably lower and stable rate of inflation, a drastic change in the sources of financing the expansion of firms in Brazil will be needed, with a reduction in their present dependence on financial capital and an increase in the participation of equity financing. Present inflation rates also reflect a lack of consistency between monetary and fiscal policy. Fiscal policy became clearly expansionary after 1975. Comparing 1976 and 1975 (first semester), government spending grew 90 percent in nominal terms, while government receipts increased only by 70 percent. Even though there was the possibility of financing this deficit through the sale of government indexed bonds, there is no doubt that the sharp acceleration of public spending generated additional inflationary pressures, particularly through its impact on the demand for additional credit.[48]

The balance of the trade account changed from a small deficit of US$244 million in 1972 and a surplus of US$7 million in 1973, to deficits of US$4.5 billion in 1974 and US$3.5 billion in 1975. The current account deficit was close to US$7 billion in both years. These deficits were partly compensated by inflows of foreign capital (mostly loans) and by losses of reserves (altogether about US$2.4 billion).

Although petroleum was an important factor in the sudden disequilibrium of the balance of payments (see Table 5 above), the strong demand for imports of capital goods and industrial inputs in real terms seems to suggest the

---

[48]From December 1975 to September 1976, Banco do Brasil loans to the public sector grew by 65.5 percent.

111

additional contributions of a loose monetary policy and of accelerating inflation, accompanied by continuing overvaluation of the cruzeiro.[49] The combination of these factors helps to explain how it was possible for the Brazilian economy to double its deficit within one year (1974) from US$6,192 million to US$12,530 million.

Brazilian strategy to adjust to these deficits has been basically: a) to create larger barriers to imports;[50] and b) to increase the incentives to exports (particularly through expansion of export financing and special credit facilities for exporting firms). The new legislation tends to be highly discriminatory and dependent on government agencies.[51]

Until 1976, the government has avoided increasing the intensity of the mini-devaluations. Furthermore, the import restrictions referred to above imply that, in practical terms, the government has been devaluating the exchange rate relevant to the trade balance more than that relevant to the capital account.

There were two main reasons for this strategy: a) price controls, and b) the ceiling on interest rates. Price controls make it difficult for firms with dollar debts to transfer part of the cost increases due to devaluations (which cannot be absorbed by productivity gains) to their final prices.

As far as interest rate controls are concerned, the monetary authorities attempted to bring interest rates down in a gradual way. The period 1969-1974 was one of deceleration of inflation and, to a certain extent, this helped the authorities to make effective the ceilings on interest rates.[52] When inflation started to accelerate in 1974, these ceilings did not allow the government to increase the mini-devaluations, since otherwise the differential between domestic interest costs and foreign borrowing costs would be eliminated, affecting the inflow of foreign capital, which was crucial for the overall equilibrium of the balance of payments.

---

[49]During 1974, while prices rose by 35.4 percent (Table 4), the devaluation amounted to 19.7 percent. The figures for 1975 are 30 percent and 22 percent, respectively. The share of oil's expenses on total imports rose from 10 percent in 1973 to 25 percent in 1975.

[50]The major measures were the following: a) a 100 percent increase in the tariffs on approximately 2,000 imports; b) a requirement of payment in cash for all imports with a tariff higher than 38 percent; c) a requirement of a 360-day deposit equal to the value of imports, without interest payments; d) administrative controls on certain items, such as steel and metals, and on all government imports, including those by its enterprises.

[51]Some administrative control of imports may be justified as the only instrument powerful enough to control imports by the government itself. The share of the public sector of Brazilian imports was recently estimated to be roughly 40 percent of the total, 16 percent represented by machinery, equipment, and raw materials (other than petroleum), and 24 percent by petroleum and wheat.

[52]Nevertheless, banks have, in some circumstances, used all sorts of devices to go around these ceilings, for example, requiring a certain average balance.

Acceleration of inflation inevitably made controls of interest rates less and less effective and, in March 1976, the government decided to free interest rates gradually. With respect to more intensive mini-devaluations, the constraints are their short-run inflationary feedback and (due to the maintenance of price controls) the increasing burden for firms which borrowed abroad. The liberalization of interest rates will also allow the implementation of a more restrictive monetary policy, since there is now a greater degree of freedom for open market operations. Furthermore, the short-run increase in interest rates will help to transfer excess cash balances to savings (instead of their being used in consumption), thus reducing the possibility of a liquidity crisis and, therefore, also closing the excess demand gap through the maintenance of a reasonable rate of expansion of aggregate supply.[53]

The lack of coordination between fiscal and monetary policy already mentioned also contributed to the difficulties in adjusting to the disequilibrium in the trade balance. The beginning of new import substitution programs and of new public investments in infrastructure had a short-run impact on imports, which could not be eliminated through conventional mechanisms (exchange rates, tariffs, etc.). In fact, the result of the constraints were mainly to raise the cost of these projects, which created additional pressure either for subsidized credit or for a direct increase in public spending. The final result would inevitably be an unavoidable increase in inflation, which by itself makes it more difficult to control the trade credit.

Until inflation and the balance of payments situation are brought under control, Brazil will have to accept a rate of economic growth which is considerably lower than that achieved in recent years. One possible risk is that the restrictive policies recently adopted to equilibrate the trade balance, instead of acting as a transitory mechanism to be disconnected gradually when the problem is over, may in fact be transformed into the basis for a revival of development strategies which will again treat foreign exchange savings as the only criterion for domestic investment, with all the well-known negative effects of such policies on efficiency and income distribution.

---

[53] For a more elaborated discussion of this process, see McKinnon (1973).

REFERENCES

1. Baer, W., Kerstenetsky, I., and Villela, A., "A Mudanca do Papel do Governo na Economia," in Painéis Internacionais sobre o Desenvolvimento Sócio-Econômico, Rio de Janeiro: APEC, 1974.

2. Bergsman, J. Brazil, Industrialization and Trade Policies. New York: Oxford University Press for OECD, 1970.

3. Bergsman, J., and Candal, A., "Industrialization: Past Successes and Future Problems," in The Economy of Brazil, (ed. H.S. Ellis), Berkeley: University of California Press, 1969.

4. Carvalho, J.L., Goncalves Porto, A.C., Lemgruber, A.C., and Neuhaus, P., "Commercial Bank Behavior and Selective Credit Policies in Brazil," mimeo, Fundacão Getúlio Vargas, Rio de Janeiro, 1976.

5. Contador, C., "Desenvolvimento Financeiro, Liquidez e Substituicão entre Ativos no Brasil: A Experiência Recente," Pesquisa e Planejamento Econômico, 4, (June 1974), 245-84.

6. Fishlow, A., "Brazilian Size Distribution of Income," American Economic Review, LXII, No. 2, (May 1972), 391-402.

7. _____, "Some Reflections on Post-1964 Brazilian Economics," in Authoritarian Brazil: Origins, Policies, and Future, (ed. A. Stepan), New Haven: Yale University Press, 1973.

8. _____, "Indexing Brazilian Style: Inflation without Tears?" Brookings Papers on Economic Activity, Washington, D.C.: The Brookings Institution, 1974: 1, 261-82.

9. _____, "Foreign Trade Regimes and Economic Development: Brazil," mimeo, University of California, Berkeley, 1976.

10. Friedman, M., "Monetary Correction," in Essays on Inflation and Indexation, Washington, D.C.: American Enterprise Institute, 1974.

114

11. Hirschman, A.O., and Rothschild, M., "The Changing Tolerance for Income Inequality in the Course of Economic Development," Quarterly Journal of Economics, 87, No. 4, (November 1973), 544-66.

12. Kogut, E.L., and Langoni, C.G., "Population Growth, Income Distribution and Economic Development," International Labor Review, 111, No. 4, (April 1975), 321-33.

13. Laidler, D. Essays on Money and Inflation. Chicago: University of Chicago Press, 1975.

14. Laidler, D., and Parkin, M., "Inflation: A Survey," mimeo, University of Manchester, 1975.

15. Langoni, C.G. Distribuição da Renda e Desenvolvimento Econômico do Brasil. Rio de Janeiro: Expressão e Cultura, 1973.

16. _____. A Economia da Transformação. Rio de Janeiro: José Olympio, 1975.

17. _____, "Income Distribution and Economic Development: The Brazilian Case," in Frontiers of Quantitative Economics, (ed. M.D. Intriligator), Amsterdam: North-Holland, forthcoming 1976.

18. Lemgruber, A.C., "O Modelo Econométrico de St. Louis Aplicado ao Brasil," Ensaio Econômico da EPGE, No. 18, Rio de Janeiro: Escola de Pós-Graduação em Economia da Fundação Getúlio Vargas, 1975.

19. Luders, R., "The Economic Commission for Latin America: Its Policies and Their Impact," Carnegie-Rochester Conference Series on Public Policy, VI, (eds. K. Brunner and A.H. Meltzer), Amsterdam: North-Holland, 1977.

20. McKinnon, R.I. Money and Capital in Economic Development. Washington, D.C.: The Brookings Institution, 1973.

21. Morley, S., and Williamson, J., "Growth, Wage Policy and Inequality: Brazil During the Sixties," SSRI Workshop Series, Madison: University of Wisconsin, July 1975.

22. Pastore, A., "A Resposta da Producão Agrícola aos Precos no Brasil," São Paulo: Universidade de São Paulo, 1968.

23. _____, "A Oferta de Moeda no Brasil: 1961-72," Pesquisa e Planejamento Econômico, 3, No. 4, (December 1973).

24. Pastore, A., and Almonacid, R., "Gradualismo ou Tratamento de Choque," Pesquisa e Planejamento Econômico, 5, No. 4, (December 1975).

25. Santos, F.P., "Oferta de Mão-de-Obra e Crescimento Econômico Brasileiro," in A Economia Brasileira e suas Perspectivas, Rio de Janeiro: APEC, 1973.

26. _____, "Desenvolvimento Econômico e o Mercado de Trabalho no Brasil," in A Economia Brasileira e suas Perspectivas, Rio de Janeiro: APEC, 1974.

27. Senna, J.J., "A Participacão do Setor Público no Comércio Exterior do Brasil," Estudos Econômicos, No. 1, Rio de Janeiro: Confederacão Nacional do Comércio, 1976.

28. Simonsen, M. Brasil 2002. Rio de Janeiro: APEC, 1972.

29. Sjaastad, L., "How to Contrive an Economic Miracle: Brazil in the 70's," mimeo, University of Chicago, 1975.

A COMMENT ON THE LANGONI AND KOGUT AND LUDERS PAPERS

Larry A. Sjaastad
University of Chicago

The two papers under discussion complement one another nicely. The Luders paper traces the evolution of thought (doctrine?) in the United Nations Economic Commission for Latin America (ECLA) during its nearly 30 years of history and provides a critique of the main ECLA positions. The Langoni and Kogut paper focuses on the Brazilian experience, their emphasis being on the post-1964 period during which the economic policies followed in Brazil have frequently been in direct contradiction to ECLA prescriptions.

Turning first to the Luders paper, one finds in it an excellent description of the economic philosophy of ECLA as well as a critique of the key ECLA proposals concerning regional integration and import substitution. For my taste, however, the critique is far too gentle in view of the positive damage that ECLA-endorsed policies have caused over the years. The simple and unvarnished truth would appear to be that the authors of the ECLA propositions--particularly Raúl Prebisch--did not understand certain fundamental elements of economic theory. In a nutshell, it seems to me that the basic errors of the ECLA propositions stem from the (implicit) assumption that both inflation and the balance of payments are real rather than monetary phenomena. It follows rather directly from these assumptions that inflation necessarily accompanies the process of development (the "structural" view of inflation) and that balance of payments "problems" can only be solved via import and/or export substitution. No theory of economic development or commercial policy, whether it be highly sophisticated or hopelessly naive, can make much sense when it is based upon such a misunderstanding of the fundamental workings of a market economy.

Although the ECLA writings were often represented by proponents as consistent with a general equilibrium approach, most of them relied, in fact, on a partial equilibrium analysis of problems whose very nature precludes the latter type of focus. Inflation, for example, became basically a problem of changes in relative prices (particularly for food), and in their analysis of the balance of payments there is little or no recognition of the obvious fact that the ultimate effect of a successful import substitution program would be to reduce exports; indeed, some strands of ECLA thought appear to favor simultaneous policies of import substitution and promotion of nontraditional exports! In short, the economics of ECLA was--and is--exceedingly poor.

One wonders, then, how ECLA doctrines became so deeply rooted in Latin American economic thinking as to dictate policy in the majority of the South American countries for nearly two decades. This query may be answered in three parts: a) ECLA economics was so simple that almost anyone could master it and become a policy "expert" in a matter of months; b) ECLA economics provided the intellectual underpinnings for the policies that the governments really wanted to pursue (or were in fact pursuing, as Luders points out); c) finally, ECLA economics exploited the idea that the developing countries--particularly those in Latin America--were somehow different from the rest of the world and, hence, needed a different brand of economics.

With respect to the first point, ECLA economics was essentially descriptive rather than analytical; inflation, for example, occurs because one or more prices rise and hence the obvious solution to the inflation "problem" is to increase supply rather than restrict demand. Containing demand via restrictions on the rate of growth of bank credit was viewed as particularly noxious because credit is essential to expansion of supply. Concerning the second point, mercantilism, for example, is always attractive politically, particularly when it is argued that the (international) terms of trade are favoring the rich and castigating the poor. Another example concerns inflation; by attributing increases in the price level to food producers, the government is free to continue inflationary finance at the central bank. The final point is crucial: by "demonstrating" that traditional economics was irrelevant to developing countries, ECLA eliminated the only competition that was around, leaving the field to itself.

Luders emphasizes the important role of regional integration in the ECLA view of development economics; this is certainly a valid point as most of the Latin American national economies are quite small. Brazil is the only country with a GNP larger than that of Switzerland, and Switzerland is every economist's example of a country that must trade to survive. Indeed, of the several regional trading blocs whose formation was inspired by ECLA, only the now all but defunct Latin American Free Trade Association (LAFTA) has a collective gross product in excess of that of Switzerland.[1] The Central American Common Market, for example, had a con.bined GNP, at the height of its success, less than Chile's. While regional integration undoubtedly can lead to economies of scale, the fact remains that the integration failed to produce even one large international trading group, and hence only modest protection could be justified. Nevertheless, regional integration was viewed by ECLA as a means of

---

[1] This statement does not apply to the Andean Group after the incorporation of Venezuela.

validating the import substitution policies, and hence, where integration occurred, it was accompanied by very substantial increases in the external tariff. In the case of the Central American Common Market, the common external tariff was set at roughly three times the average of previous national levels. In other words, the objective of integration, from ECLA's point of view, would appear to be maximization of trade diversion (rather than creation). ECLA, of course, never paid more than lip service to the traditional considerations concerning integration as developed by Viner and Meade[2]; rather, they emphasized the effects of integration on growth.

Another disservice rendered by ECLA concerns the confusion of the current account of the balance of payments with the balance of payments proper which was, of course, a natural by-product of Prebisch's overriding concern with the terms of trade and his peculiar "center-periphery" conception of the world. As a consequence, the "balance of payments" became a key concern, and every policy had to be examined in terms of its effects on the balance of payments. Despite the fact that the absorption approach was developed while ECLA was still young, there appears to have been little appreciation of the direct relationship between the current account of the balance of payments and the level of expenditure relative to income. It is most unfortunate that to this day most Latin American economists confuse the current account with the balance of payments and also confuse expenditure-switching with expenditure-reducing policies. Indeed, there is evidence of this confusion in both the Langoni and Kogut and the Luders papers.

In his critique of ECLA's commercial policy, Luders emphasizes the ECLA idea that because of technical progress and low price and income elasticities of demand for the exports of developing countries (Prebisch's "periphery"), "one of the main development problems most Latin American countries faced were continuous balance of payments crises." That balance of payments crises have occurred with high frequency in Latin America cannot be denied; it is another thing, however, to attribute them to adverse changes in the terms of trade and an uneven distribution of the fruits of technical progress. In my view, the so-called balance of payments crises arose because the development policies were usually expenditure increasing in nature, whereas the foreign exchange market policies were such that foreign capital simply could not be attracted in sufficient quantities to close the gap. Indeed, there seems to be little recognition of the fact that policies aimed at compressing imports without reducing expenditure (relative to income) can only succeed in reducing the volume of both imports and exports. Luders' set of alternatives to ECLA's commercial policy proposals is, however, very sound.

[2]See, for example, Viner (1937) and Meade (1951).

Turning to the paper by Langoni and Kogut, I find it to be a very clear exposition of developments in Brazil through 1973, but somewhat lacking in its analysis of the 1974-76 period. As noted above, the economic policies of Roberto Campos and Delfim Netto were in sharp contrast with certain ECLA positions, particularly with respect to commercial policy. During the 1967-1973 period, the main emphasis in Brazil was on the opening of the economy both in terms of trade and capital flows. Import substitution was largely replaced with export promotion; as a consequence, trade, measured as a fraction of national income, rose dramatically from the mid-1960s to the early 1970s. In the terms of the doctrines of ECLA, the most important aspect of the Brazilian "miracle" during this period was a very rapid and sustained growth without the emergence of a balance of payments "problem"; it is also notable that the rate of inflation was actually reduced during this period. This experience has probably done more to discredit ECLA than all the attacks of academic economists over a period of nearly two decades.

Brazilian economic policy changed in 1974. Apparently not deliberate, this change was rather the consequence of a decentralization of economic policy formation that permitted certain institutions--the Banco do Brasil in particular-- a degree of independence not experienced during the period of Campos' and Delfim Netto's influence. The most dramatic development consisted of an enormous capital inflow beginning in 1974, which appears to have been induced in large part by the Banco do Brasil. As a consequence, the dollar volume of imports doubled in 1974, the increase being several times the hike in the cost of imported petroleum. The policy response to this "balance of payments" problem has been to turn in the direction of the pre-1967 policies--that is, protectionism, import substitution, greater controls over international capital transactions, etc. In short, Brazilian economic policy now appears to be closer to that of ECLA than to that devised by Campos and Delfim.

Brazilian economists, including Langoni and Kogut, have been slow to reach an agreement concerning the causes of the deterioration in the economic situation of Brazil since 1973. Not only has the trade deficit increased enormously, but the rate of inflation has more than doubled. Much of the difficulty in reaching a common diagnosis of the nature of the problem lies, I believe, in a failure to appreciate the degree to which the Brazilian economy has opened during the past decade. For example, Brazilian economists still speak in terms of monetary policy, targets, and budgets, even though it is becoming quite clear that the money supply has become more endogenous in that economy. In addition, the Central Bank has largely lost control of credit creation, that function having been usurped by the Banco do Brasil which continues to engage in massive borrowing abroad, the proceeds of which are lent in the private sector in Brazil. In both 1974 and 1975, for example, nominal credit in Brazil increased by about 60 percent, whereas the increase in the money supply was little more than half that percentage. The difference is accounted for by the huge current account deficit in the balance of payments which, by "recycling" the credit inflow, prevents growth in foreign reserves (and hence money) at the same rate as the expansion in credit.

The expenditure-increasing policies of 1974 and 1975 in Brazil did not, of course, significantly affect the demand for money, and the inflationary potential of those policies was largely tapped via the current account deficit in the balance of payments. This permitted the government to maintain its claim that the money supply growth was "on target"; moreover, the erroneous preoccupation with money diverted the attention of both officials and economists from the real cause of the deficit--the credit expansion based on foreign borrowing.

In the course of 1976, several measures were taken which had the effect of closing the economy and, hence, reducing the endogeneity of the money supply. I would attribute the rapid increase in the rate of inflation during 1976 to growing import restrictions which have caused the continued credit inflow to be reflected to a greater degree in the quantity of money. Unfortunately, there is as yet little recognition of this relationship in Brazil.

It is ironic that the full acceptance of inflation as a monetary phenomenon took place in Brazil at precisely the time that the economy had become sufficiently open so as to cause the money supply to be demand determined (as a first approximation). By extrapolation, one might imagine that by the time the Brazilians fully realize that the money supply in a small open economy (with fixed exchange rates) is endogenous, the current policymakers will have succeeded in closing the economy to a degree sufficient that the old model applies once again.

In its final version, the paper by Langoni and Kogut recognizes the important difference between credit and money creation in Brazil. The authors present what I believe to be a correct diagnosis of the current balance of payments and inflation problems in Brazil. There is little evidence, however, that a change of policy can be expected in the near future.

Both the Langoni and Kogut and the Luders papers are extremely useful documents despite their limitations. The Luders paper provides the most comprehensive compilation of ECLA thought that exists to date and also a good, if rather uncritical, analysis of that body of thought. The final version of the paper by Langoni and Kogut represents the beginning of a reexamination of monetary policy in Brazil--one that is long overdue.

REFERENCES

1. Langoni, C.J., "Development Policies and Problems: The Brazilian Experience," Carnegie-Rochester Conference Series on Public Policy, VI, (eds. K. Brunner and A.H. Meltzer), Amsterdam: North-Holland, 1977.

2. Luders, R.S., "The Economic Commission for Latin America: Its Policies and Their Impact," Carnegie-Rochester Conference Series on Public Policy, VI, (eds. K. Brunner and A.H. Meltzer), Amsterdam: North-Holland, 1977.

3. Meade, J.E. The Balance of Payments. London: Oxford University Press, 1951.

4. Viner, J. Studies in the Theory of International Trade. New York: Harper and Bros., 1937.

LAND REFORM AND AGRICULTURAL EFFICIENCY IN MEXICO:
A GENERAL EQUILIBRIUM ANALYSIS

Arthur De Vany

Texas A&M University

Mexico's agricultural production increased at an annual rate of 4.6 percent between 1940 and 1965, a rate which exceeds that experienced by nearly every other Latin American country. This growth was sufficient to raise per capita output nearly 1.5 percent in spite of an annual rate of population growth of 3.2 percent. Judged by the performance of per capita agricultural production in the less developed world, Mexico's performance is a spectacular success. This success has attracted the attention of other countries which would emulate it and of analysts who would explain it. Among the factors that analysts have identified as sources of increased productivity are the policies of the Mexican government which have increased the quantity and quality of agricultural land through heavy investment in irrigation and rural roads, and a land reform program which has expropriated some 46.5 million hectares of land from large farms and distributed it to 2.3 million landless peasants. There is little doubt that agricultural investment has raised production, though one could question whether the returns exceeded the costs. There is, however, a very substantial question as to whether land reform has increased or lowered productivity.

There is a large literature addressed to this latter question, including studies by Castillo (1956), Dovring (1968), Hertford (1971), Reynolds (1970), and Simpson (1937). While sharp distinctions are difficult to make, most of the studies conclude that the land reform program has, on balance, promoted a gain in productivity. The measurement of productivity is itself a very difficult empirical task. I show in this paper that the distinctive institutional features of Mexico's Agrarian Reform Program further complicate this task and require amendment of the procedures that have been used to evaluate productivity, which assume a competitive equilibrium devoid of these crucial institutional features. A general equilibrium competitive model of Mexican agriculture is constructed, which incorporates the fact that land tenancy rights differ in the reform and private sectors. The usual comparisons of factor productivity are shown to be meaningless in this institutional setting in that they do not measure the efficiency gain or loss associated with an allocation of more land from the private to the land reform sector.[1]

Land tenancy rights in the reform sector are limited to use (usus fructus), and the peasant is not legally entitled to sell, lease, or otherwise alienate rights to the land. The quantity of land available to peasants on this basis is set by government policies, but there is relatively free mobility of peasants between the private and land reform sectors. Incorporating these institutional features into the competitive process shows that the land reform program is inefficient and that the existing productivity comparisons are meaningless since a second-best setting applies. Furthermore, the econometric studies of production have generally not used a model which is appropriate to the study of production under usufruct land tenancy. More fundamentally, these studies do not really address the basic question: What are the consequences of a further extension of the land reform program? The model developed is a greatly simplified representation of Mexican agriculture; yet it indicates that there are some surprising complications involved in answering that question. In the setting modeled, it is found that increasing the amount of land eligible for reform reallocates labor from the private to the land reform sector, raises the wage rate, lowers the rental rate on land, and decreases the intensity of cultivation in both sectors. Under these same circumstances, agricultural output may rise or fall. Unfortunately, these implications are difficult to test, although the general features of Mexico's agrarian development are consistent with the model. Nonetheless, the model does have empirical content, and certain of its central implications are supported by the econometric studies reviewed below.

While the analysis is carried out in the context of the Mexican institutional structure, the results hold generally for land tenure structures which mix private property land tenure with usufruct land tenure. Such a structure of land tenure is common throughout Latin America, parts of Africa, and Asia. The model developed here would apply in many agricultural settings in which an element of private agriculture is mixed with agricultural practices limiting the farmer's rights in the land to use and prohibiting sale or lease.

---

[1] There is a parallel between this issue and the debate concerning the efficiency of share tenancy. This parallel is instructive as well since it suggests that the same kind of equilibrium approach which has sharpened the analysis of share tenancy might also be useful in the analysis of usufruct tenancy. Indeed, the institutional features of Mexico's land reform program require a general equilibrium approach if they are to be modeled faithfully.

I. THE INSTITUTIONAL SETTING

Article 27 of the Mexican constitution states that "all lands and waters in the national territorial limits belong to the Nation which has the right to transfer their domain." A series of 16 amendments to the constitution has established the basic machinery of Mexico's Agrarian Reform Program. The provisions of interest to this study are as follows.[2]

A "dotación" or outright grant of land may be made, regardless of previous ownership of the land if: (a) a request is submitted by 20 or more native-born Mexicans; (b) there exists "affectable" land within a radius of four miles of the land village in which the requestors reside. "Affectable" land is privately owned property exceeding 200 hectares of unirrigated cropland, or 100 hectares of irrigated land; (c) the request is granted by all concerned agencies, including the President of the Republic.

The group applying for land is called an "ejido" and an individual member of the ejido is an "ejidatario." Some ejidos hold and work the land as a collective. Most reform land, however, is assigned to individual ejidatarios by a committee elected by members of the ejido. Under the law, the ejidatario has the right of use of the land, but he may not lease, sell, encumber, or otherwise alienate rights to the land. If he should fail to work the land for two consecutive years, his right of use can revert to the ejido or to the Mexican government.

There are two features of the program which are of central interest to this study: the nonalienation laws and the terms of eligibility. The implications of the nonalienation laws, developed in detail below, are that the ejidatario has a finite time horizon for investments fixed to the land, and that he is willing to become or remain a member of an ejido so long as the total returns to his labor on the land exceed or equal his alternative earnings.[3] I consider the eligibility provisions as the setting of the conditions for entry into the ejido sector, and treat the transactions costs of forming a group and applying for land as negligible. In effect, I assume free entry into the ejido sector, subject to the governmentally determined constraint on "affectable" land.

In the period 1930 to 1960, a sizable amount of land was redistributed from private hands to ejidatarios. In 1930 small private farms and ejidatario units represented 85 percent of Mexico's farms and worked about 8 percent of all workable land. A few large private farms worked over two-thirds of the

---

[2]There are many sources of information on the features of the Mexican Agrarian Reform Program, e.g., Reynolds (1970). A good brief account is Hertford (1971), on which my discussion is largely based.

[3]This point is also made by Hertford (1971).

farmland. According to Hertford (1971), "by 1960, ejidatarios had acquired 29 percent of Mexico's arable land, 43 percent of the cropland, about half the publicly irrigated land, and 54 percent of all farm units" (p. 8). The earliest and most sizable redistributions occurred in the central mesa, where the density of the population was greatest, making a large fraction of the land area eligible for conversion. The pace of conversion has slackened. Slightly more than half of the 46.5 million hectares of land which have been converted were expropriated by 1940.

II. THE EJIDO SECTOR

The construction of the two-sector model begins with a simple model of the ejido sector. Assume that the Mexican peasant is free to choose employment in the private sector at a wage w, and that the length of the work period is t. I assume that the peasant's choice to become an ejidatario is an all-or-nothing decision; he must choose between full-time employment as a paid agricultural laborer or as a self-employed ejidatario.[4] There are several reasons underlying this assumption. First, the land reform code specifies that the ejidatario is to work the land as his full-time employment; such is typically the case, as noted by Hertford, since when the surrounding area is converted from private lands to ejidatario, few local employment opportunities remain. Second, the fragmentary evidence reviewed below suggests that this assumption affords the best explanation of the data. Third, the assumption simplifies the model with little loss of information.[5]

Let $f(\cdot)$ be the agricultural production function; then the ejidatario's income is $pf(t, h^e)$, where p is the competitively determined market price of agricultural output, and h^e is the quantity of land worked. Profits of the ejidatario are $pf(t, h^e) - wt$, and the peasant leaves private employment for the ejido sector whenever profits are positive as an ejidatario.[6]

---

[4] Typically, the ejidatario works his farm full-time and hires only 10 percent of the total labor expended on the farm; see Table 1 following, and Castillo (1956).

[5] See footnote 6.

[6] Suppose the ejidatario may find part-time employment in addition to the time he works his farm. Then the equilibrium conditions become: (a) $pf_1^e - w = 0$; (b) $pf_2^e - \lambda = 0$; (c) $pf^e (t_1, h^e) + wt_1 = 0$, where t_2 is outside work; and t_1 is the length of the full-time work period in the private sector. From the zero profit condition (c), it can be seen that the availability of outside work cannot increase average ejido farm size relative to the case where the ejidatario works his farm full-time.

Suppose the government determines the amount of land available for the formation of ejidos, and let the number of qualified applicants be in elastic supply. Then if H^e hectares are available, the equilibrium number of ejidatarios N^e is the solution to

(1) $pf(t, H^e/N^e) = wt.$

Ejidatarios apply for the available land until the average plot size $h^e = H^e/N^e$ is driven down to the point where the value of the average product of labor in the ejido sector equals the wage paid in the private sector. That is, $\frac{pf(t, H^e/N^e)}{t} = w$.

This condition is equivalent to zero profits in the ejido sector. What one must imagine is a kind of Walrasian auction. Suppose amount H^e of land is offered free to all eligible takers, to be divided equally among them. Individual applicants submit their request for a parcel; then the auctioneer announces the size of the parcel to be awarded after all applications are processed. On the basis of this size, individuals either add their names as applicants if the plot size is too big, or withdraw their names if it is too small. Equilibrium is reached when the plot size discovered by the auctioneer neither adds to nor substracts from the list of applicants.

There is evidence that the market gropes to the labor allocation implied by the auction. Indirect evidence comes from the econometric studies reviewed below which show that the marginal product of labor in the private sector (i.e., the real wage) approximately equals the average product of labor in the ejido sector. Other evidence comes from the abandonments of ejido land which have taken place. One would expect abandonments where the average plot size is too small; it is the mechanism whereby bidders withdraw from the auction. Moreover, the Mexican government has attempted, with little success, to keep individual plot size above some minimum, with the full understanding that the competitive pressure for the land presses plot size down. Presently, about three-fifths of the ejidatario plots are smaller than the minimum size established by the Mexican government (10 hectares of irrigated or 20 hectares of unirrigated land). In addition, the requirements for eligibility make for a very elastic supply to the ejido sector. Males qualify at age 16 if unmarried, and at 12 if married. Females qualify if they are widowed or are the primary source of support for their families. It is not unusual for many family members to suddenly "appear" when application for land is made by villagers. Indeed, since each family wants a bigger share of the land to be expropriated, it has an incentive to put forth as many eligible applicants as possible.[7]

III. THE PRIVATE SECTOR

Assume a competitive agricultural market, with each firm able to sell all the output it wishes at the going market price p. These firms produce a single, homogeneous product which is identical to that produced in the ejido sector. Each individual firm produces with the same production function, and the production function is the same among private and ejido firms. Let $q = f(n, h)$ represent output q, when n is the number of workers hired, and h is the number of hectares of land employed by the firm.[8] The firm hires factors in a competitive market and takes the wage w and the rental on land γ as given.

The firm's profits are $\pi = pf(n, h) - wn - \gamma h$, which are to be maximized by choice of labor and land. Equilibrium occurs when

(2) $pf_1 - w = 0$;

(3) $pf_2 - \gamma = 0$.

In addition, profits must equal zero.

The firm's supply and factor demands may be derived in the usual way and written as:

$$q^s = q^s (p, w, \gamma);$$

$$n^d = n^d (p, w, \gamma);$$

$$h^d = h^d (p, w, \gamma).$$

The industry totals are determined from these functions and from the number of firms.

---

[7] See De Vany and Sanchez (1975) on this point; the fertility implications of the land reform program are also explored therein.

[8] Since the length of the work period has been fixed at t in the model, one need only consider n, the number of employees hired by the firm, in order to determine its use of labor. Recall that the ejidatario also works the same number of hours, so that the model has a fixed labor supply in total; I am here concerned with the mechanisms by which this supply is allocated between the two sectors.

IV. MARKET EQUILIBRIUM

Let agricultural production be subject to long-run constant returns to scale at the <u>industry</u> level in both the ejido and private sectors.[9] This common production function is denoted $F(\cdot)$, and output of the ejido sector is $Q^e = F^e(N^e, H^e)$, where N^e is the total number of ejidatarios, and H^e is the total amount of land allocated to ejidos. Private sector output is $Q^p = F^p(N^p, H^p)$, where N^p is total private employment, and H^p total private land use. The function $F(\cdot)$ is concave contoured and homogeneous of degree one.

Total industry profits of the ejido sector are

$$(4) \quad pF^e(N^e, H^e) - wN^e \,,$$

and total private profits are

$$(5) \quad pF^p(N^p, H^p) - wN^p - rH^p.$$

Let the work force and stock of land be given and equal to $\overline{N}$ and $\overline{H}$, respectively, so that the total resource constraints on the economy are

$$\overline{H} = N^e + N^p \,;$$

$$\overline{H} = H^e + H^p \,.$$

It can be supposed that both the ejido and private sectors are competitive in the sense that each unit within the sector is a price-taker and that there is free entry. There are two interpretations to be placed on this supposition. The first is that the region modeled is an area within Mexico whose output is a small enough share of Mexico's total agricultural output as to exert no influence on the market price. In this interpretation the unit of analysis is an agricultural "valley" within Mexico, and a competitive equilibrium will obtain whenever labor mobility between the ejido and private sectors and between the valley and the rest of Mexico is unrestricted. The second interpretation is to take as the unit of analysis the entire country of Mexico. It is then necessary to assume that Mexico is a price-taker in the world market, that there is free mobility between the ejido and private sectors, and that the stock of land and labor resources is fixed. It is primarily this latter interpretation I consider.

---

[9] At the firm level, each farm has eventually rising average cost so that the size of farms is determined. The constant returns at the industry level simply say that existing firms may be replicated by farms having the same costs.

129

The complete model may now be set forth as follows:

(6) $pF^e(N^e, H^e) - wN^e = 0$;

$pF^p_1 - w \qquad\qquad = 0$;

$pF^p_2 - \gamma \qquad\qquad = 0$;

$\bar{N} - N^e - N^p \qquad = 0$;

$\bar{H} - H^e - H^p \qquad = 0$;

$Q^e - F^e(N^e, H^e) \quad = 0$;

$Q^p - F^p(N^p, H^p) \quad = 0$.

The first equation is the zero profit equilibrium condition for the ejido sector. The second and third equations are the profit maximization conditions for the private sector. These conditions also ensure a zero profit equilibrium for the private sector since, with a first-degree homogeneous production function, if the factors receive their marginal products, total product is exhausted. The remaining equations characterize the resource setting and output. Together, there are seven equations in the seven variables, Q^e, Q^p, w, γ, N^e, N^p, H^p. The exogenous variables are H^e, $\bar{H}$, N, and p.

Using the constraints the model may be reduced to three equations in the three variables, N^e, w, γ, of the following form:

(7) $pF^e(N^e, H^e) - wN^e = 0$;

$pF^p_1(N - N^e, H - H^e) - w = 0$;

$pF^p_2(N - N^e, H - H^e) - \gamma = 0$.

The fact that the number of equations matches the number of variables does not ensure that a solution exists. However, the Jacobian of the system is non-vanishing if the labor market has a stable equilibrium. Stability requires that profits in the ejido sector be falling with entry. From (6), then, must follow

$pF_1^e - w - N^e \dfrac{\partial w}{\partial N^e} < 0$. But, from (6), $\dfrac{\partial w}{\partial N^e} = -pF_{11}^p$, so that stability requires

(8) $pF_1^e - w + N^e F_{11}^p < 0 .$

Since this last expression is the Jacobian of (6) or of (7), a unique solution exists if the labor market equilibrium is stable in a neighborhood of equilibrium.

The equilibrium of the ejidatario and private farm is shown in Figure 1. Curve MC represents the competitive firm's average cost curve.[10] The average cost curve of the ejidatario lies somewhere between the private firm's average cost curve and the private average cost curve less the rental payment on the land used (AC - γH). As the stability condition implies, the ejidatario equilibrium occurs on the downward sloping portion of his average cost curve, AC_e. His profits would rise if he could obtain more land, but he cannot since the competitive pressure of entry drives farm size to the zero profit level. This equilibrium creates the false appearance of economies of scale.

V. EXTENSIONS OF LAND REFORM AND AGRICULTURAL EFFICIENCY

It is apparent that the equilibrium described in system (6) is inefficient; neither the marginal product of labor nor the marginal product of land is equalized among all farms. The source of inefficiency is the labor allocation mechanism under the incentive provided by the usufruct form of land tenure. Under this system, so long as there is free entry, labor enters the ejido sector until its average product therein equals its marginal product in the private sector. I now want to consider the effect of extending the amount of land subject to agrarian reform.

To consider this question, the system (7) must be displaced with respect to the policy parameter H^e; that is, the effect of a policy change which allocates more land to the ejido sector while taking it from the private sector must be examined. Differentiating (7) fully with respect to H^e gives the system

---

[10]In contrast to the usual competitive case, the point where AC = MC may not be the social cost of output in the present setting because of the factor use distortions introduced by the land reform program. As will be shown below, the program raises the wage rate relative to the rental rate on land and encourages private firms to use a socially inefficient factor mix.

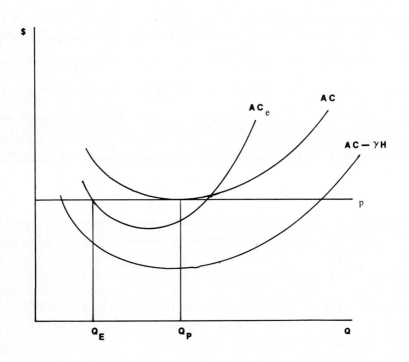

FIGURE I

$$(9) \quad \begin{bmatrix} pF_i^e - w & -N^e & 0 \\ -pF_{11}^p & -1 & 0 \\ -pF_{21}^p & 0 & -1 \end{bmatrix} \begin{bmatrix} \dfrac{\partial N^e}{\partial H^e} \\ \dfrac{\partial w}{\partial H^e} \\ \dfrac{\partial r}{\partial H^e} \end{bmatrix} = \begin{bmatrix} -pF_2^e \\ pF_{12}^p \\ pF_{22}^p \end{bmatrix}$$

By Cramer's rule we obtain

$$(10) \quad \frac{\partial N^e}{\partial H^e} = \frac{-p(F_2^e + N^e F_{12}^p)}{\det A};$$

$$(11) \quad \frac{\partial w}{\partial H^e} = \frac{(w - pF_1^e)\, pF_{12}^p + pF_{11}^p\, pF_2^e}{\det A};$$

$$(12) \quad \frac{\partial \gamma}{\partial H^e} = \frac{F_{22}^p\, [\det A] + pF_{21}^p\, [1 + a]\, F_2^e}{\det A},$$

where det A is the determinant of the matrix in (9), and a is the fraction of land allocated to the ejido sector. Since det $A = (pF_1^e - w) + pF_{11}^p\, N^e$, it is negative by the requirement for labor market stability; see (8) above. If we assume a concave production function, the F_{11} and F_{22} are negative, and if we assume complementarity of inputs, F_{12} is positive. Then, since $w > pF_1^e$, we obtain the following signs of the derivatives:

$$\frac{\partial N^e}{\partial H^e} > 0, \quad \frac{\partial w}{\partial H^e} > 0, \quad \frac{\partial \gamma}{\partial H^e} < 0.$$

The first derivative indicates that more ejido land will attract more ejidatarios, that is, will induce people to leave private employment and become ejidatarios. The second indicates that this shifting of land and people into the ejido sector will raise wages in the private sector. The last points to a surprising conclusion, which is that land rent in the private sector falls as land is allocated from the private to the ejido sector. One might expect private land rents to rise as more land is removed from private hands. But, since the stock of land is fixed and immobile, if the wage rises, rent must fall in order to keep average production cost from rising above the world price.

The preceding analysis demonstrates that the equilibrium ratio of land to labor depends on the fraction of available land which is allocated to the ejidos. To understand this dependence requires additional work. Let

$$\ell^e = \frac{H^e}{N^e} \; ; \quad \ell^p = \frac{H^p}{N^p} \; ; \quad \text{and} \quad a = \frac{H^e}{H} \; .$$

Then, writing $AP^e_N = MP^p_N$ in real terms and using the first-degree homogeneity of the production function, we may obtain from (6) the equation

$$(13) \quad F^e_1 (1, \ell^e) + F^e_2 (1, \ell^e) = F^p_1 (1, \ell^p) = F^p_1 (1, \frac{\ell - \ell^e a}{1 - a}) \; ,$$

which gives the equilibrium land/labor ratio in the ejido sector, ℓ^e, as a function of a, the proportion of total land allocated to the ejido sector. Then we may find

$$(14) \quad \frac{d \ell^e}{da} = \frac{F^p_{1\ell^p} \; [-\frac{\ell - \ell^e}{(1 - a)^2}]}{[F^e_{1\ell^e} + F^e_{2\ell^e}\ell^e + F^e_2] + \frac{a}{1-a} F^p_{1\ell^p}} \; ;$$

$$(15) \quad \frac{d\ell^p}{da} = \frac{1}{(1-a)} \; [F^p_{1\ell^p} \ell^e + (F^e_{1\ell^e} + F^e_{2\ell^e}\ell^e + F^p_2) (1 - a \, \ell^e)],$$

which are the derivatives of the equilibrium ejido and private land/labor ratios with respect to the fraction of total available land allocated to the ejido sector. As a consequence of the linear homogeneity of the production functions, both $\frac{d \ell^e}{da}$ and $\frac{d \ell^p}{da}$ may be shown to be positive.

The argument to this point is easily illustrated through use of the Edgeworth box. In Figure 2 output of the ejido sector is shown by isoquants running from the lower left-hand corner to the upper right-hand corner and by isoquants for the private sector running in the opposite direction. Labor quantities run on the horizontal and land on the vertical axes; the length of these axes is the total amount of each resource. The locus of isoquant tangencies is the locus of efficient allocations. It is a straight line given identical, linear homogeneous production functions. At each point on the efficient locus, the land/labor ratio is a constant.

Now, the locus of equilibrium allocations is the curved line lying beneath the efficient line. Every point on the equilibrium line corresponds to the equality of the average product of labor in the ejido sector to the marginal product of labor in the private sector. Accordingly, the ratios of marginal products of land and labor for the two sectors are not equal at equilibrium, and there is an efficiency loss associated with the Mexican land reform program.[11] The equilibrium locus is upward sloping, as (14) and (15) say it must be, and a horizontal movement to the right, which increases a, raises the land/labor ratio in both sectors. Notice that the end points of the equilibrium locus share a point with the efficiency locus at the corners of the box. This is because there is no factor use distortion if the two sectors do not coexist. The left-hand corner corresponds to the competitive outcome when all land is privately owned. The upper right-hand corner corresponds to the competitive equilibrium when land is rent free.[12]

It is necessary to distinguish between the effects of the existence of land reform and the effects of changes in the amount of land in the reform sector. Relative to the efficiency locus, the land reform locus is inefficient, and is characterized by too low a land/labor ratio in the ejido sector, too high a land/labor ratio in the private sector, lower land rents, higher wage rates, and less

---

[11]Notice that the distortion operates in both sectors, causing too high a land/labor ratio in the private sector and too low a ratio in the ejido sector. On optimal resource allocation in imperfect markets, see David and Fishlow (1961).

[12]However, if we drop the assumption that land is fixed in supply, then the equilibrium resulting in the case where all land is held on a usufruct basis would not be efficient, owing to the reduced incentive to maintain and improve the land. Technically, this equilibrium would seem to correspond to a complete lack of property rights in land or to government ownership.

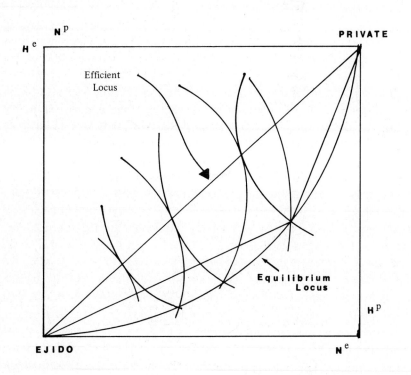

F I G U R E II

output relative to the efficient outcome. From a starting point at which some amount of land is in ejidos, a further allocation of land to the ejidos will raise the land/labor ratio in both the ejido and private sectors, raise the wage rate, and lower land rents, but may increase or decrease the amount of output. Whether output increases or decreases with further land reform has nothing to do with efficiency because all outcomes are inefficient except when zero or 100 percent of the land is in the ejidos.

VI. ANALYSIS AND INTERPRETATION

A central implication of the preceding analysis is that the marginal product of labor on private farms should equal the average product of labor on ejido farms. As a corollary it is easily shown that the land/labor ratio in the private sector will exceed the ratio in the ejido sector. Hertford's study allows us to check these implications and others against the evidence.

Hertford estimated logarithmic production functions on cross sectional data from the 1960 Mexican Agricultural Census. His observations were averages per farm in each county and the data set is partitioned into four groups: private sector, outside irrigation districts; ejido sector, outside irrigation districts; private sector, inside irrigation districts; ejido sector, inside irrigation districts. The results of his study are summarized in Table 1. The standard errors of the regression coefficients are given in parentheses below the coefficient. All average and marginal products as well as the land/labor ratio were evaluated at the means of the data.

The empirical estimates conform rather well with the implications of the model. The land/labor ratio is higher on private farms than on ejido farms, as predicted. The major implication asserting the equality of the marginal product of labor in the private sector with labor's average product in the ejido sector is also supported. Outside irrigation districts, the marginal product of all private labor is 1.71, which closely approximates the 1.60 average product of all labor in the ejidos. Inside irrigation districts, the relevant figures are $MP_N^p = 2.38$; $AP_N^e = 2.17$. The average product of all labor in the ejido sector is below its level in the private sector whether the comparison is made inside or outside irrigation districts.

Table 1

Comparison of Production in Mexican Agriculture for Ejido and Private Sectors
Inside and Outside SRH Irrigation Districts*

	Outside Irrigation District		Inside Irrigation District	
	Private sector	Ejido sector	Private sector	Ejido sector
R^2	0.794	0.690	0.727	0.649
Regression coefficients				
Family labor	0.112 (0.029)	- 0.121 (0.024)	0.195 (0.075)	- 0.041 (0.069)
Hired labor	0.237 (0.018)	0.154 (0.014)	0.065 (0.058)	0.041 (0.037)
All labor	0.349 (0.033)	0.033 (0.022)	0.260 (0.082)	0.000 (0.056)
Land	0.418 (0.024)	0.488 (0.027)	0.503 (0.054)	0.235 (0.043)
Means				
Output	14.939	2.907	22.646	4.280
Family labor	2.069	1.791	1.948	1.931
Hired labor	0.981	0.024	0.525	0.034
All labor	3.05	1.82	2.47	1.97
Land	20.025	5.013	27.910	6.456
Average products				
Family labor	7.221	1.623	11.623	2.217
Hired labor	15.226	121.632	43.164	123.841
All labor	4.90	1.60	9.17	2.17
Land	0.746	0.580	0.811	0.663
Marginal products				
Family labor	0.809	- 0.191	2.266	- 0.091
Hired labor	3.608	18.731	2.806	5.077
All labor	1.71	0.05	2.38	0.00
Land	0.312	0.283	0.408	0.156
Land/labor	6.56	2.70	11.29	3.27

*Based on regression 4, Tables A-4, 5, 6, and 7 of Hertford (1971, Appendix A, pp. 59-62).

VII. <u>AN EXTENDED MODEL WITH CAPITAL</u>

Most of the conclusions of the preceding model stem from the nonalienation provisions of the land reform law and their effect on the allocation of labor to the two sectors. I have ignored, to this point, another crucial aspect of the nonalienation provision, which is that the ejidatario's investment horizon is truncated. Because he cannot sell the land, he cannot capture the full returns on any capital improvements made to it which extend beyond his expected time horizon.

To consider the implications of this issue, let us define an implicit interest rate which shows the rate of return the ejidatario must earn on investments if they are to "pay off" in his horizon. Let the expected horizon be T years, and let the capital market be competitive, with i, the real rate of interest, a parameter. Then, on a stock of capital with a value K, the value of the annual flow of services is iK. Let K be infinitely durable with no loss of generality. The present value of the capital must be equal to its price, so the real rate of return the ejidatario must earn is i^e which satisfies

$$(16) \quad K = \sum_{\tau=1}^{T} \frac{i^e K}{(1+i)^\tau} .$$

Solving for i^e in terms of the private return on capital from (16) gives

$$(17) \quad i^e = \frac{i(1+i)^T}{(1+i)^{T+1} - 1} ,$$

which, as can be easily verified, implies $i^e > i$. For example, if $i = .10$ and $T = 15$, then $i^e = .12$; and if $T = 20$, then $i^e = .105$. The longer the horizon, the closer i^e is to i.

Now, let firms in the private and ejido sectors choose capital in addition to the other choices considered above. By analysis similar to that in section V, we obtain the following equilibrium conditions:

(18) $pF^e(N^e, H^e, K^e) - wN^e - i^e K^e = 0$;

$pF_1^p - w$ $= 0$;

$pF_2^p - \gamma$ $= 0$;

$pF_3^p - i$ $= 0$;

$pF_3^e - i^e$ $= 0$;

$\bar{N} - \bar{N}^e - N^p$ $= 0$;

$\bar{H} - \bar{H}^e - H^p$ $= 0$;

$Q^e - F^e(N^e, H^e, K^e)$ $= 0$;

$Q^p - F^p(N^p, H^p, K^p)$ $= 0$,

where all symbols are as previously defined, and K^e and K^p are the values of capital in the ejido and private sectors, respectively.

It is evident that another source of inefficiency is present in that the marginal product of capital is not equalized among sectors. What we have is $pF_3^e = i^e > i = pF_3^p$, so that the marginal product of capital is higher in the ejido than in the private sector. Since this is already a second-best setting, owing to labor misallocation, it is not possible to say whether the capital misallocation improves or worsens the situation.

By following the procedure of section VI, we may displace the equilibrium of the system. The following results emerge from such an exercise:

$$\frac{\partial N^e}{\partial H^e} > 0, \quad \frac{\partial w}{\partial H^e} > 0, \quad \frac{\partial \gamma}{\partial H^e} < 0, \quad \frac{\partial K^p}{\partial H^e} < 0, \quad \frac{\partial K^e}{\partial H^e} > 0.$$

Since the interest rate is a given, the marginal product of capital in both sectors will be unaffected by land reallocations, and the efficiency of capital allocation is also unaffected. The total amount of capital employed in agriculture is affected by land allocations, but, once again, one must distinguish between the effects of the existence of the program and the effects of a change in the land allocated to the ejido sector. Any initial allocation of land to the ejido sector will distort capital allocation and reduce efficiency; however, further allocations may increase or decrease efficiency.

Evidence bearing on the issues raised in this more complicated model can be found in the careful study of agriculture in the Celaya district by Castillo (1956). Because of the size of the study area, Castillo was able to make a careful survey and to estimate the inputs and outputs of both sectors. He then fitted a log linear production function to the data for each sector. The coefficients of these regressions, as well as the marginal and average products of land, labor, and capital are presented in Table 2. The results differ somewhat from the Hertford study, partly because of the lower level of aggregation and possible differences in measurement error, and also because of the greater attention paid to capital. Nonetheless, the two studies complement one another and generally agree in their substantive findings.

Note first that Castillo finds economies of scale in the ejido sector and constant returns to scale in the private sector. I have demonstrated that this finding is not evidence that production would be increased by allocating resources from the private to the ejido sector. It is, in fact, evidence which substantiates the prediction of the model that the individual ejidatario farm is in an equilibrium such as is depicted in Figure 1.

As in Hertford's study, the marginal product of labor is lower in the ejido sector than in the private sector. However, the average product of ejido sector labor exceeds the marginal product of private sector labor. This is to be expected when capital is introduced into the model, for now the equilibrium condition is

$$(19) \quad \frac{pF^e(N^e, H^e, K^e) - i^e K^e}{N^e} = pF_1^p \ .$$

The average net product of labor in the ejido must now equal the marginal product in the private farms. Castillo's estimate of the marginal product of labor, including family labor, is 144.84 pesos. On the other hand, the income,

Table 2

Comparison of Production in the Celaya District of Mexico
for Ejido and Private Sectors*

Inputs	Private sector	Ejido sector
	Regression coefficients	
Land	0.147	0.215
Labor	0.198	0.077
Machinery and equipment	0.699	0.739
Animals	- 0.404	- 0.059
Expenses	0.169	0.069
Irrigation water	0.117	0.145
Vehicles	0.043	--
Average product		
Land	900.71	896.86
Labor	731.56	476.90
Machinery and equipment	1.20	2.93
Animals	8.51	8.83
Irrigation water	1744.29	1092.54
Marginal product		
Land	132.40	192.82
Labor	144.84	36.72
Machinery and equipment	0.83	2.16
Animals	- 3.43	- 0.52
Irrigation water	204.08	75.38

---

*Based on regressions in Table 124 of Castillo (1956, p. 132).

after all expenses, per man-month of labor on ejido farms is 156.48. For all practical purposes, the average income per unit of family labor on ejido farms equals the marginal product of labor on private farms.

A comparison of marginal products of machinery and equipment in the two sectors indicates that the marginal product of this form of capital is higher in the ejido sector. This is supportive, but hardly crucial, evidence for the model. It is interesting to note that Castillo's estimates of the rates of return in the two sectors generally conform to the analysis: 6.35 percent in the private sector and 7.69 percent in the ejido sector. From (17), we can calculate, by iteration, the implied value of T, the time horizon. It is about 24 years, which seems a reasonable number, given life expectancy in rural Mexico.

VIII. SOME FURTHER ISSUES AND CONCLUDING OBSERVATIONS

Stepping back from the detail of the econometric studies of productivity to examine Mexican agriculture within the framework provided by the model provides some more general insights. I will conclude by discussing briefly some qualitative aspects of Mexican agriculture such as income distribution, public investment programs, and the role of property rights in the "dual" structure of agriculture.

First, there is the question of whether the ejidatario is "better off" than the small private land holder and the paid, landless agricultural worker. Hertford suggests that the ejidatario is better off, in terms of income, than the small private land holder who has about one hectare of land and annual production of $120 (U.S.). The ejidatario, on the other hand, has a net income of $180 annually (in 1960). Yet, the ejidatario typically works full-time, whereas the small private holder works about three months part-time, for an income of $85. The relevant comparison is, therefore, $120 + $85 minus the rent on one hectare for the private holder versus $180 for the ejidatario. A rental value of $25 per hectare for private land would equalize these incomes. Castillo found that private land rents were of the order of $3 - $5 per year in the Celaya district. It is certainly difficult to conclude, as Hertford did, that the ejidatario is better off than the small private farmer on the basis of these figures. Furthermore, from Castillo's study, the net income per man-month of labor in the ejido sector is 180 pesos, which is very close to the earnings per man-month of paid agricultural workers of 190 pesos. If there is free entry into the ejido sector, which is consistent with the stated goals of the land reform program, then one would be surprised if incomes were not equalized across all three categories of Mexican "campesino": the ejidatario, the small private land holder, and the paid agricultural worker. The fragmentary evidence I have found does not suggest a great discrepancy in incomes among these occupations. Moreover, to the extent that the ejidatario places a high value on having land (in the limited, usufruct sense), then this should be reflected in his willingness to earn a lower income than he could earn as a landless, paid agricultural worker.

There is a more important question to ask. Rather than compare the ejidatario's income with the income of other campesinos, one should ask how a marginal change in the extent of land reform will affect the quantity and distribution of income. There is efficiency or income loss associated with land reform of the Mexican kind; a marginal change may increase or decrease that income loss. When capital is introduced into the analysis, the same conclusion holds. There are, however, strong distributional aspects of the program. Increasing the proportion of land allocated to the ejido sector increases the wage rate, lowers the rental rate on land, and increases the land/labor ratio in both the private and ejido sectors. Reform reallocates income from landowners to non-land holding peasants. Landowners are harmed in two ways. If the land is expropriated without compensation, they bear this direct loss; the rent they receive on their remaining land declines as well.

According to the model, an increase in the land allocated to the ejido sector will be accompanied by an upward drift in wages and in the average size of private and ejido farms. The evidence indicates that private farms did increase in size from 1940 to 1960 in spite of the 200 hectare upper limit on nonexpropriable land. While much of this may be attributable to changes in technology, it may also be true that the reallocation of some 20 million hectares of land from the private to the ejido sector during this period exerted some force in this direction. Consistent with this upward drift of private farm size has been an increase in the average size and government minimums for ejido plots.

To highlight the distributional and efficiency aspects of the land reform program, one can depict the trade-off curve between these two goals. In Figure 3, point A is an initial point showing output and income distribution under the private property, competitive equilibrium. At this point, the distribution of land holdings might be highly uneven. The competitive distribution of land would depend upon the optimum firm size and the relative advantages of rental versus ownership of land from the point of view of firms and landowners. Nonetheless, the distribution of wealth at this starting point will be uneven if the distribution of land is so. Now consider the point B at which private property ceases to exist, and all land is distributed, in equal size plots, to ejidatarios. Since land and labor are assumed to be homogeneous, income is equally distributed at this point. But, we know from the second model, that output at point B is less than at point A because of inefficient use of capital in the two sectors owing to the nonownership provisions of the land reform

$Q = Q^e + Q^p$

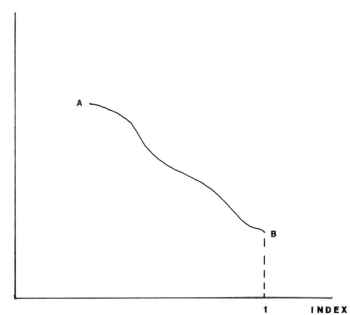

FIGURE III

law. So point B has less income but greater equality than point A. The locus of trade-offs between A and B is not necessarily smooth but would tend to be concave, reflecting the slope of the equilibrium locus in Figure 3. Even if there were a well-defined social welfare function in which income and equality were arguments, one should not expect a unique, global optimum. In some respects, Mexico's heavy investment in agriculture can be viewed as an attempt to improve the trade-off between output and distribution, since irrigation projects would shift the trade-off curve to the right. Furthermore, since agricultural land is not fixed in supply but depends on clearing, terracing, irrigation, and other costly improvements, one must recognize that the supply of agricultural land is diminished in two respects by the land reform program. First, since land reform lowers rent on agricultural land, it reduces the quantity supplied. Second, the threat of expropriation raises the rate of return required by owners of agricultural land and causes this land to be diverted to other uses.

A further implication deserves comment at this point. It has been noted by many authors, for example Lewis (1954), that agriculture in less developed countries has a "dual" structure, with efficient, private firms existing alongside small, family firms which produce inefficiently. It is argued that family farms produce where the marginal product of labor is essentially zero. The model developed here suggests that the nature of the tenancy rights of these families is important. If these families hold the land on a usufruct basis, as do the ejidatarios, then they will equate the average product of labor with wage, and drive the marginal product of labor close to zero. If they owned their land outright, they would never drive the marginal product of labor below the wage, even if they were to pool income to maximize average income per family member. It is clearly important, therefore, to examine the form of land tenancy rights enjoyed by families in the traditional sector before drawing any conclusions about the efficiency of the traditional agricultural sector.

REFERENCES

1. Castillo, C.M., "Eficiencia en el Uso de los Recursos," ch. IX of "La economía agrícola en la Region del Bajío," Problemas agrícolas e industriales de México, VIII, Nos. 3-4, (1956), 127-54.

2. David, P.A., and Fishlow, A., "Optimal Resource Allocation in an Imperfect Market Setting," Journal of Political Economy, LXIX, No. 6, (December 1961), 529-46.

3. De Vany, A., and Sanchez, N., "Property Rights, Uncertainty and Fertility: An Analysis of Land Reform and Fertility in Rural Mexico," mimeo, Texas A&M University, October 1975.

4. Dovring, F., "Reforma Agraria y Productividad: El Caso Mexicano," Investigacion Economica, XXVIII, Nos. 11-12, (June-December 1968), 167-88.

5. Hertford, R. Sources of Change in Mexican Agriculture Production, 1940-65. Economic Research Service, U.S. Department of Agriculture Foreign Agricultural Economic Report No. 73, Washington, D.C., August 1971.

6. Lewis, W.A., "Economic Development with Unlimited Supplies of Labour," The Manchester School, 22, No. 2, (May 1954), 139-91.

7. Reynolds, C.W. The Mexican Economy: Twentieth Century Structure and Growth. New Haven: Yale University Press, 1970.

8. Simpson, E.M. The Ejido: Mexico's Way Out. Chapel Hill: University of North Carolina Press, 1937.

LAND REFORM AND AGRICULTURAL EFFICIENCY IN MEXICO:
A COMMENT

David R. Henderson*
University of Rochester

De Vany sets out to explain relative marginal and average productivities of land and labor in the private and ejido sectors. He produces a general equilibrium model to do so. My criticisms are under three headings: (1) the applicability of the model; (2) the consistency of the empirical results with the model; and (3) the author's welfare conclusions.

However elegant the formal model, it is not applicable to Mexican agriculture. To show why, I shall cast De Vany's general equilibrium model in a more familiar partial equilibrium framework. De Vany models the ejido sector as a common resource. The analysis of the ejido sector is then the same as the analysis of fishing in a common lake which no one owns. Recall in the fishing example that the only way to have a property right in a fish is to catch the fish.[1] As long as the fish goes uncaught, no one owns it. The fisherman "bids" his labor for the fish. When he decides to fish on the lake, he does not take into account the effect his fishing has on the catch of the other fishermen already there. In Figure I is plotted a marginal product of labor (MP_L) curve and an average product of labor (AP_L) curve as a function of the amount of labor engaged in fishing. The efficient amount of labor in fishing is given by the intersection of MP_L and the wage which the fisherman can earn in some alternative employment, with fish as the numeraire. This efficient amount would be the equilibrium amount of labor if the lake were privately owned. Since the lake is not privately owned, this will not be the solution. Since each fisherman gets the average catch, the average catch is each fisherman's marginal product. Since fishermen enter until their marginal product is driven down to the wage, and their marginal product is the average product of all fishermen, then fishermen will enter until the average product equals the wage. There will be "too much" labor input in fishing on the lake. Notice in Figure I that the marginal product could be negative when the average product equals the wage, a fact which De Vany, in his conclusion, seems to deny.

*I am indebted to Sam Kazman for helpful comments. Financial support from the Center for Research in Government and Business, University of Rochester is gratefully acknowledged.

[1] I am using "property right" in a nonnormative sense. That is, "property right" is the "expectation a person has that his decision about the uses of certain resources will be effective" (Alchian and Allen, 1969, p. 158).

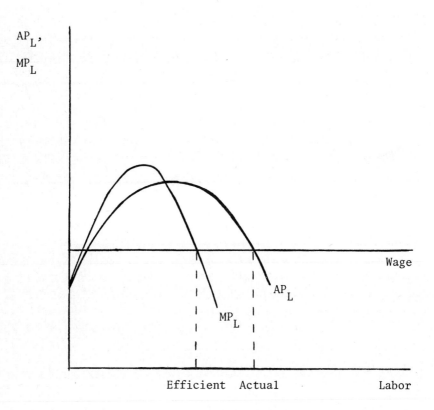

FIGURE I

The paper on Mexican agriculture tells a similar story about the ejido sector. Instead of a lake, there is a fixed quantity of land in the ejido sector, and the product produced is crops, not fish. The land has a zero pecuniary price. At this zero price, there would ordinarily be an excess demand for land. However, there is not. Farmers are not legally allowed to bid a money price for the land. Therefore, they "bid" labor for the land. Or, more correctly, they bid promises to apply a certain amount of labor to the land.[2] In order for the market to clear, as the paper implies it does, the equilibrium amount of labor bid will be an amount such that its value at the alternative wage just equals the value of the crop. Thus equation (4), and thus the result that the wage just equals the value of the average product, rather than the marginal product of labor. The result is the same in the farming as in the fishing case.

But this is not satisfactory. The story does not end where De Vany says it does. Once the farmer obtains the land, he will have an incentive to "shirk." That is, he will have an incentive to decrease the amount of labor he applies to the land to the point where the marginal product equals the wage. It is here that the analogy with the unowned lake breaks down. As long as the farmer has the right to the fruit of the land, then the land is not a common resource, and there will not be too much labor used. The only way there could be too much labor used is if the government forced the farmer to apply the amount of labor to the land that he promised to do. Such enforcement would be almost impossible. It would require constant government surveillance of ejidatarios. De Vany produces no evidence that such enforcement takes place. On the contrary, he gave evidence in an earlier draft that ejidatarios do indeed reduce the amount of labor below the amount promised. He pointed out that some adult males migrate from ejidos once they have obtained the land, leaving their children to farm it.

If the government does not succeed in enforcing the labor commitments, then ejidatarios must be earning rents on the land equal to the difference between the total product (which equals the integral of the marginal product) and the alternative wage. This means that either there is an excess demand for land (since the legal price of land is zero) or that ejidatarios compete for the land by bribing government officials.[3] There is suggestive evidence for the second possibility. The Wall Street Journal of April 5, 1976 reports that a private landowner in Mexico had to bribe a government official to prevent his

---

[2] De Vany does not make it clear that promises of a set amount of labor are being bid. However, this is the only way to make sense of the model.

[3] In a frictionless world, the amount of the bribe would equal the rent which the original landowner would have received.

land from being confiscated for an ejido. There is no reason to expect government officials to be less loath to take bribes from potential ejidatarios.[4]

I turn now to the empirical evidence. Some of the most important empirical evidence is supportive of De Vany's model. The marginal and average products of labor in the ejido sector are lower than in the private sector, as the model predicts, except in the category of hired labor where the reverse is the case. De Vany does not attempt to explain this anomaly. Another result consistent with De Vany's model is the higher labor/land ratio in the ejido sector. However, this could be the result of the fact that labor is not homogeneous. Compared to the private sector, a much higher percentage of the labor on ejido farms is child labor. Therefore, an average laborer in the ejido sector would be some fraction of an average private sector laborer. Counting each child as a laborer would overstate the amount of effective labor in the ejido sector. One would expect a higher reported labor/land ratio in the ejido sector whether De Vany's model is right or wrong.

Another empirical result which seems anomalous is that the private land/labor ratio is higher inside the irrigation district than outside. If the irrigated land has a higher price than the nonirrigated land (and the figures in Table 1 on the marginal products of land suggest that irrigated land does have a higher price), then one would expect the opposite result. That is, one would expect a lower land/labor ratio in the irrigated districts. The anomaly could be explained if a laborer in the irrigated sector is more skilled than a laborer in the nonirrigated sector. However, if this explanation is accepted, then one would have trouble understanding why hired labor has a higher marginal product in the nonirrigated sector (see De Vany's Table 1). The empirical evidence does not strongly support De Vany's model. There are too many unexplained empirical results. A more careful analysis would require at the very least that the labor units be adjusted for quality differences.

Moreover, a discussion of constraints placed on ejidatarios by the government is noticeably absent, and the paper suffers thereby. In trying to understand why the ratio of labor to land is higher in the ejido sector, it would be helpful to know whether ejidatarios are prohibited from pooling their land. If they are so prohibited, and if large-scale capital equipment is used in Mexican agriculture, then one might be closer to understanding the higher labor/land ratio. It could result from the fact that the ejidatarios are prevented from

---

[4]However, if the government official is indifferent to the source of a given bribe, one would expect the present landowner to retain the land. He would be willing to bid more than a potential ejidatario because he would value the land more. That is why he is the present landowner.

taking advantage of economies of scale which exist with large capital equipment, and must instead use cruder, more labor-intensive methods of farming.[5] This might not matter in the case of Mexican agriculture because capital equipment might not be important in any case. However, if this is true, it should be so stated.

My last empirical criticism relates to De Vany's more complicated model in which capital is introduced. De Vany states that because land in the ejido sector cannot be resold, the time horizon which the ejidatario considers in making the capital input decision is truncated. I presume that this is the standard claim made by economists who have studied the usufruct system. In itself, the claim is unexceptionable. However, when it comes to estimating empirically the length of the truncated time horizon, matters get more difficult. De Vany estimates the ejidatario's time horizon by estimating the implicit interest rates in the ejido and private sectors and deriving the time horizon in the ejido sector. To do this, however, he assumes that the time horizon in the private sector is infinite. I find this assumption unreasonable. One would expect farmers in the private sector also to have a truncated time horizon precisely because of the ejido program. That is, because of expropriations of private land in the past, private farmers would place a positive probability on the occurrence of further expropriation in the future. According to De Vany's data, there are many big farms left. Since all land over a few hundred hectares in size is eligible for expropriation, owners of firms would have a healthy fear of expropriation. Therefore, I would expect these large farmers to invest less in long-lived capital than otherwise. There is no way of knowing a priori which sector, ejido or private, would have the more truncated time horizon.

I have argued that De Vany's model is inapplicable to Mexican agriculture. Though I believe this to be so, I shall now criticize his welfare conclusions from the standpoint of his own model. De Vany claims (section V) that it does not matter for efficiency whether the agriculture sector is organized entirely as private farms or entirely as ejidos. This conclusion follows from his assumptions that the amounts of land and labor are fixed, and that the private and ejido sectors have the same production function. However, the amounts of land and labor in Mexican agriculture are not fixed. If all the land were converted to ejidos, the result (in De Vany's model at least) would be entry of labor from nonagricultural occupations. The labor dimension of the Edgeworth production box would expand. There would be too high a labor/land ratio in

---

[5]Note that I am implicitly assuming a significant transactions cost for renting such large-scale equipment. Otherwise, a specialist could simply run the equipment for hire as is done with combines in the U.S.

agriculture. Therefore, organization of agriculture entirely as ejido land would not be as efficient as organization entirely as private land.

Finally, a clarifying comment on De Vany's output-equality trade-off is called for. De Vany claims that under the usufruct system there will be a negatively sloped trade-off between output and equality of wealth, due to the distortion in the use of capital caused by the usufruct system. There is nothing incorrect about this claim in itself. This conclusion follows whether one accepts his or my modeling of the labor input decision. However, his claim is misleading. It leaves the reader with the false impression that there is necessarily an output-equality trade-off even though in fact this trade-off arises only under the usufruct system.[6] Under a private-property system, there is no necessary trade-off between output and equality. If one starts off with a high degree of inequality due to highly unequal land holdings, then one could maintain the same output but increase the amount of equality by redistributing land from the "haves" to the "have-nots." If the have-nots are less efficient farmers than the haves, then the haves would value the land more than the have-nots and would buy it back. Output would be maintained and equality increased. However, as noted above, expropriation creates fear of further expropriation. Consequently, there could be some efficiency loss, and therefore output loss, from the redistribution of land. The size of this loss, however, would depend on whether the Mexicans believed this to be a one-time transfer, or a portent of transfers to come. In the former case, there would be no efficiency loss. There is some reason to believe, on the basis of Mexican history, that such a transfer could take place without its being construed as an ongoing process. The reason is that the transfer could be interpreted as a portent of a stronger official respect for property rights just as easily as it could be interpreted as an omen of an official disrespect for property rights. How can that be so? The reason is that many of the existing large landowners inherited their land from people who used state power to grab land from small landowning Indians.[7] Therefore, as well as increasing equality, a transfer of land from the large landowners to descendants of the dispossessed Indians could be seen as a strengthening of property rights.[8]

---

[6] I do not claim that De Vany meant to leave the reader with this impression, only that the reader is left with this impression.

[7] A descendant of one of these Indians, Emiliano Zapata, led the Mexican revolution of 1910. The expropriation of land by the large landowners was Zapata's main grievance. See Simpson (1937).

[8] This point should not be stretched too far however. Even if the Indians and the present owners regard the transfer as a portent of stronger respect for the original property rights, the transfer might still introduce uncertainty. Economic actors now realize that the government is willing to be moved by issues of justice. They might wonder to themselves what would happen if a new government with a different view of justice came to power. Therefore, the time horizon might still be truncated. I am indebted to Bill Meckling for stressing this point.

Note that I am not contradicting my earlier contention that an ongoing redistribution program would have inefficient effects.[9] If the program I suggest were carried out over time, there would still be a distorted capital input decision on the part of large landowners. For the program to have no adverse efficiency effects, it would have to be carried out in one fell swoop. Note that this contradicts the conventional wisdom that gradualism in economic reform is always to be preferred to haste.

---

[9] "Redistribution" is an inappropriate word in this context. "Return" would be more applicable.

REFERENCES

1. Alchian, A., and Allen, W. Exchange and Production. Belmont, Calif.: Wadsworth Publishing, 1969.

2. De Vany, A., "Land Reform and Agricultural Efficiency in Mexico: A General Equilibrium Analysis," Carnegie-Rochester Conference Series on Public Policy, VI, (eds. K. Brunner and A.H. Meltzer), Amsterdam: North-Holland, 1977.

3. Simpson, E. The Ejido: Mexico's Way Out. Chapel Hill: University of North Carolina Press, 1937.

ECONOMIC GROWTH: WHAT HAVE WE LEARNED FROM THE PAST?*

Douglass North
University of Washington

This paper argues that the institutional framework _implicit_ to theories about economic growth must be made a _formal_ part of the theory if economic theorists are to make further substantive progress in this field.

During the past half-century, accumulating quantitative data and theoretical developments variously emphasizing the role of physical capital, human capital, or technological change have together cleared a good deal of the underbrush from theories of the nature of economic growth. It is now possible at least to specify some of the issues. Neoclassical growth theories provide a varied menu of the interrelationships among productive factors in the growth process; and growth accounting, building on such models, offers explicit numbers to account for the contributions of human capital, economies of scale, or technological change in the process. Recently, evolutionary theories of economic growth have harked back to Schumpeter and attempted to delineate the dynamic nature of economic change.[1] This approach blurs the distinction between movements along a production function and shifts in the production function. Whatever the theoretical problems in the latter models, they are intuitively appealing to economic historians. The careful historical studies of technological change by Landes (1969), Rosenberg (1972), and David (1975) provide reinforcement for theories that suggest a more complex process of technological change than do the straightforward neoclassical accounts.

The immense literature so briefly referenced in the preceding paragraph takes as a given the incentive structure. It is true that the evolutionary theory modifies the maximizing postulate of neoclassical theory by offering a "behavioral" approach to firm decision making, but it still adheres to "the orthodox view that some form of the profit motive is the dominant motivational consideration."[2] Yet even the most casual appraisal of the economic past makes clear that incentives to engage in productive activity have varied enormously and frequently have been completely absent. Moreover, even when the incentives have provided positive inducement for productivity increase, their _specific_

---

*Yoram Barzel, Elisabeth Case, and Robert Higgs made valuable contributions to earlier drafts of this essay.

[1] For a summary of the literature on both neoclassical and evolutionary theories, see Nelson and Winter (1974).

[2] Nelson and Winter (1974, p. 892).

characteristics have fundamental implications for the theoretical superstructure which might be erected.

In the sections that follow, I shall first explore what I believe to be some major turning points in institutional organization in the history of the Western world and then suggest the implications of this approach for the study of economic growth.

I. THE FIRST ECONOMIC REVOLUTION

I begin by exploring one of the great turning points in economic history-- the development of settled agriculture. The so-called Neolithic revolution has been exclusively the province of anthropologists and archeologists and has not been explored by economic historians. Yet it clearly deserves their attention.[3] This revolution was a critical turning point in human history because in the total chronology of man's time on earth, this revolutionary event occurred in the last ten minutes or so of that period; that is, man became distinguishable from other primates anywhere from one to four million years ago, but the development of settled agriculture occurred somewhere between approximately 8 and 10,000 B.C. In the brief chronological period since then, human development has occurred at a rate that bears no comparison with the millions of years before. The models that have been developed by anthropologists and archeologists provide no convincing clues as to why this development should have made an inflectional change in the rate of progress for mankind.

Several archeological models, developed by Childe (1951) and Braidwood (1960), focus either on changing environment and climate or on regions where the biological characteristics of plants and animals made them peculiarly suited to the development of cultivation and domestication. Neither of these models makes population growth and diminishing returns to hunting and gathering a key explanation. The reason is the widely held assumption among anthropologists and archeologists that populations were homeostatic, that is, that they tended to reach an equilibrium with the resource base such that they did not expand and produce diminishing returns. But, both theory and empirical evidence run counter to this view. Theory predicts that population in the face of common property resources would have no tendency to develop a homeostatic relationship.[4] A leading demographer (Coale, 1974) maintains

---

[3] This section briefly summarizes an essay on the subject by North and Thomas, "1ne First Economic Revolution," (forthcoming).

[4] See Smith (1975).

that population growth and migration did take place. Moreover, there is widespread evidence that from about 20,000 B.C. there was significant change in the hunting and gathering patterns of tribes which clearly suggests diminishing returns.[5] In addition are the clues provided by the extinction of over two hundred species of animals during this period.[6] Moreover, it is clear that no new knowledge was needed to cultivate plants.[7] Man already knew the relationship between seeds and plants and the characteristics that led to plant growth and to the breeding of animals.

A more plausible model than those of Childe and Braidwood, one developed by Binford (1968 and 1971) and Flannery (1969), is that population growth led to diminishing returns to hunting and gathering so that ultimately these activities became less productive than the cultivation of plants and the rearing and breeding of animals. Yet the anthropologists who have developed and explored this promising model have ignored the most fundamental aspect of settled agriculture which is that it required exclusive property rights. Indeed, some anthropologists make the argument that the domestication of plants and animals did not occur where there were rich and abundant harvests, but rather occurred where the harvests were less rich and abundant. For example, in the Fertile Crescent there would have been so much wild emmer or einkorn wheat to be gathered that man would not have bothered to cultivate plants. This argument simply ignores the fundamental dilemma of growing population pressure and the common property resource problem. It is far more likely that man found rich areas with an abundance of wild grain to be harvested with a sickle and then began to defend these areas against intruders. I would speculate that the experience of the semisedentary Natufian culture in Palestine based on intensive wild cereal cultivation provides a more likely lead toward a theory of the development of domestication than does the alternative procedure of growing seed on more marginal land.[8]

The distinction between cultivation and domestication is a subtle one. Cultivation implies nothing more than the planting, cultivating, and harvesting of agricultural products, whereas domestication implies some genetic change that improves the value of the agricultural product for man. In the absence of the exclusive property rights resource, it would never have been worthwhile to devote labor to cultivation or to improve yields by domestication since the

---

[5] See Flannery (1969).

[6] Smith (1975).

[7] See Flannery and Coe (1968).

[8] See Perrot (1966).

output would be appropriated by others. Once exclusivity was established, however, weeding, primitive irrigation, seed selection, and the gradual trial and error process of learning by doing, all to improve yields and the genetic characteristics of domesticated animals, became worthwhile. A common property resource provides no incentive for the acquisition of superior technology or learning. In fact, in a world of fixed resources, greater efficiency at hunting and gathering is ultimately self-defeating since it simply implies that the resource base will be drawn down more rapidly. In contrast, exclusive or communal property rights which reward the owners provide a direct incentive to improve efficiency and productivity or, in more fundamental terms, to acquire more knowledge and new techniques. The first economic revolution was not a revolution because it shifted man from hunting and gathering to settled agriculture but because there was an incentive change for mankind of fundamental proportion which was responsible for the progress that mankind has made in the last 10,000 years, in contrast to the long era of primitive hunter-gatherer man.

II. PROPERTY RIGHTS IN THE ANCIENT WORLD

The distance both in time and economic development between the primitive Neolithic settlement, with its fields and livestock based on a structure of communal property rights, and the complex civilization that developed in Mesopotamia, Egypt, Greece, and Rome is a distance that not only spans 8,000 years but also records as remarkable a transformation as any that has occurred in human history. The most striking economic features are the enormous expansion in aggregate output and the clearly long periods of rising per capita income.[9] Very little is known about the structure of early property rights, but simply delineating the difference between tribal existence and the requirements of settled agriculture will illustrate some of them.

First, the development of a set of property rights around animals and plants involves some form of organized defense. It is necessary to exclude outsiders from the fruits of labors of those of the group. Second, if the agriculture involved irrigation, as some of the early archeological remains in Palestine and the Tigris-Euphrates suggest, coordination and a high degree of organization were necessary in order to secure the benefits of irrigation. Canals have to be dug and maintained. Drainage has to be systematically organized and sluices and floodgates arranged so that the water is distributed over the area to be irrigated. Third, settled agriculture involves a far greater division of tasks

---

[9]For evidence in the case of the Roman Empire, see Gunderson (1976).

than in a hunting-gathering society. In the latter, there is little more specialization than that hunting is usually done by men and gathering by women. In contrast, with settled agriculture, there is not only an increasing division of tasks among workers--and perhaps specialized warriors for protection, as well as priests to direct the rationalizing of man with his environment--but also, purely within the economic organization, increasing differentiation as skills emerge as a natural product of more specialized functions. By the second millenium B.C. craft specialization was well developed. Potters, metalworkers, weavers, masons, carpenters, shipbuilders, bronzesmiths, and goldsmiths are just some of the specialized occupations listed in Linear B tablets of Minoan civilization.[10] This specialization and division of labor marks an enormous change from the relatively undifferentiated society that hunting and gathering produced. Fourth, such a differentiated organization inevitably requires the development of a system of distribution of the output among individuals. A simple task in a hunting-gathering society, distribution involves far more coordination and regulation in a society in which specialization and division of labor exist. Fifth, a settled society producing a wide diversity of products has the opportunity to store goods against periods of famine or drought. The inventorying of goods also necessitated coordination and storage facilities. Finally, the pattern of specialization and division of labor implies the growth of trade between units, not only trade within the community but trade among communities in order to enhance the benefits of specialized production.

What are the implications of these changes? First, they imply a larger trade area than a single village; some minimum efficient size is required to maximize the advantages of such specialization and division of labor. Therefore, the size of the political-economic unit will of necessity increase. This is particularly true where irrigation exists, since there are typically economies of scale in such projects. Second, these changes involve the emergence of an explicit third party--a state--as an essential and necessary organization. There must be a part of the society that specializes in specifying and enforcing the rules and distributing the proceeds. The basic functions are (a) protection; (b) the adjudication of disputes which inevitably arise in a world of specialization and division of labor; and (c) the provision of public or semipublic goods in addition to protection and justice, and frequently the organization and administration of an irrigation system. A shift has occurred from an organization characterized by anthropologists as bands to one described by them as tribes and in the direction of what they call the state. The most striking aspect of this transformation is the increasing degree of control that the political unit, the

---

[10]See Renfrew (1972, p. 341).

state, will have over resources. Under its control will come the overseeing of specialized groups such as warriors, as well the inventorying and storage of foodstuffs, and ultimately their distribution.

What sorts of property rights will emerge under these changed conditions? There is a long-standing dispute among classical economic historians on this subject. A number of historians professed to see in the ancient world the emergence of markets and property right structures with close parallels to those of modern times. Others, notably Polanyi,[11] have argued that earlier historians had been misled by taking nineteenth- and twentieth-century models and applying them indiscriminately to the ancient past. Polanyi in particular argues that organized markets do not appear to have been characteristic of the ancient world and cites evidence from Babylonia and other areas (in addition to more modern counterparts in primitive societies) to suggest that markets were not a necessary part of such organizing activity. Polanyi may be correct in this regard but for a different reason. Polanyi regards markets and "economizing" behavior as synonymous and uniquely characteristic of modern western societies. But, there is no reason to believe that in a world in which information and transactions costs are high, markets will be the most "efficient" solution; to the contrary, there must have been other ways of organizing economic activity under those conditions which would have produced more efficient results.[12] One can have a world without organized markets and still have economizing behavior on the part of participants. This explanation makes more sense in accounting for the past than Polanyi's interpretation.

By the time of the Roman Empire, the Mediterranean world had become a trading unit. Roman Law provided an elaborate structure of property rights to encourage trade and commerce, and Pompeii's earlier sweep of the Mediterranean to eliminate pirates had insured enforced protection of trade routes as Rhodes had done earlier. The key to this remarkable development must have been the innovation by government of more efficient property rights. Relatively little is known about the structure of property rights in earlier times. Such bits of evidence as Hammurabi's Code provide some clues, as does Roman Law of which much more is known. But, the revision of classical economic history from the Neolithic period to the end of the Roman Empire must focus on the creative role that government played in innovating the basic rules of the game which provided incentive for economic expansion.

---

[11] In Polanyi, Arensberg, and Pearson (1957).

[12] A suggestive framework is Alchian and Demsetz (1972).

III. ECONOMIC DECLINE IN THE ANCIENT WORLD

Ultimately, all of these civilizations declined: some were destroyed or devastated by war; others display a mixed picture of economic decline and ultimate conquest and enslavement. A convincing explanation for the decline of these civilizations is elusive, but two economic themes run through the history of the ancient world. One can be called "The Barbarians at the Gate" story; the second strand describes population expansion and recurrent diminishing returns to agricultural and natural resources. These two themes are obviously related. It is known that population grew in the ancient world and that a wide variety of efforts were made to combat the consequences of population pressure on resources. There was widespread colonization by the Greeks and Phoenicians, for example, as pressure upon population led them to migrate and conquer areas with still relatively abundant land and resources. Sometimes in the face of growing population pressures, property rights were restructured. In some cases there may have been decline in fertility through delays in marriage or through infanticide, which helped to ease the problem. But, one should note that, even if one country through institutional change, the reorganization of property rights, and fertility decline, resolved its problems, it still might not survive unless all other societies were equally successful. The story of barbarians at the gate is a reminder of that.

While not in any way providing a complete explanation for the decline of the Roman Empire, the following brief description is a recurrent theme in the histories of that decline.

The barbarians at the gates of Rome is an oft-repeated story. It is well known that the line of defense of Rome along the Rhine and the upper Danube imposed an increasingly heavy burden on Rome as time went on. Not only were larger and larger payments in gold made to barbarian groups to bribe them not to invade, but the expenses of the legions rose. The army under Diocletian may have numbered 350,000 men. Gold payments to barbarians and the increasing costs of maintaining the army created strains on the economy due to the harsher tax structure. At the same time, Rome was feeding 120,000 of its citizens free. While expenses rose, the tax base was being eroded away. Those who enjoyed good political ties increasingly were freed from taxation, thereby further burdening the groups with little access to political favoritism. Increasingly, townsmen and peasants were apathetic as to which side they belonged in the struggle between Romans and barbarians.[13]

---

[13] Jones (1966, p. 368).

It is important to note that increased taxation per se is not necessarily the cause of economic decline if increased spending results in more private and public goods. But, in the case of Rome, it required continually increased taxation to provide the same amount of defense. Moreover, the increase in the burden of taxation eventually eroded the tax base, ultimately providing such a disincentive to economic activity that it was self-defeating. In effect, property rights had been so altered as no longer to found a viable economic system.

IV. THE EVOLUTION OF PROPERTY RIGHTS IN THE WESTERN WORLD

The medieval world presents a number of puzzles.[14] The size of the political-economic unit is one. For almost a thousand years following the demise of the Roman Empire, the size of political-economic units in the West was small. Even the brief period of the Carolingian empire only reinforces the view that larger political-economic units were inherently unstable, although one is reminded that both the Byzantine and Islamic empires persisted to the east and to the south. The feudal-manorial systems were an "efficient" solution to a world in which chaos persisted, land was abundant, and labor scarce.[15] The feudal-manorial systems produced islands of order in a sea of chaos and, as some degree of stability revived, population growth revived as well. This led to a frontier movement as population expanded and filled out the empty areas between manors and between the settled area and the frontiers northward and westward in Europe.

Population growth produced two diametrically opposed pressures for institutional change. On the one hand, as population spread through Europe and towns developed, the factor endowments were increasingly differentiated both spatially and in terms of human capital. As a result, the gains from trade increased substantially and led to the flowering of international commerce in the twelfth and thirteenth centuries. In order to realize the gains from trade, it was necessary to innovate institutional arrangements that would enable transactions costs to be lowered in trade. Everywhere, kings and princes were guaranteeing safe conduct to traveling merchants, protecting alien merchants (and providing them with exclusive trading privileges), enforcing the enactment

[14]This section summarizes a part of North and Thomas (1973).

[15]No effort has been made in this paper to explore property rights in man over time although some hypotheses are derivable from the propositions advanced in this paper. For a brief discussion of serfdom and slavery and the essential characteristics of each, see Engerman (1973), Domar (1970), and North and Thomas (1971).

of commercial courts, and granting and delegating property rights to the burgeoning towns. Fairs such as those in the Champagne country of France were encouraged. Banking revived, and instruments of credit expanded and were created.

But, while population growth provided positive incentive for institutional rearrangements in the commercial sector, it produced pressure of a different kind in agriculture. As settlements filled out in western Europe, ultimately diminishing returns set in, producing pressure to modify the common property aspect of landholding. The beginnings of enclosures are seen and also the development of English land law, which was the foundation piece of English common law. However, the transformation of property rights in land was a slow process and nowhere kept pace with the population growth. The difference between private and social returns on having children widened and ultimately led to the crisis of the fourteenth century, beginning with the famine of 1315-17, and ultimately being realized in the terrible plagues that swept Europe from 1347 onward and reduced population for another century.

The thirteenth to fifteenth centuries also bore witness to a series of major technological changes in military warfare. The longbow, pike, and gunpowder, and in consequence the cannon and the musket, were the most important ones. Whether the development of an exchange economy was a sufficient condition for expanding the optimum scale of warfare or was augmented by the aforementioned innovations is not clear. However, the overall consequences were that the conditions for political survival were drastically altered, entailing larger numbers for an army of effective size, more training and discipline (particularly important for an effective pikeman), and more costly equipment in the form of cannons and muskets.

At this point I can usefully pause in the historical narrative to offer an analogy from economic theory. Take the case of a competitive industry with a large number of small firms. Introduce an innovation which leads to economies of scale over a substantial range of output so that the efficient size firm must be much larger. The path from the old competitive equilibrium to a new (and probably unstable) oligopoly solution will be as follows. The original small firms must either increase in size, combine, or be forced into bankruptcy. The result is a small number of large firms of optimum size, but even then the results are unstable. There are endless efforts toward collusion and price fixing, but equally ubiquitous is the advantage that will accrue to the individual firm to cheat on the arrangements. Periods of truce are punctuated by episodes of cutthroat competition.

165

Applying the above description to the political world of this era gives a very close analogy. Between 1200 and 1500, the many political units of western Europe go through endless expansions, alliances, and combinations in a world of continuing intrigue and warfare. Even as the major nation-states emerge, the periods of peace are continually interrupted. In short, it was a period of expanding war, diplomacy, and intrigue. The magnitude of the increasing costs of survival was staggering. A year of warfare represented at least a fourfold increase in the cost of government, and most years were characterized by wars, not peace. Monarchs were continually beset by an immense indebtedness and forced to desperate expedients. The specter of bankruptcy was a recurring threat and for many states a reality. The fact of the matter is that princes were not free--they were slaves to an unending runaway fiscal crisis.[16]

It is in this context that one can begin to understand a basic dilemma with respect to the evolution of property rights. In all of western Europe, changes in relative prices were inducing pressure for institutional change. But, in several of the countries, notably the Netherlands and England, the relative price change produced a set of institutions that led to sustained economic growth, whereas in others, such as Spain, it produced stagnation and economic decline for centuries.

In England the development of land law, the gradual ascendancy of parliament over the crown, and the ultimately successful effort to evolve a body of property rights that would be far removed from royal whim and fancy were successful. The ascendancy of parliament reflected the gradual exchange of control over property rights in return for tax revenues. In contrast, in Spain the reverse occurred.

While land was still abundant in Spain, the King of Castile had granted to the shepherders' guild, the Mesta, the exclusive right to drive sheep across Spain from summer pastures high in the Pyrenees to winter pastures in the lowlands of western Spain. In return for this monopoly grant, the King received a major part of his fiscal revenues from the Mesta. This posed no problem in the period when land was abundant and labor scarce, but with the growth of population the persistence of the Mesta's privileges prevented the development of exclusive property rights and the growth of more efficient agriculture.

In England the development of efficient land laws, exclusive property rights, and enclosure were ultimately to lead to substantial productivity change in agriculture, which was an essential prerequisite to the Industrial Revolution. In Spain the persistence of the monopoly of the Mesta prevented the growth

---

[16]To the best of my knowledge, Schrumpeter (1954) gives the first description of the changing fiscal characteristics of the early modern state.

166

of exclusive property rights in land and ultimately led to a stagnation and decline in agriculture. There is more to the story of Spain than this. In spite of an inefficient agriculture, the Spanish crown had, through marriage, inheritance, and conquest, managed to receive substantial fiscal revenues from the Netherlands and the New World; but, persistent wars on the part of the Hapsburgs led to increasing needs for tax revenue and confiscations. The result was revolution and ultimately independence for the Netherlands. At home the destruction of existing property rights produced stagnation and decline.

V. THE INDUSTRIAL REVOLUTION

As the name suggests, the Industrial Revolution is considered a major turning point in economic history, yet there is agreement neither about what it was nor about how it came about. Clearly, there was an increase in the rate of innovation, an acceleration in population growth, growth in output per capita, and eventually a systematic wedding of scientific with technological advance. Yet neither the sources nor timing of these changes is matter for agreement.

In the terms of this paper, I would speculate that the capturability of returns to innovation rose as a consequence of events that followed upon some of the developments described in the preceding section. First, agricultural productivity increased both as a result of development of exclusive property rights in land and, specifically, as a consequence of the enclosure movement. Second, the long struggle of the seventeenth century between parliament and the Stuarts led to the emergence of a set of property rights that was not subject to royal whim, including the patent law as part of the Statute of Monopolies, 1624. But, probably more important than any single law governing patent rights was the gradual accumulation of an impersonal body of law which attempted to reduce those margins where potential income was being dissipated in innovation.

Still a further source of increasing the rate of return on innovation was a widening of the market which produced results, with which economists have been familiar since Adam Smith; that is, specialization and division of labor led to a pattern of production which lowered the cost of discovering new ways of undertaking economic activity. This whole process is consistent with the detailed findings of Rosenberg (1972) with respect to the incremental nature of the innovation process in contrast to the emphasis on the discrete grand innovations. It is also consistent with the framework advanced by David (1975) in which widening markets, economies of scale, and learning by doing produced an intricate pattern of cumulative expansion. In short, the brief history I attempt here is one in which there was an intermixture of increasing incentives and a pattern of innovational development that is consistent with the careful historical studies that have been undertaken on the nature of technological change.

Even less is known about the causes of growth in scientific knowledge. This represents the case of increased investment in a pure public good. Whatever its origins, the timing of the development of scientific knowledge and its relationship to innovation are matters of controversy. In a widely publicized recent book, Rostow (1974) has maintained that it was this wedding of scientific knowledge with innovation that accounts for the Industrial Revolution in England. Yet even Rostow himself acknowledges that he can find very little direct connection between scientific knowledge and the succession of innovations in textiles, iron, and machinery which characterized the classic Industrial Revolution. The evidence suggests much more strongly that another century elapsed before pure scientific knowledge played an important role in innovation. By the latter part of the nineteenth century, this wedding had occurred and had produced a basic change in the character of innovation in modern time.

The question of timing aside, there is still another implication of Rostow's model: the wedding of science with technology implies that sustained economic growth is built into the system. The implication of this view is not only that future growth of economies is assured, but also that past experience, however interesting it may be, is in effect obsolete. The conclusion depends upon two very crucial assumptions. The first is that there are no diminishing returns to the acquisition of new knowledge and, therefore, to the sustained productivity increase of revolutionizing science and technology. The second is that society has the ability to modify institutions to adjust to this set of changes.

No evidence permits me to make any definitive statements about the first proposition with respect to diminishing returns to new knowledge, but it seems to me that past experience raises important issues with respect to the second. History has witnessed the creation of an urban, industrial society with a degree of interdependence--local, national, and international--of unprecedented scope. Tension has developed within the structure of property rights which was derived from a primarily agrarian, decentralized world. The property rights inherited from this earlier time have permitted the ubiquitous development of pollution, congestion, and other environmental effects. The consequent problems of restructuring property rights to take account of these environmental problems are a critical issue of these times. There is nothing new about this dilemma. Past history records endless crises that were a product of economic changes which required institutional modification in order for the society to survive. History equally has provided witness to the demise of many, if not most, of the societies that faced these tensions. The adaptation of institutions and the modification of property rights to meet new needs is a function of the state, and, as I have attempted to demonstrate above, there is no guarantee that those who run the state will be in a position to make the necessary modifications. Economic history reveals that most societies have never developed a structure of property rights that encouraged economic growth, and that, in those that did have initial development, changes over time ultimately led to their demise because they were unable to modify these property rights in the face of changing economic conditions. The development and maintenance of a body of property rights that will assure sustained economic growth ultimately depends on the political structure and organization of the society, and both a theory of economic growth and policy prescriptions for economic growth necessitate a theory of the state in order to explain how economic growth occurs.

VI. THE THEORETICAL ISSUES

The foregoing historical vignettes do little more than reveal the historian's ignorance. But, they make clear that a systematic theory of historical growth and, therefore, a theory prescriptive of economic growth require the development of a theory of demographic change, a theory of technological change, a theory of the evolution of property rights, and, finally, a theory of the state. However, these requirements bear little resemblance to the models described briefly above. Theories of demography, property rights, and the state are usually absent. Only technological change is a standard part of the theories– but typically with incentives as a fixed parameter. However, the biggest gap in the necessary theoretical apparatus is a theory of the state. Ultimately, it is the state that provides a set of rules of the game and, therefore, the incentive structure that influences decision making with respect to fertility, technological change, and property rights.

Recent work in demographic theory, building on earlier studies by Leibenstein (1974) and Easterlin (1968), offers the promise of filling a major gap in economic knowledge. The new economics of the household focuses on the complex structure of incentives and disincentives resulting from the opportunity costs of time and human capital of the participants in the household.[17] Unfortunately, the major focus of this work has been on the transition; little work has been done on explanations of demographic change for earlier periods or even for present underdeveloped areas.

---

[17] For a summary and somewhat caustic appraisal of the new literature, see Leibenstein (1974).

169

It is more difficult to explain why there has been so little work on the incentive structure of technological change. Nothing is new with respect to the awareness of the income that is dissipated through the inability to capture the returns from both pure scientific knowledge and applied innovation. But, the controversies over patent systems and their effects have been singularly lacking in careful detailed empirical studies of the structure of contractual relationships that exist around innovation. Such research would provide basic understanding of the degree to and direction in which income gets dissipated in the course of innovative activity.[18]

The evolution of property rights is equally obscure. There has been promising initial theoretical work by Demsetz (1967) and Cheung (1970); some initial historical studies on enclosures by McCloskey (1975); Umbeck on the California gold rush;[19] and the article (1971) and book (1973) by North and Thomas cited above. However, these offer only initial clues to a much more complex process.

I can perhaps highlight the theoretical issues most clearly by restating what seem to be the implications of these brief historical examples.

It appears evident first that fertility has tended to exceed mortality. Sometimes the rate of change has been glacial and at other times much more rapid. It is also evident that since very early times there has been reciprocity between economic well-being and fertility, so that periods of rising incomes have led to expansion in fertility and periods of falling income have led to efforts at readjustment either by delay of marriage, infanticide, or primitive forms of contraception. Yet it is also clear that this feedback process has been imperfect. That is, the difference between private and social costs of having children has persisted sufficiently with the result that the adjustment process has not prevented crises of a Malthusian character.

Population growth has produced two sets of tensions to induce institutional change. On the one hand, the growth of population and its expansion over the face of the earth taken together with differential human capital, emerging with the development of concentrations of populations in towns, have encouraged trade by increasing the gains from trade as factor endowments have become increasingly differentiated. Not only has exchange itself been a major source of productivity increase but the growth of trade has induced a variety of new institutional arrangements which have encouraged productivity.

---

[18] An ongoing research project by my colleague Steven Cheung is intended to remedy this oversight and provide basic insights into the nature of technological change.

[19] Umbeck's (1975) study is a contribution both to theory and to history.

The other side of the coin, however, is that expanding population has ultimately led to diminishing returns to agriculture and to pressure on existing institutions to alter property rights to meet the dilemma of diminishing returns.[20]

There is no guarantee that property rights will become more efficient in the face of these tensions for institutional change because the ultimate dispenser of property rights is the state. As shown in section III, the creation of a state is an essential prerequisite for economic growth. Without it, anarchy prevails. When growth has occurred, it has reflected the creation of a more efficient system of property rights by the state. But, the historical past equally bears witness to the innumerable occasions when the state has failed to create property rights that would provide incentives for productive activity.

On the face of it, this is an anamolous result. Whether one regards the political decision maker(s) as a wealth maximizer or, as the more recent public choice literature would have it, as one who maximizes the likelihood of his staying in office, one would expect that, in either case, he would choose to modify property rights to make them as efficient as possible. More efficient property rights would increase the income and wealth of the society and make more likely either the politician's survival or increased wealth. However, there have been two fundamental constraints upon the decision making process of those who run the state which limit very severely their alternatives. One is a competitive constraint and the other is a transactions costs constraint.

By a competitive constraint I mean that the political decision maker(s) will not alter property rights so as to antagonize powerful groups of constituents which might thereby go over to an alternative potential ruler. Constituents whose opportunity costs allow low-cost access to alternative possible rulers thus will inhibit political policy makers from antagonizing them. The history of the Mesta is a case in point.[21]

The transactions costs constraint is quite simple. Efficient property rights will produce greater wealth and output for the society, but the costs of monitoring the system in order to collect taxes may in fact produce lower income for the state than a more inefficient structure of property rights. A

---

[20] A much neglected study in this connection is that by Boserup (1963). In the main Boserup's study has been dismissed by economists because it appeared that she did not understand simple Ricardian economics, and it is true that she confuses conceptually movements along a production function from shifts in the production function. Yet her intuition clearly was the right one. She focused on the tensions that population pressure produces in a society and on the efforts to escape that pressure by innovation and institutional adjustment. It is true that she ignores the property rights implications, but her analysis seems to me to be an important one, with useful historical illustrations.

[21] The analogy from economic theory that seems to be most appropriate is that developed by Demsetz (1968), in which potential competition forces those with "a natural monopoly" to behave in a competitive fashion.

frequent example in history is of the granting of a monopoly by the state. This gives the state low-cost ability to monitor output and, therefore, to tax wealth and income as compared to creating conditions of a more competitive market structure, which in turn would encourage factor mobility and induce technological change. However, the dispersed character of economic activity might result in much higher costs of monitoring and collection and, therefore, lower realized tax rates for the state.

It seems likely that both of these constraints have been powerful influences in the persistence of inefficient property rights, which has either prevented economic growth or, in growing societies, altered incentives in directions opposite from those that would increase productivity, and ultimately induced stagnation.

Let me emphasize, however, that while population growth and diminishing returns to agriculture have been a dominant influence in the historical past in inducing institutional change and in putting pressure on the state, they are certainly not the only causes of the instability in the state's dispensations of property rights. A more general explanation would surely focus on the phenomenon that the state as a third party to every contract and as the enforcer of the rules and regulations of society has ultimate coercive power. That coercive power inevitably means that the various groups of its constituents have a stake in getting access to political power in order to redistribute wealth and income in their own interests. There is nothing new about this fundamental paradox of the political system. James Madison's clear and concise statement in his celebrated Federalist Paper No. 10 bears quoting again.

> The most common and durable source of factions has been the various and unequal distribution of property. Those who hold and those who are without property have ever formed distinct interests in society. Those who are creditors, and those who are debtors, fall under a like discrimination. A landed interest, a manufacturing interest, a mercantile interest, a moneyed interest, with many lesser interests, grow up of necessity in civilized nations, and divide them into different classes, actuated by different sentiments and views. The regulation of these various and interfering interests forms the principal task of modern legislation, and involves the spirit of party and faction in the necessary and ordinary operations of the government. . . .

172

The inference to which we are brought is, that the causes of faction cannot be removed, and that relief is only to be sought in the means of controlling its effects.

If a faction consists of less than a majority, relief is supplied by the republican principle, which enables the majority to defeat its sinister views by regular vote. It may clog the administration, it may convulse the society; but it will be unable to execute and mask its violence under the forms of the Constitution. When a majority is included in a faction, the form of popular movement, on the other hand, enables it to sacrifice to its ruling passion or interest both the public good and the rights of other citizens. To secure the public good and private rights against the danger of such a faction, and at the same time to preserve the spirit and the form of popular government, is then the great object to which our inquiries are directed.

In order for a state to provide stability in the provision of property rights requires that there should be no changes in the opportunity costs of its constituents. That is, the bargaining strength of the various groups of constituents vis-à-vis the state would remain constant. This implies that there should be no change in the potential supply of competitors offering the services of the state, on the one hand, and no changes in the relative strength of those demanding the services of the state, on the other. Such a condition would imply no changes in relative factor shares or in factor and product prices over time. To take a single illustration from the past two centuries, the enormous change in the relative shares of incomes going to rents versus wages of necessity paralleled a transformation of the relative power of constituents away from landlords and in the direction of wage-earning groups.

Still another condition for political stability would appear to be the absence of technological changes in warfare, thereby leaving unchanged the efficient, i.e., survival size of the state. Technological changes that produce changes in the size of the state through warfare will obviously change the composition of constituents and, therefore, induce further instability.[22]

---

[22] This very summary set of propositions about the state are elaborated in a forthcoming paper of mine on the subject, "Towards a Theory of the State in History." For a similar approach see Reder (1974).

This brief description of forces for instability is certainly incomplete. It ignores noneconomic forces such as changes in the relative religious composition of the population, for example. It stands as an initial catalog of our ignorance of the most fundamental element in any theory of economic growth--and that is a theory of the state.

REFERENCES

1. Alchian, A.A., and Demsetz, H., "Production, Information Costs, and Economic Organization," American Economic Review, LXII, No. 5, (December 1972), 777-95.

2. Binford, L.R., "Post-Pleistocene Adaptations," in New Perspectives in Archeology, (eds. S.R. and L.R. Binford), Chicago: Aldine Publishing Co., 1968, reprinted in S. Struever, Prehistoric Agriculture, Garden City, N.Y.: Natural History Press, 1971.

3. Boserup, E. The Conditions of Agricultural Growth. Chicago: Aldine Publishing Co., 1965.

4. Braidwood, R.J., "The Agricultural Revolution," Scientific American, 203, No. 48, (September 1960), 130-48.

5. Cheung, S.N.S., "The Structure of a Contract and the Theory of a Non-Exclusive Resource," Journal of Law and Economics, XIII, No. 1, (April 1970), 49-70.

6. Childe, V.G. Man Makes Himself. New York: New American Library, 1951.

7. Coale, A.J., "The History of the Human Population," Scientific American, 231, No. 3, (September 1974), 40-51.

8. David, P. Technical Choice, Innovation and Economic Growth. Cambridge: Cambridge University Press, 1975.

9. Demsetz, H., "Toward a Theory of Property Rights," American Economic Review, LVII, No. 2, (May 1967), 347-59.

10. _____, "Why Regulate Utilities?" Journal of Law and Economics, XI, (April 1968), 55-66.

11. Domar, E.D., "The Causes of Slavery or Serfdom: A Hypothesis," Journal of Economic History, XXX, No. 1, (March 1970), 18-32.

12. Easterlin, R. Population Labor Force and Long Swings in Economic Growth: The American Experience. New York: Columbia University Press, 1968.

13. Engerman, S., "Some Considerations Relating to Property Rights in Man," Journal of Economic History, XXXIII, No. 1, (March 1973), 43-65.

14. Flannery, K., "The Origins and Ecological Effects of Early Domestication in Iran and the Near East," in The Domestication of Plants and Animals, (eds. P.J. Ucko and G.W. Dimbledy), Chicago: Aldine Publishing Co., 1969.

15. Flannery, K., and Coe, M., "Social and Economic Systems in Formative Mesoamerica," in New Perspectives in Archeology, (eds. S.R. and L.R. Binford), Chicago: Aldine Publishing Co., 1968.

16. Gunderson, G., "Economic Change and the Demise of the Roman Empire," in Explorations in Economic History, 13, No. 1, (January 1976), 43-68.

17. Jones, A.H.M. The Decline of the Ancient World. London: Longman, Green and Co., 1966.

18. Landes, D. The Unbound Prometheus. Cambridge: Cambridge University Press, 1969.

19. Leibenstein, H., "An Interpretation of the Economic Theory of Fertility: Promising Path or Blind Alley?" Journal of Economic Literature, XII, No. 2, (June 1974), 457-87.

20. McCloskey, D., "The Persistence of Open Fields," and "The Economics of Enclosure," in Economic Issues in European Agrarian History, (eds. E.L. Jones and W.N. Parker), Princeton: Princeton University Press, 1975.

21. Nelson, R.R., and Winter, S.G., "Neoclassical vs. Evolutionary Theories of Economic Growth: Critique and Prospectus," Economic Journal, 84, No. 336, (December 1974), 886-905.

22. North, D.C., and Thomas, R.P., "The Rise and Fall of the Manorial System: A Theoretical Model," Journal of Economic History, XXXI, No. 4, (December 1971), 777-803.

23. _____. The Rise of the Western World: A New Economic History. Cambridge: Cambridge University Press, 1973.

24. _____, "The First Economic Revolution," Economic History Review, (forthcoming).

25. Perrot, J., "Le Gisement Natufied de Mallaha ('Eynan), Israel," L'Anthropologie, 70, (1966), 437-84.

26. Polanyi, K., Arensberg, C.M., and Pearson, H.W., eds. Trade and Market in the Early Empires. New York: Free Press, 1957.

27. Reder, M.W., "An Economic Theory of Imperialism," in Nations and Households in Economic Growth: Essays in Honor of Moses Abramowitz, (eds. P.A. David and M.W. Reder), New York: Academic Press, 1974.

28. Renfrew, C. The Emergence of Civilisation. London: Methuen Co., 1972.

29. Rosenberg, N. Technology and American Economic Growth. New York: Harper and Row, 1972.

30. Rostow, W. How It All Began. New York: McGray-Hill, 1974.

31. Schrumpeter, J., "The Crisis of the Tax State," International Economic Papers, 4, (1954), 5-38.

32. Smith, V.L., "The Primitive Hunter Culture, Pleistocene Extinction, and the Rise of Agriculture," Journal of Political Economy, 83, No. 4, (August 1975), 727-56.

33. Umbeck, J., "A Theoretical and Empirical Investigation into the Formation of Property Rights: The California Gold Rush," Ph.D. dissertation, University of Washington, 1975.

INVENTION AND ACCUMULATION IN AMERICA'S ECONOMIC GROWTH: A NINETEENTH-CENTURY PARABLE*

Paul A. David

Stanford University

It is the historian's business to tell true stories. Being an economic historian by trade, I propose in what follows to relate a story of our nation's economic progress in an era now beyond the personal recall of living Americans. But, perhaps because I am also an economist, what I have to offer will be no literal narrative. It is, more precisely, an allegorical macroeconomic account of the growth process in the United States economy of the nineteenth century—a figurative representation in which meanings are conveyed symbolically, if at all. For these purposes it is most suitable for me to employ the symbolism of growth models, as the latter provide a natural vehicle for macroeconomic reasoning. Before embarking on the narrative, however, several prefatory remarks may be in order concerning the varied uses of allegory in such connections as this.

I. GROWTH PARABLES AND REALITIES

The principal virtue of macroeconomic analysis applied to questions of long-run economic development is that it seeks to summarize and condense the features of a general equilibrium system so as to focus on relationships among a few crucial markets. This is also its principal defect. Obviously, much may be lost if users of this approach are seduced into forgetting the realities of economic life, particularly when (as a syndrome of incompleted economic development) markets remain so badly fragmented that conditions within them defy accurate summary by reference to single price and quantity indicators.

Yet only those who think themselves (or others) most easily beguiled into fatal error will wish to eschew all the risks inherent in aggregation. After all, even to consider as an entity the collection of local and regional American economies that were (in the course of the nineteenth century) to become only more or less fully integrated within a national market economy of continental

---

*This paper is based on research supported under NSF Grant SOC75 0844 and draws heavily upon the findings of unpublished collaborative work with Moses Abramovitz. I have benefited immeasurably from discussion of this material with him, as with my other Stanford colleagues, Alex Field, Jonathan Pincus, Warren Sanderson, Nathan Rosenberg, and Robert Willis. But they must all be exonerated from responsibility for any of the unsatisfactory aspects of the argument advanced herein. I am grateful too for many perceptive comments and suggestions made by participants at the Conference; they have helped me to make improvements on an earlier draft of the paper.

dimensions is to begin by embracing a fiction. And, if we further seek a level of abstraction at which simple analytical propositions can be advanced concerning the economic forces manifested in the complex and imperfectly understood processes of agricultural commercialization, urbanization, and industrialization, then the figurative content of the historical narrative will necessarily be increased. It seems inevitable that macroeconomic storytellers--whether concerned with the demand side of the drama or with the supply side, as I am in this paper--should take as their license the famous aphorism of Voltaire: "History is a fable agreed upon."

Whereas discussions of economic development from the macroeconomic vantage point virtually oblige the participants to traffic in fables, it does not follow that all fables should be accepted as having equal claim to attention. Surely the storyteller's art is to select among the many conceivable allegorical plots those that do rough justice to the particular historical realities with which the audience has been acquainted, while furnishing useful "moral lessons" in the form of pragmatic inspiration for future research, if not general instructions for the guidance of current policymaking.

Abramovitz and I (1973) have tried to respond to this challenge by suggesting that despite the obvious fictions incorporated in the neoclassical model of growth, this analytical apparatus, even when applied to the simplest case of a one-sector economy, remains a vehicle for some instructive parables about important and insufficiently appreciated aspects of the historical experience of economic growth in America. Proceeding in that spirit, we thought it admissible to avail ourselves freely and fully of the assistance that the notion of a well-behaved aggregate production function (and its factor price dual) can provide in rationalizing and drawing out some meanings from the historical record.

I intend to continue employing the aggregate production function metaphor for the same purposes here. To do so, one need not harbor any delusions that this fabulous neoclassical beast's behavior must be mimicked by the workings of a "real world" economy comprising many production activities, each of which is free to select among techniques characterized by different degrees of roundaboutness.[1] In such a world the possibility of "reswitching" means that the rate of return in general will not order techniques uniquely according to their respective capital intensities; there is then nothing to guarantee that a comparison of equilibrium states would in reality find

---

[1] Such a justification for the neoclassical "parable" was proposed by Samuelson (1962).

techniques that are more mechanized or more roundabout being employed where the rate of profit or interest was lower.[2] But, as it turns out that long-run trends in the American economy of the nineteenth century, when viewed at a suitable level of aggregation, give an appearance of compatibility with the capital theories deriving from Jevons, Wicksell, Böhm-Bawerk, and J.B. Clark-- something which those observers of the nineteenth-century scene would not have found remarkable--it will be a tolerable simplification to speak as though there were a single substance called "capital" which, along with an equally homogeneous thing called labor, could be put into a single nicely behaved production function to obtain total output.

Resorting to the convenient expository device of a growth parable involving a neoclassical production function will not automatically lead to the more blatant fallacies of reification. In this paper, as in previous work in the same genre, I have no intention of suggesting that the production function has an independent historical reality of its own, an existence that would warrant literally regarding "it" as a causal determinant of the temporal path traced by the economy. Instead, it is possible to regard the appearance of a set of stable or regularly changing supply relationships as an historical consequence which emerged at the macroeconomic level--a final resultant of growth processes that in reality were played out on the microeconomic plane.[3] As such this ex post statistical construct can be a source of significant clues, indicating which sorts of microeconomic processes, among the myriad that might catch the attention, proved to be dominant in shaping the long-run course of economic evolution.

In choosing among the many allegorical plots that could be developed around the production function metaphor, however, Abramovitz and I (1973) departed from firmly established conventions by spurning the "steady state" temptation to which the many good minds engaged on growth theory have succumbed. Some succumbed only for a while, but the true visionaries persist to this day in seeking to assert the existence of a direct correspondence between

---

[2]On reswitching and its significance, see Bruno, Burmeister, and Sheshinski (1968) and other contributions to the same Quarterly Journal of Economics symposium on "Paradoxes in Capital Theory." Harcourt (1972) surveys the literature from the vantage point of the other Cambridge. The recurrence of the same techniques at widely differing rates of return (reswitching) equally suffices to vitiate the strict economic meaning of the obverse proposition which the neoclassical tradition supported; we really cannot justify statements to the effect that if two economies are in steady state equilibrium and have access to a common array of techniques, the economy in which the interest rate is lower must have the most "capital" per unit of labor input.

[3]See Nadiri (1970, p. 1146) for a similar statement on the relationship between reality and the ex post statistical construct of an aggregate production function.

"the stylized facts of capitalistic development" and fables of economies in steady state growth.[4] In that vision of the past, the establishment of a "modern" rate of increase of per capita product came about by virtue of the economy having attained a balanced growth path along which capital accumulation kept pace with output expansion; the real rate of return on capital and the savings rate remained unchanged; and steady (Harrod neutral) technological progress continued to raise the efficiency of labor--thereby carrying the capital/labor ratio and the productivity of labor ever upwards.

There is no denying that this is a comforting and aesthetically pleasing conception. By refusing to avail himself of it, the economic historian will almost inevitably lose the sympathy of some portion of his audience. The great story-tellers have long displayed the power to evoke in their listeners a predilection for the revelation of "steady states" in the Universal Design: "As it was in the beginning, is now, and ever shall be: world without end. Amen."[5] So it is not surprising that modern growth theory has been preoccupied with generalizing upon and working out the implications of von Neuman's vision of an economy undergoing "balanced," "quasi-stationary," or steady state expansion. For the neoclassical mind not the least attractive feature of this vision was von Neuman's demonstration that, in an economy in steady state growth, the prices of inputs and outputs would be determined without reference to demand conditions. And in some measure, faith was rewarded. In the context of macroeconomic models which distinguish only one or two productive activities, it has been possible to preserve the essential spirit of the von Neuman steady state solution while showing its existence to be compatible with technological change (so long as the latter is of a purely labor-augmenting character); with the presence in the system of a scarce (nonproduced) resource such as land (or alternatively in some models, labor); and with savings propensities that do not require all the income thrown off by capital to be ploughed back into accumulation.

On the other hand, the greater aspirations of many who embarked on this theoretical mission were ultimately frustrated. The conditions required to prove the existence of a steady state path in a realistically disaggregated economy, and for economies in which there are heterogeneous (and not continually malleable) capital goods, turned out to be so stringent as to offend even the

---

[4]Samuelson (1976, ch. 37, esp. pp. 738-42) presents an explicit elementary exposition aimed at showing the correspondence between the "approximate facts of modern development" in the U.S. since 1900 and a model of an economy in steady state growth. No special importance is attached to the 1900 starting date, and the implication is clear that the basic trends might well be traced back into the nineteenth century if one were to assemble the figures.

[5]A set congregational response following the singing of the Psalms in the Anglican Church service.

growth theorists' sense of realism. As a result, some economists whose intimate knowledge of growth theory leads them to identify the latter as the theory of steady state expansion, rather than exposing their work to the carping remarks of "realists," prefer not to venture even tongue-in-cheek references to the empirical usefulness of parables; instead, they insist that this branch of dynamic analysis has scarcely anything to do with economic history.[6]

In at least one sense it is easy for economic historians to agree that if and when an historical theory of growth begins to be formulated, the extant growth literature may be of some use but the bulk of the work will remain to be done.[7] Certainly narrow considerations of professional self-interest urge historians to shrink from the conception of steady state growth. Henry Adams, perhaps America's greatest historian, saw this clearly enough when he wrote: "A society in stable equilibrium is--by definition--one that has no history and wants no historians." But, on further reflection, it seems that it is too modest of the "realistic" growth theorists to declare that their accomplishments have no relevance for empirical studies of the subject of economic development, past or present. At the very least, something may be learned by formalizing the notion of steady state growth so as to understand better why the dynamic processes of the real world do not and, more strongly, cannot conform to its requirements.

There is an honorable tradition of using steady state growth theory in this self-denying way. Such, of course, was Harrod's (1948) intention when he argued that short-run speculative behavior in the money market might make it impossible to keep interest rates as low as would be required to allow planned investment to absorb savings when output was growing at the natural (full employment) rate. We have subsequently witnessed what Hahn deftly characterized as the "headlong retreat" of growth theorists from this point of view, and I do not wish here to lament the rejection of that particular (thoroughly Keynesian) usage of steady state growth theory.[8] Whatever one may say about the political and ideological meaning of economists' waning interest in demand-dominated dynamic models, it is fair to observe that during the 1950s this shift received deserved impetus from the dawning perception that

---

[6]See Hahn (1971, esp. p. vii), where a collection of theoretical papers is introduced with the disclaimer: "The theory of growth is not a theory of economic history. It is of no help in answering Max Weber's famous question and only of marginal use in understanding, say, the Industrial Revolution."

[7]On the distinction between neoclassical and historical theories of long-run growth, and special consideration of the modeling of technological change in the context of such theories, see David (1975, pp. 10-16, and 31-86).

[8]See Hahn (1971, p. xiii). For the interpretation of Harrod's position in the context of a neoclassical specification of production relations, see Eisner (1958); Burmeister and Dobell (1970, pp. 38-43) provide a more recent restatement.

disappointed expectations, unwanted capacity, and speculative hoarding were not crucial phenomena in the difficulties encountered by poor countries attempting to force the pace of their economic development. Whereas the questions on which Harrod focused derived from the vision that there was nothing in the workings of capitalist economies to ensure compatability between the demand side and the supply side requirements for sustaining growth at full employment, from a long-run vantage point it may prove more illuminating to consider whether there are secular forces which work to disrupt steady state growth and--under suitable circumstances--recurringly propel the economy toward new and different equilibrium paths.

Models built around the notion of a steady state equilibrium path, whether of the static or dynamic variety, do not oblige the analyst to draw a correspondence between the configurations indicated as the equilibrium solution(s) of the model and the configurations of prices and quantities actually observed. We are free to try to sort out the historical record for any particular economy by distinguishing phases of equilibrium motion from phases marked by motion(s) that may be interpreted--within the chosen analytical frame of reference--as a response to the disruption of some antecedent equilibrium state. This is simply a way of applying the method of comparative dynamics to organize and perhaps rationalize the available data about very long-run macroeconomic trends. I do not regard it as a daring innovation to try to use this methodology, or to show how, with the help of the simplest of the familiar neoclassical growth models, one can reexamine the central problems of inter-pretation that are posed by the broad record of secular economic change in America during the nineteenth century. These are problems of truly "classical" proportions, for they concern the respective roles of Thrift and Invention, and the underlying relations between them, in shaping the course of economic progress.

One of the reasons why it is appropriate to cast nineteenth-century American growth experience in terms of such (classical and neoclassical) theories is that these focus immediately upon the crucial relations governing the accumulation of tangible capital, which is exactly the emphasis demanded by the broad outlines of the available quantitative record.[9] The central fact to be grasped in this connection is that whereas the crude total factor productivity residual has loomed so large in growth accounting exercises carried out for the U.S. economy in the twentieth century, it does not figure correspondingly in

---

[9]The following paragraphs recapitulate the survey in Abramovitz and David (1973, pp. 429-30), with due attention to the minor revisions of the estimates indicated in the notes accompanying Tables 1 and 2, below.

the story of the preceding epoch. During the nineteenth century (see Table 1), the pace of increase of the real gross domestic product was accounted for largely by that of the traditional, conventionally defined factors of production: labor, land, and tangible reproducible capital. The long-term rate of growth of total factor productivity lay in a low range from 0.4 to 0.6 percent per annum, representing no more than a tenth to a seventh of the persisting 4.0 percent annual rate of increase in real gross domestic product, and less than two-fifths of the prevailing rate at which per capita output was rising. In the twentieth century, by contrast, the crude productivity residual has been of at least the same order of magnitude as the per capita output growth rate, has accounted for upwards of one-half of the total output growth rate, and represents more than two-thirds of the average rate of increase in real output per man-hour.

In the U.S., the long-term per capita output growth rate underwent acceleration between the first and second halves of the nineteenth century. To be precise, between the extended trend periods 1800-1855 and 1855-1905 (shown in Table 1), it increased by roughly 0.5 percentage points, reaching the 1.7-1.9 percent per annum level which has been maintained in the U.S. economy throughout the last 100 years. This acceleration, which implied the doubling of per capita real output approximately every 40 years rather than every 60 years, was entirely attributable to the quickened growth of real product per man-hour—the first discernible phase of a secular step-up of the pace of conventional labor productivity growth that continued into the present century. The proximate cause of this portentous movement is not to be found in the behavior of the trend rate of total factor productivity advance. The latter underwent an acceleration in the opening quarter of this century, but the estimated rate for the period 1855-1890 is the same as that for 1800-1855, and between the latter period and the complete half-century, 1855-1905, there was no really appreciable rise in the residual (see Tables 1 and 2).

Indeed, between the antebellum era (1800-1855) and the following half-century (1855-1905), there occurred a decline in the relative contribution made by total factor productivity growth to the growth rate of real product per man-hour—a fall from 54 percent to 42 percent, with a corresponding rise in the relative contribution being made by the growth of reproducible and

Table 1

Growth in the U.S. Private Domestic Economy*

(Percentage Average Annual Growth Rates)

Conventional Factor Input Measures:	1800-1855 "Crude"	1855-1905 "Crude"	1905-1927 "Crude"	1927-1967	
				"Crude"	"Refined"[a]
Real Gross Product[1]	4.2	3.9	3.3	3.2	3.2
Per Capita Real Output	1.1	1.6	1.7	1.8	1.8
Labor Input Per Capita	0.5	0.5	-0.3	-0.9	0.2
Output Per Unit of Labor Input[2]	0.6	1.1	2.0	2.7	1.6
Total Conventional Factor Productivity[2]	0.4	0.5	1.5	1.9	1.3

[a]Growth rates refer to the 1929-1967 period, rather than to the 1925/29 – 1965/69 interval -- denoted as "1927-1967."

Notes and sources:

[1]The output measures for the 1800-1905 period refer to GDP inclusive of land improvements and home manufacturing; "crude" measures for 1905-1967 relate to GDP in the private economy (Commerce Department definition); "refined" measures refer to gross private domestic product inclusive of services of durables owned by households and institutions, after Christensen and Jorgenson (1970, Table 12).

[2]The "crude" factor input measures are man-hours and the net capital stock (Divisia index distinguishing unimproved land and all reproducible capital for 1800-1905, simple aggregation of all capital for 1905-1967). The "refined" input measures accept the work of Christensen and Jorgenson (1970, Table 7) as far as concerns their corrections for aggregation biases in undifferentiated man-hours and simple aggregate capital estimates.
  "Crude" residual factor productivity growth rates have been computed for 1800-1855 and for 1855-1905 from the estimates made for shorter trend intervals, e.g., 1853/57-1869/1873, 1869/1873-1889/1892, 1889/1892-1903/07, using the estimated factor shares (in gross product) as the weights appropriate to each shorter period. The "refined" productivity calculation has been made using the input and output growth rates, and average factor share weights from Christensen and Jorgenson (1970, Tables 2, 7, 12).

*Extracted from: Abramovitz and David (1973, Table 1), with revisions of the estimates in lines 3, 4, and 5 for the period 1800-1855.

nonreproducible capital in relation to labor inputs.[10] During the transitional period, c.1835 to c.1890, the average growth rate of labor productivity was maintained at 0.83 percent per annum, of which three-fourths (or 0.63 percentage points) must be ascribed to the growth of capital inputs per man-hour of labor employed. The contribution being made to labor productivity growth by the growth of total capital intensity[11] was thus raised in this transitional period by roughly 0.4 percentage points above the rate (0.22 percent per annum) that had obtained during the preceding trend interval 1800-1835. Thus, it may be seen that the equivalent of almost the entire 0.5 percentage point acceleration of the trend growth rate of per capita real product recorded in the mid-nineteenth century was purchased by additional sacrifices in raising the amount of conventional tangible capital with which the American worker was endowed.

How and why did this unspectacular but eminently successful transition to a modern rate of economic progress come about? These are hard questions which ultimately may resist satisfyingly deep answers. Nevertheless, as the "why" of the matter can only be understood by first clarifying its "how," the problem may be approached by way of a story--a parable of an economy that managed an extended traverse to a new equilibrium growth path characterized by twice the degree of roundaboutness of production as that which formerly had obtained.

----

[10]The average annual percentage growth rates of labor productivity $(\tilde{Y} - \tilde{L})$ are 0.65 for 1800-1855, 1.13 for 1855-1890, 1.19 for 1855-1905. These may be compared with the total factor productivity residual $(\overset{*}{E})$ shown in Table 2 to obtain the ratios reported in the text. Figures for $(\overset{*}{Y} - \overset{*}{L})$, corresponding to each of the trend periods distinguished in Table 2, are not reported explicitly but may be derived as the following magnitude: $[\overset{*}{E} + \theta_K(\overset{*}{K} - \overset{*}{Y}) + \theta_R(\overset{*}{R} - \overset{*}{Y})]/\theta_L$.

[11]The contribution of capital intensity to the average labor productivity growth rate may be obtained from the entries in Table 2 as the magnitude(s):
$$(\theta_K + \theta_R)(\overset{*}{C} - \overset{*}{L}) = [\theta_K(\overset{*}{K} - \overset{*}{L}) + \theta_R(\overset{*}{R} - \overset{*}{L})] = [(\overset{*}{Y} - \overset{*}{L}) - \overset{*}{E}].$$

II. THE GRAND TRAVERSE OF THE NINETEENTH CENTURY

As the growth fable now to be related is but a slight embellishment of an oft-told tale, relatively few words describing the analytical schema are required to set the scene.

I ask you to picture a perfectly competitive closed economy in which labor (L), capital (K), and land or nonreproducible resources (R) are all kept fully utilized in churning out a flow of constant dollar gross domestic product (Y). For the purposes of this narrative, the factors of production are defined quite conventionally. The natural units in which L is measured are full-time equivalent man-hours. R is the constant dollar value of nonreproducible tangible assets and, analogously, K is the constant dollar resource cost of the net stock of reproducible capital available to the domestic economy. This embraces all tangible nonhuman assets other than consumer durables, and so includes the constant dollar value of improvements made to (farm) land. Additions may be made to the reproducible stock simply by forgoing consumption of some portion of the real domestic production; but the stock also undergoes physical depreciation at an exponential rate (δ).

Production in this one-sector economy is governed by a twice-differentiable constant returns to scale production function of the Uzawa form:

$$(1) \quad Y = [a(E_L L)^{1-1/\sigma} + \beta(E_K K)^{1-1/\sigma}]^{\frac{\sigma(1-\theta_R)}{\sigma-1}} [E_R R]^{\theta_R}.$$

The ease of substitution--strictly, the elasticity of substitution--between the reproducible capital and labor inputs is set by the constant parameter σ. Between the services of land and those of the bundle of reproducible capital and labor inputs, there is also a constant elasticity of substitution, but as the value of the elasticity parameter in this instance is fixed at unity, the competitive share of unimproved land in the gross output, θ_R, becomes an unchanging parameter of the production system along with the "distributional" coefficients a and β. The comparative stability of the U.S. gross domestic production share imputed to the unimproved component of the stock of land, which may be observed from the (θ_R) estimates presented for consecutive trend intervals in the nineteenth century by Table 2, provides some rough support for ascribing this particular (separable) form to the mythical aggregate production function.

Table 2

Factor Shares and Growth Rates of Capital, Output and the Residual: 1800 to 1905

Trend Intervals	Average Gross Factor Shares			Average Annual Percentage Rates of Growth					
	θ_R	θ_K	θ_L	$\overset{*}{R}$	$\overset{*}{K}$	$\overset{*}{K_T}$	$\overset{*}{C}$	$\overset{*}{Y}$	$\overset{*}{E}$
1800 - 1834/36	.09	.23	.68	2.81	4.52	3.66	4.04	4.21	0.58
1834/36 - 1853/57	.11	.27	.62	3.41	5.54	4.80	4.92	4.15	- 0.05
1853/57 - 1869/73	.12	.34	.54	2.47	4.44	3.90	3.92	2.96	0.35
1869/73 - 1888/92	.10	.35	.55	3.62	5.57	5.16	5.14	4.90	0.84
1888/92 - 1903/07	.09	.37	.54	1.95	3.94	3.60	3.55	3.78	0.84

(Bracketed aggregate $\overset{*}{E}$ values: rows 1800–1853/57 = 0.35; rows 1853/57–1903/07 = 0.50.)

Notes and definitions: All observations for 1800-1903/07 refer to U.S. domestic economy. The "real" magnitudes are expressed in constant 1860 prices.

R : Land exclusive of farm improvements.

K : Reproducible capital stock (net basis), including improvements made to farm land.

K_T : Net stock of reproducible and nonreproducible capital, i.e., $K_T = R + K$, by simple aggregation.

C : Divisia index of reproducible and nonreproducible capital stocks, i.e., $\overset{*}{C} = (\theta_R \overset{*}{R} + \theta_K \overset{*}{K})/(1 - \theta_L)$.

Y : For 1800-1903/07, real gross domestic product including improvements to farm land and home manufacturing output.

E : Total factor productivity, "crude" residual measurements: for 1800-1903/07, $\overset{*}{E} = \overset{*}{Y} - [(1 - \theta_L) \overset{*}{C} + \theta_L \overset{*}{L}]$. The labor inputs are measured in (L)man-hours, and the share weights employed are those indicated for the corresponding trend intervals. Growth rates for periods spanning more than one trend interval are computed as weighted averages of factor productivity growth rates within the constituent intervals.

L : Man-hours of (full-time equivalent) labor service. $\overset{*}{L}$ can be computed from the entries in the Table for $\overset{*}{E}$, $\overset{*}{Y}$, C, θ_L, and $\overset{*}{K_T}$. Revisions in the underlying L estimates have resulted in revisions of the figures presented for $\overset{*}{E}$ originally in Abramovitz and David (1973).

source: Extracted from Abramovitz and David (1973, Table 2), with revisions noted above.

Innovations in techniques of production and social organization, which economic writers in the latter part of the nineteenth century referred to under the broad rubric "the Progress of Invention," and which in this context can more simply be referred to as changes in technology, are assumed to manifest themselves by altering the efficiency of the three primary factors of production.[12] The function described in (1) restricts technological change to a purely factor-augmenting form, making it possible for the inputs measured in efficiency units ($E_L L$, $E_K K$, $E_R R$) to grow at rates that differ from their respective growth rates when measured in natural units. This kind of technological change, however, does nothing to alter the elasticities of substitution among the factors of production.

The general class of aggregate production functions with factor-augmenting technological change–of which (1) is a special case--gives rise to the familiar growth-accounting relation:

$$(1a) \quad \overset{*}{Y} = (\theta_L \overset{*}{E}_L + \theta_K \overset{*}{E}_K + \overset{*}{E}_R R) \ + \ \theta_L \overset{*}{L} + \theta_K \overset{*}{K} + \theta_R \overset{*}{R} \, ,$$

where the asterisks denote proportionate growth rates of the variables in question; θ_L and θ_K are interpreted as elasticities of output with respect to L and K, analogous to the elasticity (parameter) θ_R already defined. The expression in parentheses on the right-hand side is "the residual," $\overset{*}{E}$.

Now suppose that a generalized version of the condition of Harrod neutrality governs the relationship among the rates of factor augmentation-- the sum of elasticity weighted rates of land augmentation and reproducible capital augmentation is then always identically zero:

$$(2) \quad \theta_R \overset{*}{E}_R = - \, \theta_K \overset{*}{E}_K \, .$$

---

[12]For a proper conception of the breadth of the developments which the term "technological change" is here meant to evoke, one cannot do better than to quote a true neoclassical like Sidgwick (1887, pp. 115-16):

> In considering Invention as a source of increased production, we must extend the meaning of the term to include all expedients. . . ; whether introduced in particular departments of industries, or in the great social organization of industries through exchange; and whether introduced with full deliberation by single individuals, or through the half spontaneous and unconscious concurrence of many.

This condition amounts to a stipulation that Progress of Invention does not alter the efficiency of a Divisia index aggregate comprising all forms of capital, because its effects (say) in lowering the marginal productivity of land are precisely counterbalanced by its effects in raising the marginal productivity of reproducible capital.

The immediate virtue of the foregoing specification is that it enables us to interpret the rate of total factor productivity growth (which will be found as the residual in an ordinary growth-accounting exercise for this economy) purely as the reflection of labor augmentation at the rate $\overset{*}{E}_L$. Remembering the constant returns to scale assumption $(1 - \theta_R = \theta_L + \theta_K)$, equations (1a) and (2) give rise to an expression for the rate of growth of output as a linear function of the growth of labor measured in efficiency units, and of the growth of the land/output and reproducible capital/output ratios:

$$(3) \qquad \overset{*}{Y} = \overset{*}{L} + \overset{*}{E}_L + \frac{\theta_R}{\theta_L}(\overset{*}{R} - \overset{*}{Y}) + \frac{\theta_K}{\theta_L}(\overset{*}{K} - \overset{*}{Y}).$$

This in turn suggests a decomposition of the real product growth rate along lines somewhat different from the established conventions of growth accounting, but one that is familiar nonetheless in a growth-theoretic context. Under the assumption of strict Hicks neutrality, the individual rates of factor augmentation would be identical $(\overset{*}{E}_L = \overset{*}{E}_K = \overset{*}{E}_R)$, and would be measured by the total factor productivity residual, $\overset{*}{E}$. Observed changes in the capital/labor ratio measured in natural units might then be ascribed implicitly not to the influence of technological changes but rather to shifts of the savings rate in relation to the growth of the labor force. Thus, the sense behind decomposition of labor productivity growth $(\overset{*}{Y} - \overset{*}{L})$ into technical change and the contribution of capital-intensity growth $[(1 - \theta_L)(\overset{*}{C} - \overset{*}{L})]$, which Solow's (1957) paper made a commonplace growth-accounting procedure, rests squarely upon the supposition that (Hicks neutral) technical progress could not be held responsible for changes in the capital/labor ratio. Yet this constitutes only one among several quantitative representations of the Progress of Invention and Accumulation (or thrift) as orthogonal forces responsible for the growth of labor's productivity. In what follows, use is made of an alternative partitioning of observed growth rates, based on the assumption of (generalized) Harrod neutrality. This latter variant associates the influence of Thrift and accelerated Accumulation with changes in the ratio of capital measured in natural units to real output (or, equivalently, to labor measured in efficiency units), recognizing that along a steady state growth path the capital/labor ratio defined in natural units may be growing as a consequence of purely labor-augmenting technological change.

The suggestion deriving from growth theory, then, is that the economy's motion can be characterized (and ultimately understood) by distinguishing between two components of the observed rate of growth of output--the <u>natural rate</u> and the <u>contribution of the rate of traverse</u>.[13] By the natural rate of output growth (G) is meant the sum contributions of those secular developments which are usually cast in an exogenous role in simpler growth fables: the rate of growth of labor inputs along the full employment path; the growth rate of labor efficiency; and the rate at which the (utilized portion of) the stock of land is being increased.[14] Thus the "natural" rate at which output can grow is set by:

$$(4) \qquad G \equiv (\overset{*}{L} + \overset{*}{E}_L) \left\{ \frac{\theta_L}{1 - \theta_K} \right\} + \overset{*}{R} \left\{ \frac{\theta_R}{1 - \theta_K} \right\}.$$

The likely onset of diminishing returns in our economy (signaled by the downward drift of the ratio of land to labor measured in efficiency units) means that the foregoing natural rate cannot strictly be described as a steady state growth rate for this economy. But a quasi-steady state configuration may obtain when output is growing at G , in the sense of there being stability of the ratio of <u>reproducible</u> capital to output ($v \equiv K/Y$), and of the ratio of shares in gross product imputed to labor (θ_L) and reproducible capital (θ_K) . If this looser usage of the steady state concept is employed, the extent to which the actual growth rate of output diverges from G measures the effect of "traversing" between different quasi-steady state paths, that is to say, of altering the reproducible capital/output ratio at the rate $\overset{*}{v}$. This indicates a basic partitioning that is just as readily implemented as those to which growth-accounting exercises have accustomed us:

$$(5) \qquad \overset{*}{Y} = G + (\theta_K/\theta_L)\overset{*}{v}.$$

---

[13]On the "traverse" as a disequilibrium motion between steady state paths, see Hicks (1965, pp. 183-97).

[14]The presence of a stock of capital (R) which cannot grow indefinitely at the rate $(\overset{*}{L} + \overset{*}{E}_L)$ implies that, when $(\overset{*}{K} - \overset{*}{Y}) \equiv \overset{*}{v} = 0$ and therefore $\overset{*}{Y} = G$, diminishing returns acts as drag pulling G below $(\overset{*}{L} + \overset{*}{E}_L)$. For any constant rates $\overset{*}{R}$, $\overset{*}{L}$, and $\overset{*}{E}_L$, when $\overset{*}{Y} = G$, the latter will be constant. This follows from the fact that given (1) and (3), $\overset{*}{v} = 0$ leads to the constancy of θ_L/θ_K, and θ_R is in any case a parameter.

How does the motion of the American economy during the nineteenth century appear when described with reference to these coordinates? From Table 2 it may be seen that during the trend interval from the opening of the century to the mid-1830s the reproducible stock's growth rate closely approached that of total output; the same may be said of the fin-de-siècle interval 1890-1905. Further, within each of those comparatively brief periods, these estimates reveal no appreciable alteration of the relative shares of reproducible capital and labor in gross product.[15] The economy's motion in both phases thus bears at least an outward resemblance to (quasi-) steady state growth. But, as has been intimated, the same cannot be said of the century as a whole. During the intervals 1835-1855 and 1855-1890, the growth of the reproducible stock considerably outran that of real output, while the (absolute and relative) share imputed to property other than land grew by approximately seven-tenths its initial size.

The figures in Table 3 emphasize the contrast between initial and terminal steady state phases and the traversing motion that characterized American growth during the period from 1835 to 1890. (At least a grain of salt should be taken with the last significant digits of the growth rate estimates presented.) It is apparent that the movement toward a higher capital/output ratio not only was the dominant component (easily accounting for two-thirds) of the labor productivity growth rate, but that it also constituted the preponderant source of the quickening rise of per capita real product during the 55-year phase of development. Whereas the rate of improvement in labor efficiency contributed 21 percent of the average annual rate of growth of output per capita during 1835-1890, and increasing labor inputs per member of the population added approximately another 29 percent, the contribution of the increasing roundaboutness of production accounts for 44 percent of the total.[16]

---

[15]The underlying estimates for $(\theta_K/\theta_K + \theta_L)$ at the beginning and end of the 1800-1834/36 interval are .217 and .244, respectively; at the beginning and end of the 1888/1892-1903/07 interval the same magnitudes are .396 and .407.

[16]Increasing inputs of nonreproducible capital (land) per capita account for the remaining 6 percent. To make the calculations just reported in the text, average rates of change for each of the four components of $\overset{*}{y}$ (indicated in the notes to Table 3) were computed for the 1835-1890 interval. These components when summed yield .0146, compared to the 1835-1890 average figure that may be found for $\overset{*}{y}$ (.0137) by weighting the subperiod averages presented in Table 3 for 1835-1855 and 1855-1890. For consistency, however, the former (larger) of the two rates was taken as the denominator in reckoning the relative contributions to the growth rate of per capita output.

The reference in the text comparing "the effect of traversing" with the growth rate of labor productivity is based on the higher of the two estimates implied for the latter magnitude. Since $(\overset{*}{Y} - \overset{*}{L}) = \overset{*}{y} - (\overset{*}{L} - \overset{*}{P})$, and the average (1835-1890) rate for per capita labor inputs is .0051, accepting $\overset{*}{y} = .0146$ for the purposes of the calculation yields $[(\theta_K/\theta_L)\overset{*}{v}] / (\overset{*}{Y} - \overset{*}{L}) = .0064/.0095 = .67$; using the alternative weighted average estimate of $\overset{*}{y}$ obtainable from Table 3 gives .0064/.0086 = .74.

Table 3
The Impact of the Capital Deepening Traverse
in the Nineteenth-Century Growth of the U.S. Domestic Economy

Trend Intervals	Per Annum Rates of Growth of		Percentage	
	Real Product Per Capita * (y)	Effect of "Traversing" $[\theta_L/\theta_K]$ $(\overset{*}{v})$	Relative Contribution of "Traversing" in:	
			$\overset{*}{y}$	$\overset{*}{Y}$
"1800 - 1835"	.0117	.0010	8.5	2.4
"1835 - 1855"	.0106	.0060	56.6	14.4
"1855 - 1890"	.0155	.0066	42.6	16.4
"1890 - 1905"	.0185	.0011	5.9	2.9

Notes and sources:

Estimates of $\overset{*}{Y}$, $\overset{*}{v} = \overset{*}{K} - \overset{*}{Y}$, θ_L, θ_K are those given in Table 2. Population growth rates (per annum) for the four trend intervals in this Table are, in consecutive order, .0302, .0305, .0241, and .0191. The average annual rates of change given above for $\overset{*}{y}$ are discrete time rates computed directly from the underlying estimates of $y = Y/P$, so as to allow for interaction terms.

Note that the per capita growth rate version of (5) is $\overset{*}{y} = g + (\theta_L/\theta_K)\overset{*}{v}$, where g is the per capita analogue of the natural rate G:

$$g = [\overset{*}{E}_L + (\overset{*}{L} - \overset{*}{P})]\left(\frac{\theta_L}{1 - \theta_K}\right) + [\overset{*}{R} - \overset{*}{P}]\left(\frac{\theta_R}{1 - \theta_K}\right).$$

From Table 2 and this Table are found the following components of the average per capita output growth rate for the period 1835-1890: $\overset{*}{E}_L\theta_L/(1 - \theta_K)=$ .003; $[\overset{*}{L} - \overset{*}{P}]\,\theta_L/(1 - \theta_K) = .0043$; $[\overset{*}{R} - \overset{*}{P}]\,\theta_R/(1 - \theta_K) = .0009$; $(\overset{*}{v}\,\theta_L)/\theta_K = .0064$.

The quantitative record makes it tempting to extend this allegory by portraying the course of American growth in the mid-century as a disequilibrium movement between two steady state paths, in consequence of which the economy attained a terminal configuration characterized by a higher savings rate and a correspondingly higher reproducible capital/output ratio. As is known, maintenance of a (quasi-) steady state configuration requires that the planned savings rate coincides with a planned rate of investment that will keep the reproducible capital stock growing at the natural rate. This is expressed by the Harrod-Domar consistency condition

(6) $\quad s_G - v\delta = Gv,$

in which the left-hand side presents the real net savings rate as the difference between the real gross savings rate (s_G) and the fraction of gross output set aside to cover the annual depreciation of the reproducible capital stock.

It is only to be expected that the configurations exhibited by the American economy in the periods 1800-1835 and 1890-1905 approximately satisfied the Harrod-Domar condition, for these have been previously characterized as phases of quasi-steady state growth. (Table 4 makes this explicit by comparing the equilibrium capital/output ratio indicated by (6), i.e., $_Bv$, with the actual values of v estimated for the midpoint of each period.) If the reestablishment of Harrod-Domar consistency after a prolonged phase of non-steady state growth is not written off as mere coincidence, a more interesting question is how this came to pass. The answer to this question must, in effect, expose the mechanism underlying the movement I have called the Grand Traverse.

The simplest interpretation of events is the one suggested by remembering that stable steady state paths exist in such a model of the economy because the capital/output ratio is supposed not to be influenced directly by technological changes. Rather, it adjusts to reestablish Harrod-Domar consistency should any alterations occur in the other elements of the

195

Table 4

The Grand Traverse: U.S. Domestic Economy c.1817 to c.1897

Variables	Average Values for Quasi-steady state Periods	
	1800 - 1835	1890 - 1905
$\overset{*}{E}_L = \overset{*}{E}/\theta_L$, labor efficiency g.r.:	.0085	.0155
$\overset{*}{L}$, labor input (man-hours) g.r.:	.0342	.0243
θ_L , nonproperty share in gross product:	.68	.54
θ_R , unimproved land share in gross product:	.09	.09
$\overset{*}{R}$, unimproved land input g.r.:	.0281	.0195
$G = (\theta_L/\theta_L + \theta_R) \, [\overset{*}{L} + \overset{*}{E}_L] + (\theta_R/\theta_L + \theta_R)\overset{*}{R}$,		
the "natural" rate of growth of output:	.0410	.0369
$\overset{*}{Y}$, the actual rate of growth of output:	.0421	.0378
s_G , the real gross savings rate:	.11	.28
δ , depreciation rate on reproducible stock:	.017	.036
$_B v = s_G/(G + \delta)$, real capital/output ratio		
required for steady state growth:	1.90	3.84
v , the actual real capital/output ratio:	1.80	3.62
$v/_B v$, actual as fraction of equilibrium		
capital/output ratio:	0.95	0.94

Computation of Adjustment Speed Parameters for Subperiods of the Traverse

	1835 - 1855	1855 - 1890
G , the "natural" rate:	.0366	.0337
δ^r , the depreciation rate:	.0209	.0287
$\lambda = (G + \delta) (1 - \theta_K)$:	.0420	.0402

Notes and sources:

Growth rates and elasticity estimates are based on those in Table 2. s_G (in 1860 prices) for 1890-1905 is the estimate of gross capital formation in comprehensive GNP for 1889-1898 from Davis and Gallman (1973, Table 2, col. 4). On the stability of the average gross savings rate during 1889-1908, see Davis and Gallman (1973, Table 1). They also (pp. 437-38) suggest a procedure for estimating the (constant) level of s_G for the period 1800-1840, which is modified and applied using estimates of K, v, and δ consistent with those used here for the midpoint of the 1800-1835 interval. δ for 1890-1905 is based on the estimates given by Abramovitz and David (1965, Table V-7, Part B), for the ratio of private capital consumption to the net private reproducible domestic stock (both in 1929 prices), adjusted for the inclusion of improvements made to farm land in the present definition of K . For 1800-1835, δ was extrapolated to 1840 on the basis of the relationship between the latter estimates and figures derived from Davis and Gallman (1973, Table 8) in the period 1870-1900, making adjustments for the inclusion of farm improvements in the stock to which δ refers.

configuration.[17] This casts the average propensity to consume[18] ($c = 1 - s_G$), the depreciation rate (δ), and the natural rate of growth (G) in the role of jointly determining the steady state equilibrium value ($_Bv$) to which the actual capital/output ratio must adjust. An effort to construe the meaning of the historical record within this framework evokes a story with a thoroughly classical plot.

Although there were changes in all these variables, it would appear from Table 4 that the mid-century traverse had been set in motion basically by Thrift--that is to say by a pronounced rise in the proportion of output saved. During the initial (1800-1835) phase, consumption was absorbing about 89 percent of the gross product, and depreciation another 3 percent, leaving 8 percent available for real net capital formation.[19] By contrast, at the close of the century, the real gross savings rate stood at 28 percent, of which 13 percentage points [$(.036)(3.62) = \delta v$] represented depreciation, leaving the real net rate at 15 percent of the gross product. The implicit rise in the share of output available for net capital formation was considerably greater than this if the increase in the gross savings rate is evaluated from the vantage point of an economy on the 1800-1835 growth path, for which the required capital/output ratio was as low as 1.9. Even allowing for the higher depreciation rate that prevailed later in the century as a consequence of the shift of the pattern of capital formation to shorter lived assets, real capital consumption would have absorbed less than 7 percent of gross product [$\delta_1 v_0 = (.036)(1.9) = .068$],

[17] Solow (1970, pp. 21-23) gives a neat heuristic exposition of the stability property for the one-sector model. With CES production functions other than the Cobb-Douglas (such as in equation (1) above where $\sigma \neq 1$), a slight complication must be noticed. If a constant savings rate implies a consistent capital/output ratio outside some attainable range determined by the ease of substitution, there will be no steady state solution for the system. As it is argued below that $\sigma < 1$ is the relevant specification to adopt here, it is worth establishing that there is no cause to worry about the existence of pathological conditions in which $s_G/(G + \delta)$ required a $v = {_B}v$ which was too low to be attainable by factor substitution before labor's share was driven to zero. Given σ as low as $\bar{\sigma} = .10$, the data in Table 4 may be used to calculate that the critical limits on s_G would be $\bar{s}_G = .089$ for 1800-1835, and $\bar{s}_G = .251$ for 1890-1905. These values are obtained from the expression $\bar{s}_G = (G + \delta) v \, \theta_K^{\sigma/1-\sigma}$ (see Burmeister and Dobell, 1970, pp. 33-35, 60). One may see from Table 4 that $s_G > \bar{s}_G$, so the configurations observed for 1800-1835 and 1890-1905 could be consistently interpreted as true steady states even under this extreme specification of the production function.

[18] Recall that the government sector remained so minor in relation to the U.S. domestic economy that, for this century, taxes can safely be included with private consumption, without appealing to the sort of rationale considered by David and Scadding (1974).

[19] Identifying the gross (and net) domestic capital formation rates with the gross (and net) savings rates, and referring interchangeably to savings or investment rates along the full employment path, includes foreign lending as a source of resources flowing into the growth of the domestic capital stock. In the periods 1800-1835 and 1890-1905, however, the average rate of net imports of capital was negligibly small, although in the individual years of the century when they were of greatest relative importance (in the mid-1830s) the flow of net foreign lending represented roughly a tenth of gross domestic investment. See North (1960) and Simon (1960) for current value capital inflow estimates and Gallman (1966) for current values of gross domestic investment. The dynamic implications of the American economy's access to overseas savings are recognized somewhat more fully by the alternative model presented below.

whereas the attainment of a higher capital/output ratio meant that in the event the proportion actually claimed by depreciation amounted to 13 percent.

The century witnessed another set of developments that also tended to force the reproducible stock to grow more quickly than output after 1800-1835. By comparison with the changes in savings just examined, however, these forces appear to have been of subsidiary importance. The growth rates of labor and land inputs underwent parallel retardation during the latter half of the century, with an impact on the growth of productive potential that was not fully offset by the accelerated pace of labor-efficiency growth achieved in the terminal period 1890-1905. As a result, the natural rate declined by about one-tenth, from 4.1 percent per annum in the initial growth phase to 3.7 percent per annum in the terminal growth phase of the century. This by itself would have called for an upward adjustment of the capital/output ratio by rather less than one-tenth of its 1800-1835 equilibrium level.[20] The upper panel of Table 4 shows, however, that the entire configuration of changes entailed a full doubling of the capital/output ratio $(_Bv)$ required for Harrod-Domar consistency, and that the increase actually recorded in the degree of roundaboutness paralleled this exactly.

This simple story of the mechanics of the American Traverse may be rounded off by showing that shifts of the savings rate and the displacements of the steady state path for the economy which these implied are broadly consistent with the historical path actually traced by the (full employment) capital/output ratio during its prolonged upward movement. To do so, it is necessary to consider what is known about aggregate savings behavior in the nineteenth century, and to take account of the factors which, in the context of the model, would have determined the speed of convergence toward the ruling steady state path.[21]

In neoclassical models of the simple kind considered here, the critical determinants of the speed of adjustment turn out to be the form of the savings function, the rate of depreciation, and the magnitude of the "disequilibrium gap" between the actual capital/output ratio and the requisite steady state

---

[20]Letting only G take its 1890-1905 value, keeping δ and s_G at the levels observed for 1800-1835, we may calculate v_B = (.11) / (.0539) = 2.04, which is 7 percent greater than the 1800-1835 equilibrium value of 1.9.

[21]On adjustment time in one-sector neoclassical models, see R. Sato (1963), K. Sato (1966), Conlisk (1966), and Atkinson (1969).

ratio.[22] Since the process of asymptotic convergence toward the (new or old) balanced growth path (following a permanent or transient disturbance) involves the alteration of the actual capital/output ratio, the time required to complete a given fraction of the entire traverse depends in essence upon the flexibility in the growth rate of the capital stock. The smaller the share of output that is automatically claimed for consumption, and the faster the existing stock disappears if not replaced, the quicker a positive or negative discrepancy between the actual and the equilibrium capital/output ratio can be eradicated. This takes as given the magnitude of the natural rate of growth. Obviously enough, the less dependent the output growth rate is upon capital inputs (i.e., the smaller θ_K is), and the higher the natural rate of increase (G) is, the more rapidly the adjustment toward the equilibrium level of the capital/output ratio $(_B v)$ can proceed. The larger the positive disequilibrium gap, the more rapid the rate of growth of v can be, and hence the higher the possible rate of growth of output during the transition. This shortens the necessary adjustment time.

Denoting the completed fraction of the required adjustment by ϵ, the corresponding adjustment time can be approximated for the model economy using the expression

$$(7) \quad t(\epsilon) = [-\frac{1}{\lambda} \ln(1 - \epsilon)] + \{ \frac{1}{\lambda} \ln [1 - \epsilon (1 - \frac{v_0}{_B v})] \} \quad ,$$

where λ is simply the "adjustment speed parameter," the estimated values of which appear in the lower panel of Table 4: $\lambda \equiv (G + \delta) (1 - \theta_K)$. The first term on the right-hand side of (7) measures the time required for 100ϵ percent adjustment to an infinitesimal displacement of the "balanced" capital/output ratio, while the second term takes into account the effect of a discrete shift

---

[22] The concern here is with the trend of the full-employment capital/output ratio, i.e., with its movements between the episodes of more or less full capacity utilization around 1800, 1834/36, 1853/57, etc., with reference to which the chronology of growth intervals has been constructed. Hence, I shall abstract from the factors considered by Conlisk (1966), who showed that allowing for unemployment tends to shorten the required adjustment time.

of $_Bv$ away from the level (v_o) that initially prevailed.[23] From the former, it may quickly be seen that there is every reason to suppose the traverse to have been a rather long-drawn affair; putting $\lambda = .041$ (the general order of magnitude indicated by the figures in Table 4), the time required to complete 95 percent of the adjustment to <u>marginal</u> disturbances is found to be 73 years.

The displacements of the balanced growth path described here were hardly marginal, however. Nor can they be held to have occurred all at once, at the close of the period 1800-1835. But, if the real gross savings rate did not rise from 11 percent to 28 percent in a single mighty bound, then, as the work of Gallman (1966) and Davis and Gallman (1973) suggests, the complex historical pattern can be simplified to reveal two distinct stages in the upward shift. Having remained at average levels slightly above 10 percent during the era before 1834 (see Table 4 and notes), the real gross savings rate achieved in the decade 1834-1843 approximated the 20 percent level that was attained during the pre-Civil War decade 1849-1858.[24] During the 1860s, a second shift carried s_G upward to the higher plateau on which it remained for the remainder of the century. Davis and Gallman put the average rate of gross capital formation at 27 percent for the decade 1869-1878, essentially equal to the (28 percent) rate found for 1889-1898.

By 1834/36 the actual capital/output ratio lay in the neighborhood of 1.9, closely approximating the equilibrium ratio for the period 1800-1835. Let us suppose that on 1 January 1836 (sic) the gross savings rate jumped from 0.11 to 0.20 and $(G + \delta)$ slipped slightly from its 1800-1835 level of .058 to the .0575 level indicated in Table 4 (lower panel) as that prevailing during the interval 1835-1855. Using (7) and the estimate of $\lambda = .042$, we can calculate that by 1 January 1872, after 36 years had elapsed, the upward trajectory of the

---

[23] Equation (7) can be obtained from R. Sato (1963), taking account of the modifications introduced by K. Sato (1966) to allow for depreciation and a constant gross savings rate. Equation (6) is exact for a Cobb-Douglas model, in which θ_K is constant, but a reasonable approximation for a CES model in which θ_K changes can be obtained by estimating $\lambda = (G + \delta)(1 - \theta_K)$ for subintervals and allowing for changes in average values of all the underlying "parameters" between subintervals--as has been done in the lower part of Table 4. This turns out to be convenient in the present case because the timing of changes in s_G, and hence in $_Bv$, indicates a subperiodization of the 1835-1890 traverse. An alternative procedure would allow for the endogenous determination of θ_K, but would make the estimate of $t(\epsilon)$ depend upon the accuracy with which the elasticity of substitution (σ) could be determined. As shall be seen below, the latter route would lead one immediately to question the whole interpretation of the traverse as having been launched by exogenous shifts in s_G.

[24] From Davis and Gallman (1973, Table 2), it is found that during 1834-1843 gross capital formation <u>exclusive</u> of inventory accumulation was 16 percent of comprehensive GNP, in 1860 prices. The corresponding figure for the decade 1849-1858 is 17 percent. If real net inventory accumulations accounted for 3 percent of average real GNP during the earlier period (this being the rate Davis and Gallman estimate for 1849-1858), the inclusive gross savings rate for 1834-1843 would have been 19 percent, compared to 20 percent in 1849-1858.

capital/output ratio should have raised it to 3.31. Perhaps momentary acknowledgment of the intervening historical realities of the Civil War, the diversion of resources from capital formation, and the outright devastation incurred in these years can account for the fact that the estimate of the capital/ output ratio for 1869/1873 (i.e., the average centered on 1871) fell 6 percent below the predicted level: it was 3.12 rather than 3.31.

But to resume the story, let me suppose that the second step in rise of the ex ante gross savings rate occurred at just this point in time, 1 January 1872. The jump in s_G from .20 to .28, accompanied by shifts in G and δ, now displaced the equilibrium value of the capital/output ratio in an upward direction--to the 3.84 level required along the 1890-1905 steady state path. Once again it may be asked how far the adjustment from the initial (1871) position would have progressed, this time after the lapse of 19 years. Applying the estimate λ = .408 from Table 4, the model calls for ϵ = .585 of the requisite 23.1 percent increment in the size of v to have been completed within this time span, predicting that the latter would have reached 3.54 by the close of 1890.[25] It so happens that according to the data underlying the preceding Tables, the real reproducible capital/output ratio at that point in time (i.e., the estimate for 1888/1892) stood at 3.53!

Neat empirical fits obtained with elegantly simple models are always arresting. One is momentarily tempted to consign the results to the nearest scientific journal rather than trying to exchange them for fifteen dollars from the New Yorker magazine's "Department of Funny Coincidences." The apparent quantitative plausibility of the story just related is no exception.

It is exactly in these general terms that Temin (1971) and Williamson (1973) have sought to explain certain macroeconomic aspects of the U.S. growth experience in the era following the Civil War. Temin (1971) proposes to explain the secular price deflation of the period 1873-1896 as a consequence of recurring recessions engendered by the long-run adjustment process–here called the Traverse–set in motion by the markedly higher postbellum savings rate. The chronic downward pressure on the real rate of return (in this view) persistently forced it below the nominal interest rate. Presumably because of the slow growth of the money supply and public debt before 1896, the level of nominal interest rates could not adjust downward with sufficient speed to obviate the need for the ongoing absorption of real savings to be accompanied

---

[25]This prediction is not sensitive to the precise location in time of the hypothesized "second displacement." Essentially the same predicted value for 1890 is obtained on the supposition that the shift took place on 1 January 1866 (sic), rather than at the end of 1871.

by recession and secular price deflation.[26] Williamson (1973) likewise casts the rise in Thrift (that is, the level of the real gross savings rate) in the role of prime mover of the postbellum American growth mechanism, and holds the gradual completion of the entailed upward adjustment of the capital/output ratio to be responsible for the retardation of the rate of labor-productivity growth as the century drew to a close.[27] The main plot of the story just related seems to fit well enough with these neoclassical interpretations of postbellum events, even if it calls for more notice to be paid to the movement to a more roundabout mode of production that was occurring in the antebellum era.

Furthermore, in portraying increased Thrift as the impetus behind the Grand Traverse, the preceding narrative would furnish a needed justification for American economic historians' renewed convictions that the positive effects of government policies and institutional innovations upon the supply of savings during the nineteenth century were of critical importance in fostering the country's economic development.[28]

But, this very classical tale is not the only possible construction that may be placed upon the events of the Grand Traverse. Nor does it provide the most satisfactory explanation of all the aspects of the available macroeconomic record. Indeed, inasmuch as the rise of the reproducible capital/output ratio and the real savings rate were developments well under way by 1840, the interpretations advanced by Temin (1971) and Williamson (1973) provide no immediate assistance in understanding why chronic price deflation and retarded labor-productivity growth appeared within the period 1873-1896, but did not mark the quarter-century that preceded the Civil War. Having taken pains to

---

[26]The argument as stated by Temin (1971, pp. 73-74) is slightly elliptical regarding the mechanism of the downward adjustment of prices in the U.S. In the foregoing I have interpolated a link--recurring business recession and weak cyclical recoveries--between the hypothesized incipient gap between the real and the nominal rate of interest, on the one hand, and the observed price deflation on the other. Note that Temin's argument (as he recognized, 1971, p. 74) could not account for, and made no use of, the concurrent secular price deflation in Britain--and indeed throughout the international economy. For a recent survey of these questions, see Saul (1969).

[27]The late nineteenth-century retardation of labor productivity growth which Williamson (1973) sets out to explain appears from a comparison of the rates for the periods 1869/1873-1888/1892 (1.78 percent per annum) and 1888/1892-1903/07 (1.34 percent per annum) using the estimates Abramovitz and I have prepared (see Tables 1 and 2 above), although these differ in a number of respects from the data consulted by Williamson. On the other hand, it may be argued that the anomaly lies not in the fin-de-siècle retardation so much as in the immediate postbellum burst of growth that followed the slow labor productivity gains (0.39 percent per annum) of the 1853/57-1869/1873 interval. The trend growth rate for the complete period 1853/57-1888/1892 is maintained (without any retardation) during the fin-de-siècle period. Furthermore, in the broader sweep of American development, the whole period examined by Williamson (1973 and 1974) emerges as one characterized by a pronounced acceleration of labor productivity growth. The data underlying Tables 1 and 2 disclose the following average annual growth rates for successive 40-year periods: 1790-1830, 0.58 percent; 1830-1870, 0.60 percent; 1870-1910, 1.68 percent.

[28]See, e.g., Davis and North (1971, ch. 6); Williamson (1974); Davis and Gallman (1973). Note however that the emphasis of these discussions has tended to fall on developments in the latter part of the nineteenth century, concentrating on the trans-1860s rise in s_G, and rather ignoring the earlier increase.

provide a full and fair airing for Thrift's claim to an heroic nineteenth-century role, I must now essay an alternative version, one which denies that the supply of savings occupied the crucial causal role assigned to it by the foregoing account.

Rather than treating the average propensity to consume or the conventional gross savings rate as exogenous--or, equivalently, as having been determined by circumstances independent of those influencing the demand for investment--I shall argue that the observed rise in the fraction of the U.S. real product being devoted to the accumulation of tangible reproducible assets was itself a reflection of more deeply seated autonomous changes which were disrupting the steady state path of the economy and forcing growth to become a disequilibrium process. These more fundamental developments are related to the character of technological changes in the nineteenth century, specifically with their nonneutrality in both the Hicksian and Harrodian sense. They should be considered, therefore, as having impinged first upon the relative positions of the demand schedules for various classes of assets, rather than on the aggregate savings supply schedule. Thus, in what follows, I aim to portray the Progress of Invention (not Thrift) as the fundamental force which instigated America's Grand Traverse in the nineteenth century. The course of technological innovation is the causal factor whose particular, historically determined characteristics during that epoch must be appreciated before one may properly understand past patterns of successful economic development or hope to prescribe wisely for the future.

III. THRIFT OR INVENTION?--A SHORT WHODUNIT

There is little room for doubt that sometime during the second quarter of the nineteenth century the conventionally defined rate of real capital formation in the American economy underwent the first phase of a dramatic and sustained rise. The question is where to place the responsibility for this change, or, since responsibility for such happenings is divisible, how it should be apportioned between forces which operated mainly through the supply of savings and those which impinged upon the demand for investment.

One is here confronted with an obvious identification problem. The narrative of the Grand Traverse in the preceding section dealt with this problem implicitly, and quite arbitrarily, by treating the observed movements of the savings rate as if these reflected nothing but the shifting position of a (perfectly inelastic) savings supply schedule. Figure 1 (a) recapitulates the essence of the

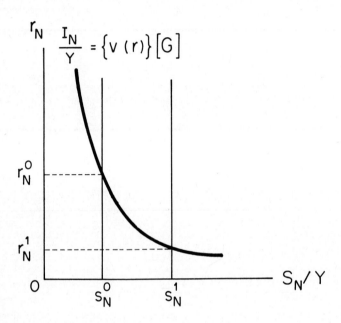

FIGURE 1 (a)

classical version of the story in compact form.[29] Relative to the level of current output, the real demand for net investment in a dynamic equilibrium situation is represented as the product of the anticipated trend rate of output growth and the desired capital/output ratio. The former is fixed by the determinants of G, the natural rate, but the capital/output ratio is free to adjust and so depends upon the real rate of return. The real net savings supply function then appears as a vertical schedule which, in shifting to the right, set in motion the Traverse: the incipient excess supply of savings forced down the rate of return until the desired capital/output ratio became large enough to restore dynamic equilibrium.

But, is there any good reason to suppose that the real savings supply schedule was so inelastic to the rate of return, or that the investment demand schedule did not shift to the right between the initial and terminal phases of the century? Figure 1 (b) presents an alternative interpretation of the historical developments underlying the Grand Traverse, one that I suggest has more to commend it than the classical version. There are three essential points of difference. First, the net investment demand schedule is shown as having been displaced to the right during the 1835-1890 period, although its elasticity with respect to the rate of return remains unaltered. In the context of Figure 1 (a), such a movement would have driven up the real rate of return unless there were an offsetting shift in the (inelastic) savings supply schedule. The second point of difference in Figure 1 (b) is that the long-run supply of savings available for conventional capital formation in the U.S. at the beginning of the nineteenth century is depicted as having been extremely elastic throughout the relevant range--although one may suppose it would become inelastic quite quickly at much higher rates of real capital formation. This suggests that a very substantial portion of the total increase observed in real net savings as a fraction of real gross product (from roughly 8 percent to 15 percent) is directly assignable to the forces underlying the investment demand shift. That portion is $\Delta s(D)$ in Figure 1 (b).

---

[29] For the sake of expositional clarity, it is desirable to formulate the identification problem by asking whether the net investment demand schedule remained stable, as in Figure 1 (a), or shifted to the right, as in Figure 1 (b). But note that net savings and net investment are measured relative to gross product Y. The gross investment demand schedule would have to be shown as being displaced to the right by the rise of $(G + \delta)$, whether or not biased technological change had altered the desired capital/output ratio, and the issue would then be how far to the right it shifted. To avoid this, I specify a net savings supply function, although in the preceding section I developed the implications of assuming the gross savings rate had shifted. While some alteration in the formulation of the argument is entailed, the same points could be made while continuing to work in terms of gross savings and investment flows.

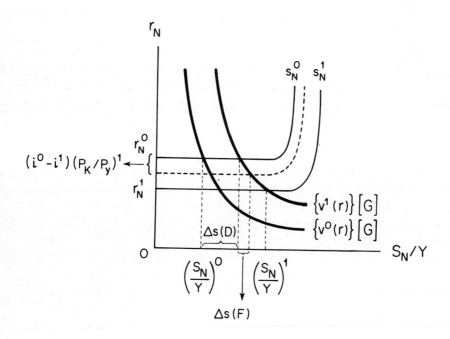

FIGURE 1 (b)

It is generally known, however, that real rates of return were lower--not higher--at the end of the nineteenth century than they had been at the beginning.[30] This implies that some shift must have occurred in the position of the savings supply curve, which directs attention to the third point of difference between Figure 1 (b) and the classical version represented by Figure 1 (a). The decline in the real rate of return is indicated as having been less pronounced than that which would have had to occur if the equilibrium-path investment demand schedule had really remained undisturbed--as in Figure 1 (a)--and the rise of the real capital formation rate had therefore to be accommodated by an <u>induced</u> movement toward more roundabout modes of production--that is to say, by factor substitution <u>along</u> the production function until a higher capital/output ratio was established. To say that the real rate of return on conventional reproducible capital did not fall as drastically as the (uniform) inelasticity of the investment demand schedule in Figure 1 (a) would require is equivalent to another statement: by accepting the form for the neoclassical investment demand schedule derived from the CES production function given in (1) above, one is obliged to accept the empirical conclusion that the investment demand schedule was not elastic. It therefore must have shifted to the right as a consequence of conventional capital-deepening bias in the progress of Invention during the nineteenth century. I shall have something further to say on this point, but to complete the story in outline form it is first necessary to account for as much of a decline in the real rate of return as did occur.

The orders of magnitude for the average real net profit rate on conventional reproducible assets which the data in Table 4 imply for the periods 1800-1835 and 1890-1905 are, respectively, 10.5 percent and 6.6 percent.[31] Adhering to the supposition that the supply schedule was extremely elastic over the relevant range, this 4 percentage point decrease would have corresponded to an exogenous drop in the real supply price facing investors seeking to accumulate reproducible capital. In Figure 1 (b) this is depicted by the downward and rightward displacement of the real net savings supply

---

[30]This is a common empirical premise in most modern discussion of savings and investment in the U.S. during the period, especially the second half of the century. See, e.g., Williamson (1973). It proceeds largely from consideration of the movements of nominal bond yields or short-term rates, such as those readily available in <u>U.S. Historical Statistics</u> (1960), and from the behavior of the relative price of investment goods, such as may be obtained from the work of Gallman (1966). See below for the average rate of return movements implied by the data in Table 4.

[31]From Table 4 one can quickly calculate that the net share imputed to the reproducible capital stock should be $(\theta_K - v\delta)$: $.23 - .03 = .20$ for 1800-1835; and $.37 - .13 = .24$ for 1890-1905. The real net rate of profit is then found using the corresponding estimates of v, as $(\theta_K/v - \delta)$, or, equivalently, ([.20/1.9] =) .105 for 1800-1835; and ([.24/3.62] =) .066 for 1890-1905.

schedule, which has been in turn decomposed into two underlying shifts. Between 1840 and the closing decade of the century, the ratio of the price index of fixed investment goods to the implicit deflator for GNP (P_K/P_Y) decreased by approximately 19 percent.[32] Since the relative demand for this class of investment goods had <u>increased</u> vis-à-vis output, it is evident that for the purposes of this discussion one can take the alteration in relative price structure as an exogenous development independent of any alleged increase in Thrift.

What caused the decline in the relative price of fixed investment goods? Looking at the behavior of the ratio of aggregate implicit deflators (P_K/P_Y) in Table 5, col. 4, one is struck by the abrupt downward shift between the pre-1860 and post-1869 levels of this series. Williamson (1974) argues that this displacement of the price structure and the concurrent upward shift of the real gross savings rate was a direct consequence of higher tariff levels, instituted by the Union government in response to the fiscal exigencies of the Civil War, and maintained thereafter by the political-economic hegemony of the North.[33] It is Williamson's (1974, pp. 657-58) essential contention that the prices of consumer goods were thus raised in relation to the general class of producer durables, and a fortiori in relation to the category of (nontraded) capital goods produced by the construction industries. Support for this exclusive emphasis on the impact of fiscal policies can be found in the movements of the relative prices of producers' durables and structures shown in Table 5--so long as attention is riveted upon the 1860-1870 interval. Yet, allowing oneself a less

---

[32] This figure is a modest estimate derived by comparing the average standing of P_K/P_Y (Table 5, col. 4) in 1889-1908 with the 1839/1849 estimate of this variable. The relative price movements during 1840-1850, in which the decline of P_H/P_C (Table 5, col. 3) carried dominant weight, indicate that the 1840 level of P_K/P_Y stood above the 1839/1844 average level.

We can express the net rental rate on capital as $r_n = (P_K/P_Y)$ (i) $= \hat{P}_K i$. The shift $(r_N^o - r_N^1) = .039$ from 1800-1835 to 1890-1905 can thus be partitioned (approximately) between $[(\hat{P}_K^o - \hat{P}_K^1) i^o = .105 - .085 =]$ .02 due to the relative investment goods price effect, and $[(i^o - i^1) \hat{P}_K^1 =]$ .019 due to the nominal cost of funds effect.

[33] Williamson (1974, pp. 640-651) also suggests that although the debt financing of the Civil War had depressed capital formation during 1861-65, the Federal policy of debt retirement contributed (during the 1870s) to raising the current value of the private savings rate. By choosing to use less comprehensive estimates than the Gallman (1966) and Davis and Gallman (1973) figures referred to here, Williamson vastly exaggerates the size of the trans-1860s rise of the nominal gross savings rate which requires explanation. The estimates considered here indicate a 2 percentage point shift in $s_G(P_K/P_Y)$, whereas Williamson (1974, Table 1) sets himself the task of explaining a 7 to 9 percentage point change in terms of Federal debt-retirement effects. A more basic problem with Williamson's formulation of the effect of government fiscal operations in terms of their impact on the position of the (private) supply of savings available for tangible capital formation lies in the implicit closed-economy assumption; Federal debt, like other financial assets, could be displaced from U.S. investment portfolios by sales to foreigners-- without having to be retired by government surpluses. And, in the case in point, this is precisely what happened. Williamson himself notes in passing (1974, p. 650, n. 25) that, as early as 1869, approximately half of the $2.2 billion Federal debt outstanding was already in the hands of European investors.

Table 5

Nineteenth-Century Trends in the Relative Prices of Fixed Investment Goods

in the U.S.

(All Price Indexes are based on 1860.)

	Investment Goods Prices Relative to Consumer Price Index:				Gross Fixed Capital Formation Deflator Relative to GNP Deflator
	Business Equipment (Producers' Durables)	Business Structures (New Factories and Stores)	Nonbusiness Structures (New Houses and Churches)		
Years	(P_E/P_C)	(P_{BS}/P_C)	(P_H/P_C)	Decades	(P_K/P_Y)
1840	109	96	123	1839/1859[a]	101
1850	120	101	100	1849/1859[a]	98
1860	100	100	100	1860	100
1870	60	60	85	1869-1878	80
1880	50	87	99	1879-1888	88
1890	44	82	121	1889-1898	84
1900	44	88	131	1899-1908	79

[a] Averages of terminal (census year) observations.

Notes and sources:

Implicit deflators P_K and P_Y were derived from estimates published by Gallman (1966, Tables A-1, A-3). Manufactured durables and new construction are aggregated in P_K.

Implicit deflators P_E, P_{BS}, and P_H, based on the work of Dorothy Brady, were from an unpublished study kindly supplied by Gallman and Howle (1965, Table D-4, lines 1 (b), 2 (b); Table B-1, col. 2, respectively). These and other related series are presented in Abramovitz and David (1965, Table V-A-2, Part A).

The Consumer Price Index P_C which serves as numeraire for the series in cols. 1, 2, 3 of this Table is described in detail by David and Solar (1977).

blinkered view, it becomes apparent that the impact of the Civil War-related change in price structure was rather ephemeral and hardly so fundamental as Williamson suggests. During the 1870s the relative price of consumption goods (including tradables and nontradables such as rents and personal services) fell in relation to those of new business and nonbusiness structures; the relative price of houses and churches of a constant size (P_H/P_C) had returned to its 1850-1860 level by 1880, and went on drifting upward--giving reason to believe that a comparison of post-1890 with pre-1840 levels of the price ratio (P_H/P_C) would show no difference worth mentioning in this connection. Surely the putative influence of the tariff changes cited by Williamson ought to have made itself felt most strongly in the movements of the relative reproduction costs of wood, brick, and stone houses (P_H/P_C), rather than in the relative prices relating to new factories and stores (P_{BS}/P_C), or producers' durables (P_E/P_C). The latter two types of investment goods made greater use of tradable intermediate inputs (such as ferrous and nonferrous metal products), which received heightened tariff protection along with textiles and other consumer goods.

Furthermore, it is evident from Table 5 that the development that underlay the maintenance of the lower relative price level for fixed capital goods as a whole (P_K/P_Y) during the postbellum era was the continuing downward course of the relative prices of business equipment (P_E/P_C). And what is known regarding the changing composition of the real stock of fixed reproducible capital (excluding improvements to farm land) during the period 1840-1900 militates strongly against the notion that this pattern of relative price movements was caused by a differentially slow rate of shift in the demand for producer durables vis-à-vis other investment goods.[34] Quite the reverse: the negative correlation between long-run relative price and quantity trends is far more readily interpreted as a set of movements along stable relative asset demand schedules—a portfolio reallocation induced by relative asset price changes. The share of the aggregate fixed reproducible stock (in 1860 prices) comprising business equipment expanded from 18.3 percent in 1840 to 39.1 percent in 1900, while between the same dates the share comprising residential

---

[34] This and the following statements are based on the estimated asset type distribution of the constant (1860) dollar values of the U.S. net stock of private domestic fixed reproducible assets, at decennial intervals from 1840 to 1900, which have been derived from the unpublished work of Gallman and Howle (1965). Abramovitz and David (1965, Table V-4, Part B) present such distributions for the following asset categories (excluding improvements made to farm land): (1) farm and nonfarm residential structures; (2) transportation structures and improvements; (3) other nonresidential structures and improvements; and (4) business equipment. Category (4), corresponding to (P_H/P_C), declines in relative importance after 1860, due to the farm dwellings' relative decline. Category (3), corresponding most closely to (P_{BS}/P_C), shows a moderate increase between its 1840-1860 level and its 1870-1900 level. Category (4), corresponding to (P_E/P_C), shows a slight contraction from 1840 to 1850, and thereafter expands in relative size in every succeeding decade.

structures contracted from 52.2 percent to 31.4 percent. It seems only reasonable therefore to attribute the secular alteration of the structure of investment goods prices to the differentially faster rate at which the supply curves for fixed business assets, and shorter lived business equipment in particular, were being shifted downward by cost-reducing technological innovations and learning effects.[35]

The foregoing argument suggests that something approaching half of the 4 percentage point fall in the real net rental rate on reproducible capital properly could be assigned to the autonomous "technological" developments that underlay the secular alteration of the relative price P_K/P_Y. This leaves "unexplained" the 2 percentage point change of the real net rental rate which came in the form of a reduction in the nominal cost of funds. One might take the latter as a reflection of the effects of the growth of bank and nonbank financial intermediation, and the integration of capital markets which began to be noticeable from the third decade of the century onward. But it is particularly important in this context to distinguish clearly between two forms of the familiar "financial intermediation" hypothesis.[36]

One aspect of the hypothesis concentrates on the presumed effect of intermediation in reducing (diversifiable) portfolio risks for ultimate asset holders and thereby increasing the total volume of resources which households would wish to divert from consumption, given the same average portfolio yield. This effect could be represented in Figure 1 (b) as a pure displacement of the real savings supply schedule to the right, and thus would become noticeable in the range when the volume of conventional capital formation began to press up against the aggregate savings supply constraint. The other aspect, however, emphasizes the role played by particular financial institutions and policies in the mobilization of savings for use in specific sectors of the economy, and it is this "mobilization effect" which is represented by the downward shift of the supply price of funds for conventional capital accumulation purposes from its original level to the intermediate level indicated along the dashed savings schedule shown in Figure 1 (b). The balance of the full change reflects the

---

[35]See Rosenberg (1963) for discussion of the way such developments were manifested in the American machine tool industry during the period 1840-1910.

[36]For a survey of salient institutional developments in the U.S., see Davis and North (1971, ch. 6). Davis and Gallman (1973) claim a very large role for the growth of financial intermediaries, citing it as the major factor responsible for the nineteenth-century increase of the real net savings rate. More generally, on the role of financial reform and capital market integration in economic development, see, e.g., Abramovitz (1952, pp. 140, 164-66), McKinnon (1973, esp. ch. 2), and Shaw (1973). For formal treatment of the effects of financial intermediation in the context of a one-sector growth model, see the interesting papers by L.J. Spellman and C. Gonzalez-Vega in McKinnon (1976, pp. 11-34). The argument of the latter papers, which have only recently come to my notice, bears close kinship to the interpretation of American historical experience developed here.

relative price structure effect displacing the savings schedule both downward and to the right, since this analysis is concerned with measuring how much in the way of reproducible investment goods could be obtained by sacrificing current consumption. Evidently were the investment demand schedule as inelastic as Figures 1 (a) and 1 (b) suggest, the pure impact of the mobilization effects of improved financial intermediation, measured as [$\Delta s(F)$], must have been quite restricted.

The preceding story hinges on two empirical magnitudes: the low elasticity of the investment demand schedule and the high elasticity of the long-run supply of funds for conventional capital-formation purposes. While neither of these parameters can be estimated with exactitude for the periods in question, I shall try to sketch some of the considerations which render these conjectures consistent with other known features of the American economy of the nineteenth century.

The question of inelasticity of the neoclassical investment demand schedule is bound up directly with the issue of whether the elasticity of substitution in the production function, equation (1), was less than unity and, if so, how much less than unity. For it is the magnitude of σ which governs the relationship between the average productivity of capital ($1/v$) and the marginal productivity of capital--which is taken here to be strictly proportional if not identical to the real rate of return.[37] Rather than appealing exclusively to econometric results obtained for the U.S. private domestic economy in the twentieth century, which put the long-run value of σ at about 0.5 and in some instances as low as 0.32, it is possible to refer to similar findings from rather tentative experiments with aggregate production-function estimation for the nineteenth century.[38]

Now, as Abramovitz and I (1973) have pointed out, both the share of capital and the capital/output ratio rose concurrently in the U.S. economy during the period 1835-1890. This being the case, finding the (constant)

---

[37] If $r = \partial Y / \partial K$ and the index of capital efficiency is E_K, it is readily shown that in two-factor CES functions (including those in which there is a separable CES part, such as equation 1) the following relation obtains: $v = \gamma(E_K)^{\sigma-1} (r)^{-\sigma}$, where γ is a constant scalar magnitude. Since Y measures gross product, r is the real gross rental rate of capital.

[38] See, e.g., David and van de Klundert (1965) for estimates pertaining to the period 1899-1960, and Abramovitz and David (1973) for a brief discussion of findings for the nineteenth century, applying essentially the same econometric approach to a smaller number of observations relating to full employment years. Some further implications of the latter findings are discussed in David (1975, pp. 55-57). From the preceding footnote it is readily seen that with $\sigma = .5$, the doubling of v (see Table 4) along a stable investment demand schedule (I_N/Y) in Figure 1 (a) would require the real gross rental rate (r) to have decreased by three-fourths of its 1800-1835 level by 1890-1905. Since the magnitude $\hat{P}_K \delta (=[r \cdot \hat{P}_K i])$ actually increased over this same interval, the implied drop in the real net rental rate would be of even greater magnitude and therefore far larger than the two-fifths reduction observed.

elasticity of substitution to have been smaller than unity implies that capital-deepening (or Harrod labor-saving) technological change was tending to lower the ratio of capital to labor when both are measured in efficiency units. In this way capital services would have become the increasingly scarce input reckoned on an efficiency basis, whose imputed share in output would be expected to grow. It is worth pointing out that the possibility of Invention's progress having operated so as to raise the rate of return on reproducible tangible capital--given the existing capital/output ratio--is entirely admissible under the generalized form of the Harrod-neutrality conditon adopted in equation (3). The latter simply requires the acceptance of the plausible implication that the course of technological change also carried with it land-augmenting effects, which worked to reduce the land/output ratio (measured in natural units) given a constant real net rate of return.

Looking backward from a fin-de-siècle perspective, Taussig (1897, pp. 7-10) was fully persuaded that his and preceding generations had lived through an era in which economic life had been reshaped by what we would call Harrod labor-saving innovations. Under the influence of Böhm-Bawerk (1896), he saw the vital part which the "successive" (as opposed to the "contemporaneous") division of labor had played in improving the efficiency of labor as a manifestation of a particular historical tendency–though not an inevitable and inherent bias--toward the lengthening of the period of production. As Taussig phrased it:

> In the past, those inventions and discoveries which have most served to put the powers of nature at human disposal have indeed often taken the form of greater and more elaborate preparatory effort. The railway, the steamship, the textile mill, the steel works, the gas works and electric plant,-- in all these, invention has followed the same general direction. But that it will do so in the future, or has always done so in the past, can by no means be laid down as an unfailing rule (1897, p. 10).

Nor was he alone in these judgments. A decade earlier, Sidgwick had reached essentially the same conclusions on the basis of the historical process he saw from his vantage point on the opposite side of the Atlantic:

Though the progress of Invention--including the developments of the great system of cooperation through exchange--
does not necessarily increase the need of capital, it has, on
the whole, tended continuously and decidedly in this
direction: the increase in the amount of consumable
commodities obtainable by a given amount of civilized labour
has been attended by a continual increase in the amount
of real capital required to furnish these commodities to the
consumer (1887, p. 133).

This view of the character of nineteenth-century technological change
makes it impossible to portray long-run economic growth as a steady state
process, or to separate cleanly the contributions made to labor productivity by
technological change on the one hand, and by the relative increase in capital
inputs on the other. But, much as one might lament the havoc this wreaks with
the sense of simple growth accounting, and with efforts to show the existence
of steady state solutions, there is consolation in the consistency between this
view and the truly neoclassical tradition in which the Progress of Invention is
seen as the autonomous force behind the increasing roundaboutness of
production.

Lest there remain an opportunity for Thrift to spring forward at the last
moment to claim the lion's share of the credit, I should reiterate a point I
have elaborated elsewhere concerning the autonomous nature of the Harrod
labor-saving drift in technological progress during the nineteenth century. When
all is said and done, it proves to be empirically quite unilluminating to attempt
to account for this bias as a relative factor-price induced neoclassical
phenomenon by invoking the apparatus of "innovation possibility frontiers"
along Kennedy-Weiszäcker-Samuelson lines.[39] The rate at which fundamental
technical knowledge was exploited, and the particular details and circumstances
of its application no doubt reflected the influences of changing relative factor
prices. It is less clear, however, that the directions in which the frontiers of that
knowledge were being extended reflected the controlling hand of profit-seeking
innovators responsive to shifts in the anticipated course of future prices, rather
than the opportunities for learning by doing which had been shaped by the past
history of relative factor prices and the legacy of irreversible capital-
accumulation decisions. And, at a still deeper level, the historian of late
eighteenth- and nineteenth-century technology finds himself returning again and

---

[39] See David (1975, pp. 31-57) for a critical discussion of the literature bearing on this basic issue.

again to the perception that the possibilities of raising the productivity of ordinary labor were closely restricted rather than boundless. These entailed an increasing degree of roundaboutness, primarily by the massive accumulation of physical structures and machinery because, in that epoch, a mastery of mechanical engineering--though not yet of chemical, biological, and electronic engineering--was already firmly established as the legacy of the scientific achievements of the seventeenth and eighteenth centuries.

Something must be said now in support of my portrayal of the long-run savings supply schedules in Figure 1 (b) as being extremely elastic to the rate of return. For the sake of brevity I shall go right to the point that the supply of savings has been defined heretofore in thoroughly conventional terms, so as to correspond with the conventional definition of reproducible capital as comprising tangible nonhuman assets. If one is prepared to broaden this concept of capital formation--urged on by Schultz (1960) and encouraged by the systematic statistical labors of Kendrick (1976)--one must correspondingly enlarge the scope of what is taken to constitute "savings." This means that the present argument does not really turn on the elasticity of savings compre-hensively defined. Rather it concerns the elasticity of the (net) flow of funds into sectors of the economy where issuers of primary debt were acquiring the particular class of assets (tangible nonhuman capital) around whose accumulation the story of the Grand Traverse revolves. It must first be shown, however, that at an early point in the nineteenth century the American people were already undertaking extensive capital-forming activities above and beyond those reflected in the conventional measures of savings and investment upon which I have focused attention until now. In other words, the picture of the rate of conventional capital accumulation as initially pressing up against a long-run aggregate savings constraint, as represented in Figure 1 (a), must be shown to be false. To do this I shall pursue the simplest course, which is to reexamine the component of output I have been calling "consumption." The alternative would require embarking upon a laborious and dubious set of imputations designed to capture sources of nonmarket production for capital-formation purposes beyond those already embraced in the gross output estimates.

The eighteenth-century legacy left the U.S. with a high per capita income level compared to most of the other regions of the world, and a per capita stock of tangible nonhuman wealth that perhaps had been rising (at 0.6 percent per annum) somewhat faster than per capita income, but not significantly so.[40]

---

[40] See Menard (1976, pp. 124-25), and the literature on colonial wealth trends referred to therein.

The wealth in question was preponderantly in the form of tangible inanimate capital, much of it nonreproducible—except that cleared and fenced land really did arise from capital-formation activities. Yet there was another important type of "capital formation" that had been going on since the seventeenth century, and which might be recognized as absorbing a substantial part of the current resources at the disposition of income receivers. Like the clearing and improving of the land, this investment was not channeled through markets, but was conducted within the households—on the farms and plantations of this predominantly agrarian economy. I refer to the rearing of children.

During the opening decades of the nineteenth century, the American population was growing at 3 percent per annum, far more rapidly than that of the European regions from which the settlers had come; c.1800 approximately half the white population was below the age of 16, and it is generally accepted that this bottom-heavy age distribution was a long-standing characteristic of the American demographic situation, reflecting high rates of natural increase dating back to the late seventeenth century. Early marriage, by the standards prevailing in western Europe since the sixteenth century, and lower rates of infant and child mortality combined to produce completed family sizes of six to eight children. (If one were disinclined to consider all childrearing costs as capital formation, it would suffice for the present argument to consider only the difference between the relative resource commitment for childrearing by the American and European populations—standardized for differences in per child cost.) The mechanisms which had brought about this differentially high fertility in the colonial population, and which sustained it in some regions of the U.S. during the nineteenth century, were intricate, and are not yet well articulated. But, in a general sense, the underlying causal nexus is clear: an abundance of improvable land established a high marginal return to labor power. This fostered the erosion of social and institutional reinforcements for patterns of individual behavior that served elsewhere, in long-settled regions, to hold fertility in check.

These same circumstances had encouraged the New World colonists to revamp and reinstitute the ancient relations of temporary servitude and perpetual bondage, the better to facilitate the direct accumulation of wealth in the form of other human beings' labor power. The obvious point is still worth stating concerning the rearing of Negro slaves. Where the stream of future revenues could be captured with greater certainty, and where the costs of raising children and maintaining adult workers were made less subject to upward pressures from the social norms established among the free members of an increasingly affluent society, this indecent form of human investment activity

216

proved to be privately profitable on the American mainland. It went on, yielding rates of return comparable to those on physical tangible capital of the types which technological changes made available during the first half of the nineteenth century.[41]

Although nowadays the merest allusion to the existence of <u>unconventional</u> capital-formation activities is sufficient to place the subject of investment in education on the agenda for discussion, it is not especially pertinent in this context. To be sure, so far as the poor statistics allow us to judge, colonial Americans and their republican offspring were probably the most literate and education-conscious people of their times.[42] And it is only reasonable to regard the comparatively high average level of educational attainment that was maintained during the course of the nineteenth century (while non-English speaking immigrants from less-schooled agrarian societies were being assimilated into the American population) as having constituted an essential ingredient of this nation's receptivity to new and better ways of doing things in the sphere of production and distribution. A generally educated population was surely a population better prepared both as workers and as consumers to adapt to, and so to adopt, the novel products and services, the altered work routines, and the new locations that technical and organizational innovations entailed.[43] Yet the conditions determining the rate of investment in <u>tangible</u> human capital were ultimately of far greater consequence in shaping the course of American growth in the nineteenth century and, in the context of the present argument, their quantitative significance far surpasses that of expenditures on schooling.[44]

---

[41] The importance of the purely redistributive aspects of slavery in sustaining the peculiar institution remains, <u>inter alia</u>, a matter on which economic historians have reached rather divergent conclusions. Compare David, Gutman, Sutch, Temin, and Wright (1976) with Fogel and Engerman (1974).

[42] See e.g., Fishlow (1966a, pp. 48-49), and Lockridge (1974). Field (1976, pp. 11-21) suggests that Fishlow's picture of the early nineteenth-century levels of educational commitment as having not been much exceeded in consequence of the Common School Revival of the 1840s is perhaps overdrawn, at least in the case of Massachusetts.

[43] See Abramovitz (1972) on the general issue of relationships between educational <u>levels</u> and realized rates of technological progress. Field (1976) raises the issue as to whether the "human capital formation" interpretation properly captures the important structural reinforcement functions fulfilled by the nineteenth-century educational system.

[44] See below for estimates of the fraction of real output representing <u>direct (net)</u> "investment" outlays in the rearing of dependent children. Until late in the nineteenth century, the magnitudes indicated below exceed the direct <u>and</u> indirect rate of <u>gross</u> investment in education, estimates of which may be derived from the work of Fishlow (1966b) and Solmon (1970).

American fertility declined steadily during the nineteenth century, as is well known.[45] The retardation in the rate of growth of the population was reflected in the decline of the labor input growth rate seen in Table 4.[46] It would require another paper, at least, to fully adumbrate the proposition that this demographic trend was an endogenous development connected with the transformation of the economy, and thus part and parcel of the process of the Traverse.[47] A significant part of the fertility decline can be accounted for by the increasing portion of the population that was being absorbed within the urban-industrial sector, for fertility levels characteristically were lower among urban dwellers than among the rural population. The extent of the fall in marital fertility within each of the urban and rural sectors has been shown to correspond closely with the adjustment that would be needed to maintain completed family sizes constant in the face of an eminently labor-saving "technological change"– the progressive decline in infant and child mortality.[48] Easterlin (1976) has linked the downward drift of completed family size observed in the demographic histories of individual farming regions with the process of adjustment to the altered costs of fulfilling the traditional accumulation plans of the early settlers. As farming regions became more densely populated and more fully integrated within the market economy, the price of land rose. It became necessary, according to Easterlin, to revise the old expectations of being able to raise numerous children and as well to endow each of the sons with the beginnings of a workable farm. But, in addition to such effects of the rising average value of farm land--much of which may be explained by the investments previously made in clearing, fencing, and related improvements, and the influence of extensive transport investments in reducing the marketing costs of agricultural outputs--part of the downward adjustment of rural fertility was probably connected with the increasing reproducible capital requirements of profitable commercial agriculture. These last were coupled with important labor-saving changes in farming technology. Not only would such investment undertakings

---

[45] For new estimates of the total fertility of the white population 1800-1920, and analysis of demographic developments underlying the decline, see Sanderson (1976).

[46] The realized reduction of $\overset{*}{L}$ was less marked than that implied by the slowed rate of natural population increase, due to the direct and indirect (labor-force participation) effects of immigration. The unrequited human capital transfer represented by overseas immigration to America helped maintain the natural rate of growth (G), and so, in the context of Figure 1 (b), contributed to the rise of the desired (I_N/Y), and to the actual nonhuman capital-formation rate on this side of the Atlantic. That story, however, must be related more fully on another occasion.

[47] For a general introduction, see the excellent survey treatment by Easterlin (1972). Sanderson (1976) presents new decadal estimates of the extent and sources of the decline in the total fertility of white women in America from 1800 to 1920.

[48] I owe this point to the unpublished work of Warren Sanderson. The underlying estimates refer to the decline in marital fertility over the period 1865-69 to 1915-19 among native white Americans.

be competitive with expenditures on childrearing, in the sense that both made claims on the income of the farm family, but, in addition, the very character of the technological changes embodied in the newly diffusing types of farm equipment would tend to reduce the relative return to the young farmer from the rearing of additional hands.

How significant was the quantitative impact of these induced demographic changes upon the supply of funds that could be mobilized for other (nonhuman) forms of capital accumulation? The retarded rate of natural increase markedly shifted the age structure of the population, raising the median age of white Americans from 16.0 to 19.2 during the first half of the century, and bringing it up to 23.4 by 1900.[49] Within the context of a life-cycle model of consumption (or savings) behavior, the implied alteration of the dependency ratio would have had a calculable negative effect upon the aggregate propensity to consume--simply because a larger proportion of the population had moved into the net asset accumulation phase of the typical household life cycle. But, one must consider in addition the effect of the reduced tangible human wealth of the individual households upon their demands for other types of wealth.[50]

Rather than estimating the parameters of these micro- and macro-level consumption functions for the nineteenth century, it is possible to assess the rough quantitative dimensions of the combined demographic effects by considering the fact that between 1800 and 1900 a 65.4 percent decrease had occurred in the ratio of the number of white dependent children (aged 10 and younger) to the level of real GNP. Actually, for purposes of comparison with the rate of net reproducible (nonhuman) capital formation at these dates, it makes more sense to consider not the entire group of white dependent children but only those in excess of the number required to replace the current population. On this basis, taking alternative estimates of the annual direct childrearing costs, which range between $20 and $40 per dependent child (in the constant prices of 1860), one may conclude that this form of net investment absorbed between 3.7 and 7.3 percent of the real GNP in 1800, but only between 0.9

---

[49] See U.S. Historical Statistics (1960), Series A-89.

[50] It is easier to think of this at the level of the individual household if one imagines the demographic change as imposed exogenously by social norms regarding family size, and costs of childrearing. Either would be tantamount to a wealth reduction, pushing the actual wealth/income ratio below the desired ratio for the household. For very low income households, a reduction in unwanted dependents would most likely result in some upward movement of the propensity to consume for the working members of the family. The comparatively high income levels of nineteenth-century (free) Americans assumes considerable significance in this latter connection, suggesting that resources released by reduction of wanted dependents would largely become available for capital accumulation purposes.

and 1.8 percent in 1900.[51] Adding the lower of these sets of estimates to the real net rates of conventional capital formation at the century's opening and close would indicate that the more inclusive measure of the potential flow of savings available for financing net additions to the reproducible stock amounted to 11.8 percent of real gross product between 1800-1835, compared with 15.9 percent in 1890-1905. The larger pair of estimates, however, still might not overstate the direct and indirect costs of rearing of dependent children. These figures yield the still more striking conclusion that the inclusive measure of real net savings hardly rose at all: the estimates for 1800-1835 and for 1890-1905, respectively, would stand at 15.4 percent and 16.8 percent. At the very least, this lends credence to the hypothesis that the Grand Traverse at basis involved a massive portfolio reallocation, largely instigated by technological change which, at least for a time, had the effect of raising the relative rate of return on tangible nonhuman forms of capital.

Of course I have presented here the long-run dénouement of a drama that was played out in a succession of short-run scenes. In doing so, it is too easy to slight the crucial role that established institutional arrangements and patterns of entrepreneurial behavior played in mobilizing potential savings, guaranteeing thereby that the long-run supply schedule facing particular sectors of the economy remained as elastic as I have argued it was.

Further, unless the realities of short-run finance constraints are appreciated, it is also easy to overlook or misapprehend the real significance of the fact that recurringly throughout the nineteenth century the U.S. exercised its ability to borrow funds from abroad. The quantitative importance of this source of savings cannot be inferred from the commonplace observation that foreign lending, preeminently by Britons, was a major source of funds channeled into the extremely capital-intensive American transportation sector. That phenomenon reflected the demands of overseas investors for certain kinds of securities. But, at no time did total net capital imports represent more than a marginal contribution--a tenth at most--to the current aggregate flow of

---

[51]The estimates of the white dependent children aged 0-10 are derived from U.S. Historical Statistics (1960), Series A71-73; and from Lee, Miller, Brainerd, and Easterlin (1957, Vol. I, pp. 519-53). Adjustments removing children required for replacement were made by approximation, using the ratios of net natural increase per 1,000 to the crude birth rate, in 1800 (.600), and in 1900 (.433). For the underlying vital rates, see Potter (1965, pp. 646, 667), and U.S. Historical Statistics (1960), Series B-20, B-130. The real GNP estimates are those described in Tables 1 and 2 above. Forty dollars per annum is roughly the 1860 dollar value of per capita consumption of perishables in the U.S., c. 1840, as estimated by Gallman (1971) from information on diets and commodity flows. It also approximates the average maintenance cost of a slave, c. 1860, as estimated by Fogel and Engerman (1974). A sample of estimates of the costs of maintaining destitute dependent children in publicly and privately supported asylums during the period 1840-1860 give figures above $40 per child (inmate) per year. See Schneider (1969, pp. 330-70); Cummings (1895, p. 59); Bremmer (1970, Vol. I, pp. 664-65). The $20 per year figure seems to establish a plausible lower bound on direct costs, i.e., excluding forgone earnings of mothers or siblings engaged in child care.

resources being devoted to tangible nonhuman capital formation in the U.S.[52]
Nor can it be said (as is sometimes maintained in regard to the situation of
developing countries in the post-World War II era) that foreign lending to
America during the nineteenth century played a critical role by removing a
foreign exchange constraint on capital formation–furnishing the wherewithal
to obtain from abroad the specific types of capital equipment that domestic
producers were unable to supply. The fact of the matter is that the flow of
manufactured and semimanufactured products being imported into the U.S.
during the nineteenth century, from the earliest date, consisted overwhelmingly
of consumer goods; investment goods, by and large, were made at home.

To appreciate properly the role played by America's access to long-term
foreign lending, one must first acknowledge the disequilibrium dynamics of the
historical growth process rather more explicitly than the strictly neoclassical
fables allow; one must recognize that the operation of the real forces that
underlay the Grand Traverse also caused it to proceed not smoothly but through
alternating phases of accelerated and retarded growth, referred to as Kuznets
cycles, or "long swings."[53] Second, it must be recalled that the U.S. was not
only an open economy, but (except during 1861-1879) a specie standard
economy in which changes in the money supply were governed ultimately by
the state of the balance of payments. The key dynamic significance of foreign
lending lay therefore in the contribution it made to alleviating pressure on the
American balance of payments during periods of especially rapid growth in
domestic demand. By covering the incipient growth of deficits, the export of
American securities would for a time prevent premature curtailment of the
periodic domestic "booms" in capital formation. It thus prolonged surges of
investment demand that were (and eventually proved themselves to be)
extremely vulnerable to check by the array of short-term financial restrictions
and conservative portfolio readjustments which unanticipated monetary
stringency almost inevitably engenders.

---

[52]See footnote 19. From the work of Gallman (1966), cited there, it is also possible to examine
the investment goods-consumption goods composition of imports, and to compare these with domestic
production in these categories.

[53]These movements occurred within the "trend intervals" considered in Table 2, for example. See
Abramovitz (1974) for the formulation of a disequilibrium dynamic model within which the role of
autonomous foreign lending is the one ascribed to it here.

IV. MORAL

In every historical epoch of significant duration, I venture to suggest, there has been a specific bias in the progress of Invention; in the absence of responses induced from the supply side, rates of return on some produced assets are systematically pushed up, while those on others are being pulled down. Embodied technological changes are not distributed uniformly across all types of investment goods. If there are learning effects in the installation of new capital, these too can be expected to be greater when the history of the type of capital has been briefer, and the total experience acquired in putting such assets into productive employments has therefore been more limited. It may also be the case, as has been suggested elsewhere, that in any particular historical epoch innovation proves to be easier where it rests on the mastery of particular ways of deriving new, directly productive assets from recent accretions to the body of fundamental scientific knowledge. The macroeconomic parables to be told about the way long-run development proceeded during these epochs should therefore be stories of non-steady state growth, of economies for which "balanced" expansion could be only an ephemeral phase soon to be disrupted by the progress of Invention.

From such Schumpterian tales as the one related here, a simple moral may be drawn. Unless domestic and foreign financial intermediaries in the public and private spheres facilitate the reallocation of a country's savings and the reshuffling of asset portfolios over time, the realized rate of return on its investments will fall farther and farther below the potential rate. This is nothing more than a familiarly classical diminishing returns phenomenon. Technological change may continually create new frontier regions which hold out the hope for sustained economic progress, but if resources become trapped in the long-exploited territories, persisting accumulation there will inexorably result in capital saturation and in the onset of the stationary state–if things go at all well.

REFERENCES

1. Abramovitz, M., "Economics of Growth," in A Survey of Contemporary Economics, Vol. II, (ed. B.F. Haley), Homewood, Ill.: Richard D. Irwin, 1952.

2. _____, "Manpower, Capital and Technology," in Human Resources and Economic Welfare, Essays in Honor of Eli Ginzberg, (ed. I. Berg), New York: Columbia University Press, 1972.

3. _____, "The Monetary Side of Long Swings," Stanford University Center for Research in Economic Growth memorandum 146, 1974.

4. Abramovitz, M., and David, P.A., "Capital Accumulation and Economic Growth," report to SSRC Conference on Economic Growth in Industrialized Countries, Saltsjöbaden, Sweden, July 26-31, 1965, Stanford University Center for Research in Economic Growth, 1965.

5. _____, "Reinterpreting American Economic Growth: Parables and Realities," American Economic Review, LXIII, No. 2, (May 1973), 428-39.

6. Atkinson, A.B., "The Timescale of Economic Models: How Long is the Long Run?" Review of Economic Studies, XXXVI (2), 106, (1969), 137-52.

7. Böhm-Bawerk, E., "The Positive Theory of Capital and its Critics," Quarterly Journal of Economics, January 1896, 121-55.

8. Bremmer, R.H., ed. Children and Youth in America: A Documentary History, Vol. I. Cambridge: Harvard University Press, 1970.

9. Bruno, R., Burmeister, E., and Sheshinski, E., "The Badly Behaved Production Function: Comment," The Quarterly Journal of Economics, LXXXII, No. 3, (August 1968), 524-25.

10. Burmeister, E., and Dobell, A.R. Mathematical Theories of Economic Growth. New York: Macmillan, 1970.

11. Christensen, L.R., and Jorgenson, D.W., "U.S. Real Product and Real Factor Input, 1929-1967," Review of Income and Wealth, (March 1970), 19-50.

12. Conlisk, J., "Unemployment in a Neoclassical Growth Model: The Effect of Speed of Adjustment," Economic Journal, LXXVI, No. 303, (September 1966), 550-66.

13. Cummings, J. Poor Laws of Massachusetts and New York. Publications of the American Economic Association, Vol. X, No. 4, New York: Macmillan, 1895.

14. David, P.A. Technical Choice, Innovation and Economic Growth. Cambridge: Cambridge University Press, 1975.

15. David, P.A., Gutman, H.G., Sutch, R., Temin, P., and Wright, G. Reckoning with Slavery: A Critical Study in the Quantitative History of American Negro Slavery. New York: Oxford University Press, 1976.

16. David, P.A., and Scadding, J.L., "Private Savings: Ultrarationality, Aggregation and 'Denison's Law'," Journal of Political Economy, 82, No. 2, Part I, (March/April 1974), 225-49.

17. David, P.A., and Solar, P., "A Bicentenary Contribution to the History of the Cost of Living in America," in Research in Economic History, Vol. II. Greenwich, Conn.: Johnson Associates, 1977.

18. David, P.A., and van de Klundert, Th., "Biased Efficiency Growth and Capital-Labor Substitution in the U.S., 1899-1960," American Economic Review, LV, No. 3, (June 1965), 357-94.

19. Davis, L.E., and Gallman, R.E., "The Share of Savings and Investment in Gross National Product During the 19th Century in the U.S.A.," in Fourth International Conference of Economic History, (ed. F.C. Lane), Paris: Mouton, 1973.

20. Davis, L.E., and North, D.C. Institutional Change and American Economic Growth. Cambridge: Cambridge University Press, 1971.

21. Easterlin, R.A., "The American Population," in American Economic Growth: An Economist's History of the United States, (eds. L.E. Davis, R.A. Easterlin, and W.N. Parker), New York: Harper and Row, 1972.

22. _____, "Population Change and Farm Settlement in the Northern United States," Journal of Economic History, XXXVI, No. 1, (March 1976), 45-75.

23. Eisner, R., "On Growth Models and the Neoclassical Resurgence," Economic Journal, LXVIII, No. 272 (December 1958), 707-21.

24. Field, A.J., "Educational Expansion in Mid-Nineteenth Century Massachusetts: Human Capital Formation or Structural Reinforcement?" March 1976, forthcoming in the Harvard Educational Review.

25. Fishlow, A., "The American Common School Revival: Fact or Fancy?" in Industrialization in Two Systems, (ed. H. Rosovsky), New York: J. Wiley and Sons, 1966a.

26. _____, "Levels of Nineteenth-Century American Investment in Education," Journal of Economic History, XXVI, No. 4, (December 1966), 418-36 (b).

27. Fogel, R.W., and Engerman, S.L. Time on the Cross: The Economics of American Slavery. Boston: Little, Brown, 1974.

28. Gallman, R.E., "Gross National Product in the United States, 1834-1909," in Output, Employment and Productivity in the United States since 1800, (Studies in Income and Wealth, 30), New York: National Bureau of Economic Research, 1966.

29. _____, "The Statistical Approach: Fundamental Concepts as Applied to History," in Approaches to American Economic History, (eds. G.R. Taylor and L.F. Ellsworth), Charlottesville: The University Press of Virginia, 1971.

30. Gallman, R.E., and Howle, E.S., "Fixed Reproducible Capital in the United States, 1840-1900," presented to the Purdue University Seminar on the Application of Economic Theory and Quantitative Techniques to Problems of Economic History, February 1965.

31. Hahn, F.H. Readings in the Theory of Growth. London: Macmillan, 1971.

32. Harcourt, G.C. Some Cambridge Controversies in the Theory of Capital. Cambridge: Cambridge University Press, 1972.

33. Harrod, R.F. Towards a Dynamic Economics. London: Macmillan, 1948.

34. Hicks, J. Capital and Growth. New York: Oxford University Press, 1965.

35. Kendrick, J.W. The Formation and Stock of Total Output. New York: National Bureau of Economic Research, 1976.

36. Lee, E.S., Miller, A.R., Brainerd, C.P., and Easterlin, R.A. Population Redistribution and Economic Growth: United States, 1870-1950, Vol. I: Methodological Considerations and Reference Tables. Philadelphia: American Philosophical Society, 1957.

37. Lockridge, K. Literacy in Colonial New England: An Enquiry into the Early Modern West. New York: W.W. Norton, 1974.

38. Menard, R.R., "Comment on 'Agricultural Productivity Change in Eighteenth-Century Pennsylvania'," Journal of Economic History, XXXVI, No. 1, (March 1976), 118-25.

39. McKinnon, R. Money and Capital in Economic Development. Washington, D.C.: Brookings Institution, 1973.

40. _____, ed. Money and Finance in Economic Growth and Development: Essays in Honor of Edward S. Shaw. New York: Marcel Dekker, 1976.

41. Nadiri, M.I., "Some Approaches to the Theory and Measurement of Total Factor Productivity: A Survey," Journal of Economic Literature, 8, No. 4, (December 1970), 1137-77.

42. North, D.C., "The United States Balance of Payments, 1790-1860," in Trends in the American Economy in the Nineteenth Century, New York: National Bureau of Economic Research, 1960.

43. Potter, J., "The Growth of Population in America, 1700-1860," in Population in History, (eds. D.V. Glass and D.E.C. Eversley), Chicago: Aldine, 1965.

44. Rosenberg, N., "Technological Change in the Machine Tool Industry, 1840-1910," Journal of Economic History, XXIII, No. 4, (December 1963), 414-43.

45. Samuelson, P.A., "Parable and Realism in Capital Theory: The Surrogate Production Function," Review of Economic Studies, XXIX, No. 80, (June 1962), 193-206.

46. _____. Economics, 10th edition. New York: McGraw-Hill, 1976.

47. Sanderson, W.C., "New Estimates and Interpretations of the Decline in the Fertility of White Women in the United States, 1800-1920," History of Contraceptive Technology Project working paper, Stanford, November 1976.

48. Sato, K., "On the Adjustment Time in Neo-Classical Growth Models," Review of Economic Studies, XXXIII, No. 85, (July 1966), 263-68.

49. Sato, R., "Fiscal Policy in a Neo-Classical Growth Model: An Analysis of Time Required for Equilibrating Adjustment," Review of Economic Studies, XXX, No. 82, (February 1963), 16-23.

50. Saul, S.B. The Myth of the Great Depression, 1873-1896. New York: St. Martin's Press, 1969.

51. Schneider, D.M. The History of Public Welfare in New York State, 1938. Reprint, Montclair, N.J.: Patterson Smith, 1969.

52. Schultz, T.W., "Capital Formation by Education," Journal of Political Economy, LXVIII, No. 6, (December 1960), 571-83.

53. Shaw, E.E. Financial Deepening in Economic Development. New York: Oxford University Press, 1973.

54. Sidgwick, H. The Principles of Political Economy, 2nd edition. London: Macmillan, 1887.

55. Simon, M., "The United States Balance of Payments, 1861-1900," in Trends in the American Economy in the Nineteenth Century, New York: National Bureau of Economic Research, 1960.

56. Solmon, L.C., "Estimates of the Costs of Schooling in 1880 and 1890," Explorations in Economic History, 7, No. 4, supplement, (Summer 1970), 538-81.

57. Solow, R.M., "Technical Change and the Aggregate Production Function," Review of Economics and Statistics, XXXIX, No. 3, (August 1957), 312-20.

58. _____. Growth Theory. New York: Oxford University Press, 1970.

59. Taussig, F.W. Wages and Capital. New York: D. Appleton and Company, 1897.

60. Temin, P., "General-Equilibrium Models in Economic History," Journal of Economic History, XXXI, No. 1,(March 1971), 58-75.

61. U.S. Bureau of Census. Historical Statistics of the United States--Colonial Times to 1957. Washington, D.C.: U.S. Government Printing Office, 1960.

62. Williamson, J.G., "Late Nineteenth-Century American Retardation: A Neoclassical Analysis," Journal of Economic History, XXXIII, No. 3, (September 1973), 581-607.

63. _____, "Watersheds and Turning Points: Conjectures on the Long-Term Impact of Civil War Financing," Journal of Economic History, XXXIV, No. 3, (September 1974), 636-61.

A COMMENT ON THE NORTH AND DAVID PAPERS

Edward F. Denison*
The Brookings Institution

North's title--Economic Growth: What Have We Learned from the Past?-- makes the actual content of the paper a surprise. Aside from a single introductory paragraph, the essay is concerned entirely with property rights and their effects on incentives and forms of government. There is no review of empirical research on amounts of growth, differences among times and places in growth rates or in <u>levels</u> of per capita output, changes in the structure of output and employment that accompany growth, sources of growth, or sensitivity of output to changes in its various determinants. There is almost nothing about income distribution and nothing about advances in living standards or other consequences of growth.

If one were to take North literally, one might conclude that economists have learned nothing at all about growth. For he indicates that the ignorance of property rights, the subject he does discuss, is abysmal while growth analysis can go nowhere without a theory of property rights and, therefore, a theory of the state--neither of which is available.

For me to discuss the subject of North's title would require a new paper rather than a comment, because he does not discuss 98 percent of what I think the title should cover. Rather, I shall treat the essay as if it had a title like "The Effect of Property Rights on Incentives and Growth." I am no expert on that subject but will offer a few comments and questions.

First, one should be grateful to North for stressing property rights and incentives. There is no question that they are important determinants of output levels and, under some circumstances, of growth rates. The historical review he provides serves to recall some of the important changes that have occurred in the last hundred centuries, and it makes interesting reading.

But, is it not necessary to specify more precisely than is done in these anecdotes who it is that property is to be defended against, if generalizations about effects on incentives are to be drawn from such a review? There is protection of the property of an entire community or nation against confiscation or destruction by another community or by "barbarians at the gates." There is protection of the property of a private individual or family

*Senior Fellow, Division of Economic Studies. The views expressed herein are my own and should not be ascribed to other staff members, officers, or trustees of the Brookings Institution.

against seizure or theft by another within the community. There is protection of the property of an individual against discriminatory treatment by the sovereign or state. There is the distinction between a system in which the individual is entitled to his own output and one in which output is pooled in a common warehouse or in which the old socialist principle of "to each according to his needs" applies. Here, there are many intermediate gradations, including those introduced by nondiscriminatory taxation--and here one must distinguish between taxation to redistribute income or wealth and taxation to provide common services--and the systems prevailing in eastern Europe, the Soviet Union, and China. Finally, there is slavery. All raise interesting questions about the impact of institutions on incentives to work and to save and invest, and hence on output, but, if one is to go beyond the blandest of generalities, must these not be considered separately?

Is it really necessary to cover all human existence in order to study economic growth? Kuznets (1966) has written of economic epochs. In Europe, the most recent before the present one was merchant capitalism. Modern economic growth, the present epoch, began in England late in the eighteenth century, spread to the U.S. and to much of western Europe in the early nineteenth century, and to most of the world by the twentieth. The delineation of an epoch, according to Kuznets, is limited by the requirement that the epoch define a stretch of human history throughout which some specified set of forces is operating and dominant, or more technically, in his terms, through which a single trend line can be drawn. Kuznets analyzes growth by studying the entire period of modern economic growth, as he dates it. My concern is not that his period is too short--much less that it does not extend to prehistory--but that it may be too long.

It is useful to bear in mind how much of all growth in output has occurred very recently. On the land area of the U.S., three-quarters of the entire increase in annual output since first habitation has occurred in the brief period since 1929, three-fifths just since 1948. In Japan more than four-fifths of the all-time increase in output has occurred since 1953. Most European countries fall between these cases. Fast growth has spread to many formerly backward areas. So fast has been postwar growth compared to past experience, not only in absolute but even in percentage terms, that it seems to demand separate study.

Much can be learned that is pertinent to the present situation by studying growth since World War II, since 1929, or for the period of "modern economic growth," without encompassing earlier times. Within these time spans, there is still much to be done.

North conceives of population pressure and diminishing returns on land as a major influence in the decline or end of civilizations. If reference is to population pressure on outsiders, particularly barbarians, as a force leading to military attack on civilizations, this hypothesis is easy to accept. But, at least part of North's argument clearly refers to <u>domestic</u> population pressure and diminishing returns. Does he also view these as persistently adverse? I am not sure, but I would venture the guess that there is no such pattern. In the ancient world, as North himself points out, population pressure led the Greeks and Phoenicians to colonize and expand, not to decline. Moreover, population shortage has seemed a problem as often as has excess population. Byzantium was repeatedly forced to offset a shortage of indigenous Greek population by admitting and civilizing barbarians to augment the native stock. In the fifteen-hundred year history of the Venetian republic, periods of weakness were those of population depletion, not population pressure.

In the modern period, land has become a progressively less important factor of production, economic rent on land a diminishing share of national income, and agriculture and mining have absorbed sharply declining shares of the labor force. Even if diminishing returns were crucial in the rise and fall of nations and in the readjustment of property rights in some periods of the past, this has not been so in recent times--despite the cries of the Axis powers for "lebensraum." Of course, there are those who believe they will become so in the future.

North's main theme, stated in his opening sentence, is that "the institutional framework implicit to theories about economic growth must be made a formal part of the theory if economic theorists are to make further substantive progress. . . ." I disagree. One can learn a great deal by analyzing a period within which relevant institutional features are believed stable enough so that changes in them can be disregarded. (Needless to say, such judgments or assumptions should be explicit, not implicit.)

North apparently feels one must be far more ambitious or know nothing at all. Economists must have a theory as to why Russia is communist and the U.S. capitalist, why the U.K. and Scandinavia have such crushing tax burdens—in short, of the reason why each nation now or in the past has or has had its peculiar governmental and institutional arrangements--and then be able to specify how these institutional differences cause growth rates and output levels to differ.

In one sense, I am more pessimistic than North; I doubt that there is a theory or model that can explain all these things. However, I am, fundamentally, more optimistic than he, believing that much is known that is useful and much more can be learned without solving the grand design of human history or even believing in its existence.

I may add that I am dubious that much of anything can be learned by examining times and places and comparing growth with any one factor (such as property rights) which influences growth. To learn from comparisons, whether of all or of a small number of countries or periods, a rather complete analysis of growth determinants is necessary, in my opinion.

Finally, I agree with North about the probable importance of incentives. I also agree that too little is known about the quantitative difference in output that results from the use of one type of incentive or institutional arrangement as against another, for example, piecework versus time wages. The effect of unemployment insurance is another example; or the effects of various average or marginal tax rates on work, savings, investment, education, etc.; or the ability to pass wealth on to heirs at death. But, I do not believe this ignorance arises because the possible importance of incentives is often overlooked. Indeed, it is hard to think of a discussion of public policy as it affects growth in which the question of incentives is not introduced. The problem is that it has been difficult to design studies that would yield dependable quantitative results.

I turn now to David's paper, which is very elegant. It is a pleasure to read a paper in which an analyst combines unusual knowledge of both theory and institutional setting, and applies it to try to explain a set of observed facts. It is nicely written—and cleverly, too, so that all necessary caveats are introduced and yet the writer can proceed precisely along his chosen course.

I would hesitate to question the logic of the argument, but a few simpler questions can usefully be raised.

Given the paucity of information about most of the nineteenth century, one wonders how much reliance to place on the "facts" that the paper seeks to explain. I am confident that David has made the best possible use here of the material available, for example from his collaboration with Moses Abramovitz. But basic data for output, capital, and labor are sufficiently sketchy as to tempt me to ask David explicitly how much confidence should be placed in the main empirical relationships that he seeks to explain.

Data aside, the problem of estimating earnings of the factors of production--used as weights and to measure elasticities and, in the case of capital, to compute rates of return—is great when proprietors' incomes were as large as they were in the nineteenth century. How sensitive are the results to possible errors resulting from this difficulty?

My next questions concern the composition of capital. At the present time, housing is nearly half of the private reproducible capital stock. When housing is mixed with other business capital in unknown and perhaps changing proportions, it is impossible to evaluate the probability of labor-saving versus capital-saving technological progress, capital/output or capital/labor ratios, rates of return, or any of the other relationships involving capital, the reasonableness of which one must appraise in order to judge this paper. Would the picture be the same for capital, total factor input, and output per unit of input, if housing and its services were eliminated or treated separately? Another question is: Would the results be different if broad components of nonresidential capital were weighted by earnings rather than by value?

David's output measure is gross of depreciation while his capital/input measure is net stock. I prefer the opposite: net output, and gross stock as an input measure. I wonder whether a switch to this choice would alter the results, but I also realize that the data probably allow no such fine distinctions to be made.

I turn now to the role of relative prices as determinants of rates of capital formation and savings, both clearly important in the nineteenth century.

I was pleased to see that David notes the 19 percent decline from 1840 to the 1890s in the relative price of fixed capital, and refers to its role as a favorable factor in the growth of real investment and capital stock. It is also discussed in connection with a fall of 4 percentage points or more than one-third in the real net rate of return; this fall was apparently only 2 percentage points on a current-price basis. But, I think it would be better, if possible, to keep changes in the various ratios in current prices separate from effects of changing relative prices. I could not tell from this paper what were the levels of or changes in gross and net saving when measured in current prices. Nor could I tell whether the saving rate inclusive of differential childbearing costs (given in section III), shown as rather stable in constant prices, would not tend to fall in current prices.

There is some similarity here with postwar Japan, and a method of presentation that Chung and I (1976) have used for gross fixed nonresidential business investment might be useful. I illustrate with Japanese numbers for 1960-1971, a period in which the capital/output ratio was rising in the nonresidential business sector. Measured in constant prices, output in the sector grew 10 percent a year, the stock of fixed capital almost 12 percent, and the stock of inventories almost 13 percent. It is a long way from the change in investment to the change in capital stock, but so rapid an increase in the stock was not attainable without a huge increase in investment. Taking 1960 as 100, the index of constant-price fixed nonresidential business investment in 1971 was 399.5. In Table 1 (which also gives comparative data for other periods), this index is viewed as the product of four other indexes. These are the indexes of the total real output available for consumption and saving, the saving rate as measured by the current price ratio of total investment to gross national product, the percentage of total investment in current prices that is allocated to fixed nonresidential business investment, and the ratio of the price of GNP to the price of fixed nonresidential business investment. From 1960 to 1971, the effect of the change in the saving rate was minor compared to the change in the price ratio. The opposite had been the case from 1953 to 1960. The table refers to fixed investment. The relative price of goods held in inventory dropped sharply in both periods, greatly facilitating the growth of the capital stock.

If one accepts David's estimates as correct, and supposes their interpretation to be unchanged by attention to detailed components and relative prices, then his main story seems plausible. That the impetus for the rise in the saving/investment ratio came mainly from the investment rather than the saving side seems likely--especially if one counts relative price change on the investment side. I would put considerably lower the odds that the pressure for more capital during the Grand Traverse stemmed mainly from biased technological progress, if that term is visualized as having anything to do with inventions; yet it may be so. Before accepting this latter hypothesis, I would like to know, among other things, how capital/output ratios, and capital/GNP price ratios, compared in the U.S. and England in nonresidential business, and for major breakdowns of this sector--particularly farm and nonfarm industries. It seems likely that England was the leading country in both technology and capital per worker in the early nineteenth century, and that the U.S. was catching up.

One part of the story that seems highly artificial to me is the suggestion that costs of childrearing should be viewed as saving and investment, and that the resultant rise in saving in the form of physical capital merely offset lower saving in the form of childrearing costs. I consider it more realistic to view children as consumption. They may even impose a responsibility for the future that requires additional saving (as suggested by David's reference to Easterlin's, 1976, view of the need to provide each son with a farm). At the very most, one might suppose that a change in expenditure for childrearing affects saving and other consumption in proportion to their sizes, which is to say that by far the main offset is in consumption.

234

Table 1

Analysis of Indexes of Fixed Nonresidential
Business Investment in Japan

Description[a]	1960/1953[b]	1971/1960[b]	1971/1953[b]
GNP (constant prices)	176.3	298.4	526.2
GPI/GNP (current prices)	152.2	106.0	161.4
FNBI/GPI (current prices)	104.3	88.1	91.9
Price ratio, GNP/FNBI	100.2	143.2	143.4
FNBI (constant prices)	280.3	399.5	1,119.8

Source: Denison and Chung (1976, p. 65).

[a]GNP, gross national product at market prices; GPI, gross private investment; FNBI, fixed nonresidential business investment.

[b]Percentages, based on fiscal year data.

235

REFERENCES

1. Denison, E.F., and Chung, W.K. How Japan's Economy Grew So Fast: The Sources of Postwar Expansion. Washington, D.C.: The Brookings Institution, 1976.

2. Easterlin, R.A., "Population Change and Farm Settlement in the Northern United States," Journal of Economic History, XXXVI, No. 1, (March 1976), 45-75.

3. Kuznets, S. Modern Economic Growth: Rate, Structure, and Spread. New Haven and London: Yale University Press, 1966.

A COMMENT ON THE NORTH AND DAVID PAPERS

John W. Kendrick
George Washington University

In his paper, "Economic Growth: What Have We Learned from the Past?" North starts out with a bang, arguing that "the institutional framework implicit to theories about economic growth must be made a formal part of the theory if economic theorists are to make further substantive progress in this field."

If, for the word "theory," he had substituted the weaker word "explanation" with reference to historical developments, I would agree. Indeed, his paper is rich with many specific instances of the interactions between institutional, especially legal, and economic changes over a long historical span.

But if, by "theory" one understands a generalized relationship among variables, with sufficient stability to permit prediction or projection, then I think that his objective is a will-o'-the-wisp. In the first place, economic changes themselves are a result of various changes in technology, natural environment, and social and personal values, which can hardly be predicted even in broad outline. Further, relationships among the more purely economic variables are subject to change over time as coefficients shift. But, even if economic changes could be predicted, the possible institutional responses are so varied that specific changes in the social superstructure of the economy, again, could not be predicted.

In a sense, North is arguing for a return to the "magnificent dynamics" of the classical economists or of the subsequent institutionalists. I need not remind him that the literature is littered with the bones of dynamic projections that were proven false for relevant time periods by subsequent developments, for example, the assertions by Malthus, Ricardo, and Mill of the law of diminishing returns as a historical tendency which would eventually produce a stationary state--"if we are lucky" (as David adds); or the Marxian projection of an increasing immiserization of the working class and increasingly severe depressions bringing on the overthrow of capitalism. One might also mention Marx's inability to foresee the institutional developments which have enabled democratic regimes to patch up capitalism to make it a continuingly dynamic and viable system; or his failure to foresee chronic inflationary pressures in high-employment free economies as a major tension-producing threat requiring further institutional changes, the nature of which can even now scarcely be foreseen. After all, inventions--whether technological or social--by their very nature cannot be forecast with any specificity; if they could, they would, in effect, already be upon us.

237

North concludes on a much weaker note than that on which he began when he says of his paper that it is merely an initial catalog of our ignorance concerning the principles of a theory of the state. To which I would add that, in my view, such a theory, or the broader theory of societal evolution of which it is a part, is an impossible dream. Nonetheless, I certainly encourage efforts to explain past evolutionary developments and to speculate about the shape of things to come.

Turning to David's paper, "Invention and Accumulation in America's Economic Growth: A Nineteenth-Century Parable," I am impressed by his ingenuity in interpreting much of nineteenth-century economic development as an extended Grand Traverse, or disequilibrium movement, between steady state equilibrium growth paths he purports to find in the early and late portions of the century. The traverse encompasses a large increase in the ratios of gross and net saving and investment to national product, and an accompanying faster growth of capital per man-hour, and consequently of output per man-hour (although there is no significant acceleration in the crude total factor productivity ratio).

Although I do not want to be the realist spoiler of his fable--which is an effective device for highlighting the role of a number of key strategic variables– I find his model a bit procrustean. Indeed, David the economic historian is somewhat uncomfortable in his role as growth modeler; in the latter part of his paper, for example, he supplements his stylized account by reference to a number of additional significant forces. I would like to point out still other significant factors that his models assume away or leave out of account. First, there must have been substantial increasing returns to scale with the remarkable expansion of local markets and the gradual emergence of a national market for many commodities in the nineteenth century. Associated with this, I would suppose that there was an increase in economic (allocative) efficiency, which probably contributed to the substantial decline in the rate of return on capital which David notes.

The assumption of constant efficiency of a bundle of reproducible and nonreproducible capital, as increases in marginal productivity of the former are assumed to offset diminishing returns to the latter, seems implausible. The volume of land and natural resources was expanding, and the progress of invention caused increasing productivity in extractive industries, as well as raising the productivity of reproducible capital.

In the latter part of his paper, David notes that his model rests on the conventional concepts of saving and investment, confined to tangible business capital formation. His rough but illuminating estimates of investments in rearing suggest that <u>total</u> saving and investment increased much less as a proportion of national product than did the conventionally defined magnitudes. It would be more satisfying, however, if he could more fully implement the total approach to include the intangible investments in research and development, education and training, health and mobility.[1] The expanded estimates would increase our understanding of the growth process, although I doubt if it would alter his modified hypothesis that "the Grand Traverse at basis involved a massive portfolio reallocation."

In his concluding paragraph, the author gives special mention to the role of financial intermediaries in facilitating "the reshuffling of asset portfolios over time," thus delaying the onset of capital saturation and falling rates of return. I would say more broadly that in a predominantly free enterprise economy, given a reasonable degree of competition plus appropriate criteria for regulation of public utilities and allocation of public investment, the allocations of savings among the alternative investment channels, by industry and type, tangible and intangible, should sustain adequate rates of return indefinitely. Certainly the rising shares of total investment and of income devoted to research and development, education, and other intangible investments have had this effect in the twentieth century. Since I must answer North's question by asserting that there are <u>not</u> diminishing returns to a growing stock of knowledge, I foresee continuing flux in the economic and social future of humankind. The challenge is, of course, to make the institutional modifications and innovations required to accommodate dynamic change with as much human satisfaction as might be experienced in the mythical stationary state!

---

[1] See Kendrick (1976).

REFERENCES

1. David, P.A., "Invention and Accumulation in America's Economic Growth: A Nineteenth-Century Parable," Carnegie-Rochester Conference Series on Public Policy, VI, (eds. K. Brunner and A.H. Meltzer), Amsterdam: North-Holland, 1977.

2. Kendrick, J.W. The Formation and Stocks of Total Capital. New York: National Bureau of Economic Research, 1976.

3. North, D., "Economic Growth: What Have We Learned from the Past?" Carnegie-Rochester Conference Series on Public Policy, VI, (eds. K. Brunner and A.H. Meltzer), Amsterdam: North-Holland, 1977.